FOR:
_____

FROM:
_____
_____

365 PRAYERS FOR THE DAD

AT THE END OF HIS DAY

DR. MARK PITTS

a division of Baker Publishing Group
Grand Rapids, Michigan

© 2025 by Mark Pitts

Published by Revell
a division of Baker Publishing Group
Grand Rapids, Michigan
RevellBooks.com

Printed in the United States of America

All rights reserved. No part of this publication may be reproduced, stored in a retrieval system, or transmitted in any form or by any means—for example, electronic, photocopy, recording—without the prior written permission of the publisher. The only exception is brief quotations in printed reviews.

Library of Congress Cataloging-in-Publication Data
Names: Pitts, Mark (Mark R.), author.
Title: 365 prayers for the dad at the end of his day / Dr. Mark Pitts.
Other titles: Three hundred sixty five prayers for the dad at the end of his day
Description: Grand Rapids, Michigan : Revell, a division of Baker Publishing Group, [2025] | Includes index.
Identifiers: LCCN 2025007954 | ISBN 9780800747220 (cloth) | ISBN 9781493451531 (ebook)
Subjects: LCSH: Fathers—Prayers and devotions. | Fatherhood—Religious aspects—Christianity.
Classification: LCC BV4846 .P577 2025 | DDC 248.8/421—dc23/eng/20250313
LC record available at https://lccn.loc.gov/2025007954

Unless otherwise indicated, Scripture quotations are from The Holy Bible, English Standard Version® (ESV®). Copyright © 2001 by Crossway, a publishing ministry of Good News Publishers. Used by permission. All rights reserved. ESV Text Edition: 2016

Scripture quotations labeled AMP are from the Amplified Bible. Copyright © 2015 by The Lockman Foundation. Used by permission. www.lockman.org

Scripture quotations labeled HCSB are from the Holman Christian Standard Bible®. Copyright © 1999, 2000, 2002, 2003, 2009 by Holman Bible Publishers. Used by permission. Holman Christian Standard Bible®, Holman CSB®, and HCSB® are federally registered trademarks of Holman Bible Publishers.

Scripture quotations labeled KJV are from the King James Version of the Bible.

Scripture quotations labeled NIV are from the Holy Bible, New International Version®, NIV®. Copyright © 1973, 1978, 1984, 2011 by Biblica, Inc.® Used by permission of Zondervan. All rights reserved worldwide. www.zondervan.com. The "NIV" and "New International Version" are trademarks registered in the United States Patent and Trademark Office by Biblica, Inc.®

Scripture quotations labeled NKJV are from the New King James Version®. Copyright © 1982 by Thomas Nelson. Used by permission. All rights reserved.

Scripture quotations labeled NLT are from the *Holy Bible*, New Living Translation. Copyright © 1996, 2004, 2015 by Tyndale House Foundation. Used by permission of Tyndale House Publishers, Carol Stream, Illinois 60188. All rights reserved.

Cover design by Chris Kuhatschek

The author is represented by Alive Literary Agency, www.aliveliterary.com.

Baker Publishing Group publications use paper produced from sustainable forestry practices and postconsumer waste whenever possible.

25 26 27 28 29 30 31   7 6 5 4 3 2 1

For my wife, Susan, who has been my best friend for forty-five years. Thank you for showing me what it means to be dedicated to an ideal. You have encouraged me throughout the creation of this prayer book, always reminding me that it's a labor of love.

FOREWORD

"Do you know of anything like this for dads?"

This was the most common question my mom and I received for three years after we began praying online nightly for moms. In November of 2015, when I was awake so many hours of the night with little kids, I knew how lonely those moments felt. I also knew that other moms were awake scrolling on their phones as well, and I wanted a place where we could all find hope even there in the dark.

The Midnight Mom Devotional online community was born out of that need, and from it, a movement of over two million moms across the world praying nightly for each other. It has been a gift from the Lord to pray with so many women through all the moments of motherhood alongside my own momma. But one thing we heard over and over those first few years as our community grew was how much women knew their husbands, fathers, sons, family, and friends needed a similar community for men.

"What about the dads?!"

My mom and I had many conversations about the need for this community. We knew exactly how to pray for moms, but many of the needs a dad experiences, the struggles he faces, and the burdens that weigh heaviest on his heart are often so different from what we know personally as mommas. We saw the need for the group to exist. We considered whether we could lead it ourselves, but the Lord made it clear that there was one specific man He had already prepared and called to lead this group of fathers—my dad, Dr. Mark R. Pitts.

My dad is a man after God's own heart, a man of integrity, wisdom, and a deep love for the Lord, who has called on God to help him in his own fatherhood. He's always been my father, but in addition to being called Dad, he has been an attorney and a successful businessman and has led in pastoral ministry for decades.

He knows the challenges of being a dad, but he also knows the strength of the heavenly Father in all the struggles a father faces. He has raised his family and continues to love his grown children and be a daily part of the lives of his grandchildren. And he always says, "Being a dad is forever."

The need was there. The man stepped into place. And when the Midnight Dad Devotional online community was created in February of 2019, it should have been no surprise that the Lord would grow the community to over 75,000 in just the first three months and triple that number six years later. The Lord called the dad who saw the gold in the grit of fatherhood and was prepared to continually point men back to their heavenly Father's wisdom, provision, and protection through prayer.

Dads, as you hold this book of prayers in your hands or read digitally on your device, know that you're holding over seventy years of wisdom, counsel, and a deep, abiding relationship with the Lord. You're holding a wealth of not only biblical knowledge but the practical daily devotion of one father's pursuit of God and all He promises.

365 Prayers for the Dad at the End of His Day will uplift and strengthen you to pray about all things always. It will remind you that there is always hope, there is always strength, and there is always more of God's goodness to discover. My dad's fervent prayer for you is for this book of prayers to lead you closer to the One we each call Father. My mom and I join my dad in that prayer for you now.

Tonight we pray for the dad who needs to know that God really cares about him and everyone he loves. Lord, he needs to know that You are strong and You make him strong. He needs to know that You provide so he can provide. He needs to know that You protect so he can protect. He needs to know that You are peace so he can share peace. He needs to know You as Father so he can be the dad You have called him to be. We ask that You'd meet him as he prays each night. In Jesus's name we pray. Amen.

Becky Thompson, creator of the Midnight Mom Devotional community; author of *Peace: Hope and Healing for the Anxious Momma's Heart*

INTRODUCTION

I am the founder of the Midnight Dad Devotional online prayer ministry. A few years ago, my daughter, Becky Thompson, created a nightly prayer ministry called Midnight Mom Devotional, which currently reaches over ten million people a month. She asked her momma, Susan K. Pitts, to join her in this ministry, and together they pray with and for women around the world, reflecting the hope of Jesus Christ. Soon, those women reached out to Becky and Susan, wondering if there was such a ministry for their husbands, fathers, brothers, and other men in their lives.

Having been a pastor for the better part of forty years, I have learned that, as fathers, we see family relationships differently than mothers do. Mothers tend to focus their efforts on care and nurture and how their families are feeling on a daily basis. We, on the other hand, have a tendency to think about and discuss our relationships with a focus on our actions, our deeds, our work. We care for our families by providing for and protecting them.

I have also discovered that men often feel separated from God, wondering if God hears their prayers. So, as a father, as a dad, I began to lift up other dads in prayer, asking God to recognize and hear them as they toiled, worked, and often struggled with the day-to-day responsibilities they faced. Shortly thereafter, I began praying for dads in a new online community, the Midnight Dad Devotional. The nightly prayers helped dads see themselves as worthy of prayer and certainly worthy of God's care and concern for their lives. Very quickly, other dads responded to the simple prayers, joining me, and together those dads became the "we" in "Tonight we pray for the dad who . . ."

In *365 Prayers for the Dad at the End of His Day*, I've provided prayers for dads, similar in style to the Midnight Mom Devotional but with an inspirational and aspirational aspect for you as a dad. Many of these prayers will seem as though they were written just for you and your circumstances. Others, on any given day, maybe not so much. In Jesus's time, men prayed three times a day and let their requests be made known to God as with one voice. Everyone knew that they were communing with God. It will be much the same in this book. We will know that we are all praying for each other.

I also wanted to add a Scripture reference for each devotion to bring a little clarity to the message of the prayer. As I was praying each one, and sometimes after I had finished the prayer, a word or phrase within the prayer would display a sense of what the Lord Himself would like to portray to each of us. But rather than interrupt the prayer itself with a Scripture reference, I wanted us to feel the Holy Spirit in the words themselves and afterward read the Scripture to cement, if you will, our understanding of what the Lord had to say. While the references are very clear at times and make a very obvious connection to the meaning of the prayer, there are also instances where the Scripture might elucidate a thought for a dad who is seeking some guidance for his own life.

I've also included a subject index in the back for when you are facing a particular situation. The prayers are intended to resonate with the situations you face as a dad. There are prayers to pray when the bills aren't paid, or the kids are sick, or you have lost your job, or you have started a new business. As dads, we tend to look forward to future success rather than reflect on past losses and failures. Just as God challenges us to be our better selves, so also will we find encouragement to be better in the face of difficulties. We encourage the dads to keep going, to build their faith, and to know God better, because that's what He wants for us.

Listen, if you take nothing else away from this prayer book, remember this: God has always intended for us to have a relationship with Him, and we can and will have success in our endeavors when we maximize our time with Him. We strive to succeed using our hands, our feet, and our strong shoulders. And it is in our nature to succeed in everything we set our hands to do. God even tells us that now is the time to succeed. In Ecclesiastes 9:10, He says, "Whatsoever thy hand findeth to do, do it with thy might" (KJV). Deuteronomy

28:8 tells us, "The LORD shall command the blessing upon thee in thy storehouses, and in all that thou settest thine hand unto" (KJV). And Proverbs 14:23 says, "In all labour there is profit" (KJV).

You are a man God can use. God knows you are imperfect. It is His desire that we exchange our imperfections for His goodness. And isn't that what you really want? To be more like Him and rest in His peace, His security, and His blessing? God has called you to the role of father, and you have God Himself as a role model. These prayers are intended to draw you closer to God's heart.

Dr. Mark Pitts

TONIGHT **we pray for the dad who really wants to be a good dad.** He may not have had any idea what it would take to be successful as a dad. Even getting his child home from the hospital required more than he imagined. Then there were broken arms and braces, and he surely didn't know how much a teenager could eat! He also didn't know that he would have to be the first and last line of defense for his family. Of course he thought he'd protect them from the outside threats of violence, but he didn't really know that he'd have to protect them from themselves. That he'd be saying things like, "No, you're not wearing that."

Being a good dad requires time, work, money, and faith, in various amounts of each. And as with just about everything, true success comes from the "want to." As long as we want to, we will be the best dad we can be.

Lord, keep this dad's heart willing and his body strong for the journey. Continue to fill his heart with love for his children, no matter what their circumstances in life. In Jesus's name we pray. Amen.

Job would send for his children and purify them. . . . For Job thought: Perhaps my children have sinned, having cursed God in their hearts. (Job 1:5 HCSB)

TONIGHT I'M PRAYING THIS FOR _____

TONIGHT we pray for the dad who believes in God's promises. They are the dad's strength and comfort and assurance that tomorrow will be better than today. He doesn't always know the plan right away, especially because it is often fulfilled over time. But because this dad trusts in God, his family knows that their lives are safe, their prosperity is within reach, and their future is assured.

God is always with us and walks with us through our sorrows. And He will strengthen us in times of trouble. The world rises up and would defeat us but for our divinely provided confidence in God. When we go it alone, we usually fail miserably. Instead, we can trust that God has a plan that is for our good and will work with us on our behalf.

Lord, this dad trusts in Your promises and will never be compromised in his dedication to his family. Be with him, strengthen him, and help him always. In Jesus's name we pray. Amen.

Fear not, for I am with you; be not dismayed, for I am your God. I will strengthen you, yes, I will help you, I will uphold you with My righteous right hand. (Isa. 41:10 NKJV)

TONIGHT I'M PRAYING THIS FOR _____

TONIGHT we pray for the dad who wonders how things are going to work out for his family this time. He's been through struggles before and succeeded. But sometimes things change so quickly that he just can't quite see the end from where he's standing.

Sometimes it takes courage just to get up in the morning. It shouldn't be that way, but it often is. Many of us have pulled the covers over our heads before rising, hoping the day would just magically become yesterday, when we were in charge. But we can have an assurance that things will work out when we trust God. Our task is to keep going the way we always have and keep trusting because God's looking out for us and our family.

Lord, this dad is wearing himself out trying to make all the right decisions. Open his eyes to see the best path, and give him the courage to walk it. In Jesus's name we pray. Amen.

Do not be afraid of them, for nothing is hidden that will not be revealed [at the judgment], or kept secret that will not be made known [at the judgment]. (Matt. 10:26 AMP)

TONIGHT I'M PRAYING THIS FOR _____

TONIGHT we pray for the dad who has put in a hard day's work. He doesn't have any grand plans about tomorrow or next year. He's making it slowly but surely, and he'd like to make this day go away for a while.

Life is so hurried and chaotic, isn't it? Remember when Jesus was walking the earth and seemingly healing every person on the planet? Before that, He was a boy just like us living in a family. It's easy to think that even He wished for the quieter times with His brothers before He began His ministry. That's probably why He retreated to the hills—to refocus and reconnect with His Father. So tonight, take time to spend a few minutes with the babies. Tonight, be the good guy for the kids instead of worrying about the job tomorrow. Your children will love it.

Lord, this dad needs You to calm his heart and mind for a while before the world crashes in. Remind him that he's a good dad making his way. Give him peace tonight. In Jesus's name we pray. Amen.

When you pray, . . . pray to your Father who is in secret. And your Father who sees in secret will reward you. (Matt. 6:6)

TONIGHT I'M PRAYING THIS FOR _____

TONIGHT we pray for the dad who is trying *real* hard, even when no one notices.

All of us look forward to being publicly rewarded for our efforts to change our own lives and perhaps the lives of others. We want everyone to see how much time and effort we have put in to change our circumstances. But that hardly ever happens because "everyone" is looking around hoping to get the same approval. Still, the Lord wants us to do our best, even when no one is watching. We're all trying to be the best dad we can be, given our circumstances, which are different from every other dad. So at the end of the day, we should just look to the Lord for His approval and receive the "well done" from Him, because it means so much more and He is much quicker to give it.

> *Lord, it's probably true that there are no books written about this dad's skills, but no one doubts how much he loves his family. He has done everything he knows to do, and he succeeds one day at a time. No flash, no dash, just the honest heart of a dad who wins when it's hardest. Lord, this dad has faith, hope, and love. Help him keep going. In Jesus's name we pray. Amen.*

Now fear the LORD and serve him with all faithfulness. Throw away the gods your ancestors worshiped beyond the Euphrates River and in Egypt and serve the LORD. (Josh. 24:14 NIV)

TONIGHT I'M PRAYING THIS FOR _____

TONIGHT we pray for the dad who believes he's going to make it. "It" might be tomorrow's rent. "It" might be the completion of that project at work or that final delivery. "It" might be a passing grade on his last online course. "It" might be the final detail in preparation for the new baby.

God has called us to do good even when doing good is not easy. Some of us are hesitant to start projects unless we are confident that we can finish them with excellence. There can be a great deal of satisfaction in completing tasks or accomplishing goals. God has many wonderful opportunities in store for His children. And the wise dad knows that when he keeps going, he can slip into the promise of prosperity and peace.

Lord, this dad is determined to complete his journey. He always looks for the way where there has been no way. Keep his heart strong so he can walk with optimism and courage toward good times. Give him fresh spiritual eyes to see the road in front of him. In Jesus's name we pray. Amen.

So now finish this, so that your eagerness in desiring it may be equaled by your completion of it, according to your ability. (2 Cor. 8:11 AMP)

TONIGHT I'M PRAYING THIS FOR _____

TONIGHT we pray for the dad who believes in himself. In good times and tough times, he has stayed true to his best self. He knows who he is, and he knows why he made the choices he made.

Our choices have consequences, and as we go through life, we'll continue to see the results of them. One of our best choices was to become a dad, and we can always be grateful for the opportunity to be a dad. Our children and family, no matter how old they are, give us joy and strength to be the dad God has called us to be. We know what success means, and we know the difference between prosperity and misfortune. For us, success as a dad means being there for our family—always there with a word of advice or a shoulder to lean on.

Lord, this dad is the picture of commitment and determination. Remind him of just how much You love his dedication to his family. In Jesus's name we pray. Amen.

Let us then with confidence draw near to the throne of grace, that we may receive mercy and find grace to help in time of need. (Heb. 4:16)

TONIGHT I'M PRAYING THIS FOR _____

TONIGHT we pray for the dad who has survived a year. The Lord has been close to this dad over the past year, enough that he has survived all the trials and keeps moving forward.

One of the hardest things for our finite minds to grasp is that God is, in fact, God. He knows the expected outcome of His words. When our circumstances change unexpectedly, we immediately wonder if He is aware that things are not going the way that would seem most convenient for us. It would be much easier for the Lord to change us into the image of His Son if things were not quite so difficult. God does not want us to suffer through trials, although He does remind us that trials do come and He will be with us when they occur.

> *Lord, this dad was working through these trials during the past year, and You were present with him so that he is still standing today. He is forgetting that which is past and is ready to meet the challenges of tomorrow. Remind him of the promises in Your Word, and make Your presence known. In Jesus's name we pray. Amen.*

The Lord sat enthroned at the flood; the Lord sits enthroned, King forever. The Lord gives His people strength; the Lord blesses His people with peace. (Ps. 29:10–11 HCSB)

TONIGHT I'M PRAYING THIS FOR _____

TONIGHT **we pray for the dad who knows the right thing to do and does it.** He's a good man, and doing the right thing is part of his DNA. He knows it's right to keep close to his family even when he is on the road or just out of town.

When we're committed to our family, we're all in. We keep in touch to ensure the family will always stay together. We take measured steps to see that all the things at home get done, and we keep track of the details. Sure, there's always way too much to do at work, and it can be easy to put our family last on the list. Yet when we're committed to them, we know keeping those relationships strong is the right thing to do. It's a heart thing, not just a task to be completed. In our heart, it's important. And prayer completes the process so that the Lord is present in our family too.

Lord, this dad counts on You for his choices. Strengthen his heart and mind tonight for doing things right tomorrow. In Jesus's name we pray. Amen.

Go to now, ye that say, To day or to morrow we will go into such a city, and continue there a year, and buy and sell, and get gain: Whereas ye know not what shall be on the morrow. . . . For that ye ought to say, If the Lord will, we shall live, and do this, or that. (James 4:13–15 KJV)

TONIGHT I'M PRAYING THIS FOR _____

TONIGHT we pray for the dad who is struggling with being a first-time dad, stepdad, foster dad, or adoptive dad. He knew from a very young age that he would have a family someday. But the newness of everything just seems overwhelming today. It seems a bit hopeless, and he wonders how he'll figure out all the right steps.

We know that fatherhood is a forever thing. Once a father, always a father. It doesn't matter how that status came about. Whether in a hospital or in a courtroom, we became a forever father. And since God is Father, He has a special place in His heart for dads.

Lord, remind this dad that he doesn't have to do everything perfectly. Show him daily how to be the dad You want him to be. Remove all hopelessness and replace it with joy. In Jesus's name we pray. Amen.

The father of the righteous will greatly rejoice; he who fathers a wise son will be glad in him. (Prov. 23:24)

TONIGHT I'M PRAYING THIS FOR _____

TONIGHT we pray for the dad who never quits. He wasn't raised to step back in adversity. He knows that failure can't be an option when his family's security is involved.

Our family is our top priority, and nothing is more important to us because they are our heart and soul. All. The. Time. When we fall short, it affects our whole family in so many ways, including having peace in the home. It's not about us, it's about them. So no matter how hard it is, how long it takes, or how much personal toll it takes, we keep going. Because if we don't keep going, our family suffers. But we can trust that the Lord has our back in all things, big and small.

Lord, this dad may be tired, but he's gotten this far by trusting You. He has tried to follow Your example of living his life for the good of those he loves. Strengthen his mind and heart tonight and his shoulders tomorrow. In Jesus's name we pray. Amen.

Whosoever will save his life shall lose it: and whosoever will lose his life for my sake shall find it. For what is a man profited, if he shall gain the whole world, and lose his own soul? (Matt. 16:25–26 KJV)

TONIGHT I'M PRAYING THIS FOR _____

TONIGHT we pray for the dad who wants to make a difference for his family. He knows that things don't come easy and hard work is the norm. He knows that coasting doesn't get it done.

Work is a full-throttle commitment to our family, and we work as hard as we can. But life is not just about the long hours we spend at work. It is also about the special time we spend with our family when we get home. It is about making the most of our time with them. We want to know that our kids will remember when their dad was there for them. Whether playing catch in the backyard or having a cup of tea from a tiny pink teacup, we create that heartfelt balancing act that a dad must live every day. And at the end of each day, isn't it really about living the way the Lord showed us to live? Let's be an example of the path of hard work and love for our family.

Lord, this dad is a difference-maker because You have prepared him for his responsibilities. Give him courage to keep going and peace when he arrives to fulfill his daily tasks. In Jesus's name we pray. Amen.

I will make my dwelling among them and walk among them, . . . and I will be a father to you, and you shall be sons and daughters to me. (2 Cor. 6:16, 18)

TONIGHT I'M PRAYING THIS FOR _____

TONIGHT we pray for the dad who is ready to lend a helping hand in almost every situation. Even after a hard day's work, he works to build his community. This dad might be a soccer coach or a youth leader.

Whether it's volunteering at the local food bank or the local Christmas dinner outreach, as a dad we can lead, guide, and, most importantly, teach our children by example that their community is a part of God's family as well. And somehow, when it seems like we've given our all to others, God multiplies our time so that it is possible to fulfill all our promises to our own family.

Lord, strengthen this dad to work as he does and yet still continue to be there for his community. In Jesus's name we pray. Amen.

Beloved, let us love one another: for love is of God; and every one that loveth is born of God, and knoweth God. . . . In this was manifested the love of God toward us, because that God sent his only begotten Son into the world, that we might live through him. . . . Beloved, if God so loved us, we ought also to love one another. . . . If we love one another, God dwelleth in us, and his love is perfected in us. (1 John 4:7, 9, 11–12 KJV)

TONIGHT I'M PRAYING THIS FOR _____

TONIGHT we pray for the dad who still has dreams. Maybe he dreams of a simple thing like a little bit bigger bank account. Maybe he dreams of a miracle to heal an illness of a family member. Maybe he dreams of overcoming a great mental or emotional struggle or maybe just getting home safely tonight.

When we have plans and goals, we would like to know that we're on the right path as we've always been before. We work hard, love our family, and want to be there for them. And when we align our plans with the Lord's vision for our life, we will flourish.

Lord, You promised that You will meet this dad where he is. Open his eyes to see that promise, give him confidence that he can achieve anything, and help him to trust in a better tomorrow. In Jesus's name we pray. Amen.

There are many devices in a man's heart; nevertheless the counsel of the Lord, that shall stand. (Prov. 19:21 KJV)

TONIGHT I'M PRAYING THIS FOR _____

TONIGHT we pray for the dad who is busy. Today the alarm clock went off and this dad started the day as he always does. He knew what his family needed, and he attacked the day in his own way. He got everything done because he almost always does.

Our responsibilities don't stop just because we're tired or because we've had a hard day. As a dad, when we say we'll be there to take care of the kids, we mean it. So we stay busy, making a way when there doesn't seem to be a way, all the while keeping our family safe when the world is huffing and puffing and threatening to blow the house down. We work hard and keep our family in financial peace. And at the end of the day, when the door is finally closed, that "I don't know how I ever made it through today" peace will wash over us like a cool autumn breeze.

> *Lord, show this dad that he's going to make it. Remind him that doing his best makes the rest that follows so much sweeter. Keep him safe for his family. In Jesus's name we pray. Amen.*

Then, because so many people were coming and going that they did not even have a chance to eat, he said to them, "Come with me by yourselves to a quiet place and get some rest." (Mark 6:31 NIV)

TONIGHT I'M PRAYING THIS FOR _____

TONIGHT we pray for the dad who is going through some issues at work. He might have seen some unexpected layoffs. Maybe the welcomed overtime that helped with finances is being changed. Or maybe there's mandatory work and it's affecting his family life.

When times are tough at work, we can still do what it takes there—but making the time to solve what's necessary at work can cause stress at home. Maybe we've always been "the man," and we don't fear change or think we're incapable of working through every problem. It's just that right now we need assurance that we're making good decisions in a tough season.

Lord, only You can bring order out of the upheaval that is in this dad's life. Help him navigate the storm, and bring him and the family You gave him to safety. In Jesus's name we pray. Amen.

The same day, when the even was come, he saith unto them, Let us pass over unto the other side. . . . And there arose a great storm of wind, and the waves beat into the ship, so that it was now full. And he was in the hinder part of the ship, asleep on a pillow: and they awake him, and say unto him, Master, carest thou not that we perish? And he arose, and rebuked the wind, and said unto the sea, Peace, be still. And the wind ceased, and there was a great calm. (Mark 4:35, 37–39 KJV)

TONIGHT I'M PRAYING THIS FOR _____

TONIGHT we pray for the dad who understands that he is responsible for his child's destiny.

As a father, we have to understand that God, as Father, has an all-encompassing plan for His children. We cannot shirk our responsibility to understand the Lord's ways when it comes to raising our children. And if the Lord has a plan for us, surely we must know that He expects us to take part in the plans for our children and never doubt that His purpose will come to pass. We get to partake in the joy of seeing its completion when we contribute our own lives to it.

> *Lord, this dad believes that he has a primary purpose to raise a family. He's pretty sure that his sons and daughters will expect him to be a leader and provide direction for them. He also knows that the example he sets will in some measure set the course for future families. Strengthen this dad's resolve to fulfill Your promises and change lives. In Jesus's name we pray. Amen.*

We speak God's wisdom in a mystery, the wisdom once hidden [from man, but now revealed to us by God, that wisdom] which God predestined before the ages to our glory [to lift us into the glory of His presence]. (1 Cor. 2:7 AMP)

TONIGHT I'M PRAYING THIS FOR _____

TONIGHT we pray for the dad who feels sandwiched between generations. He has responsibilities for aging parents and growing children. He has no time for himself because he has so many demands on his limited amount of time. They are often conflicting, and his needs frequently come last.

Our primary responsibility is to be a parent, a father, a dad. Yet it's often difficult to watch our parents struggling with the issues that come with advancing age. They're our parents, after all, and we love them. We have so much emotional capital involved in their lives that it's really hard to watch, especially if we're far away. But we can be confident that we can be the best son and father because we know that's what the Lord has called us to be.

Lord, this dad works so hard because he loves his whole family. Bless him with wisdom tonight so that he can make the right decisions tomorrow. In Jesus's name we pray. Amen.

Honor your father and your mother, that your days may be long in the land that the LORD your God is giving you. (Exod. 20:12)

TONIGHT I'M PRAYING THIS FOR _____

TONIGHT we pray for the dad who is prepared for life. He spends time with the Lord even when there is so much going on around him. He knows that things that weren't going well are now on the mend. He knows that changes in his circumstances are not worth the worry until they present themselves. He absolutely knows that he is in right standing with the Lord and can trust Him in the outcome of every trial, because the Lord has said so.

A godly dad knows that God speaks in the quiet times we have with Him. And this brings quiet assurance that God is in charge of our situations. As a dad, we do not want to withhold anything from the Lord—or the Lord to withhold anything from us. Our faith may feel small even to us, but we know that the Lord will never abandon us or refuse to provide what we need. When our family looks to us for assurance in the tough decisions, we don't worry about the outcome, and neither do they. That's the kind of peace our time with the Lord provides.

Lord, keep this dad focused on the urgent issues as well as the important issues whenever they arise. In Jesus's name we pray. Amen.

The heavens declare the glory of God. . . . Day to day pours out speech, and night to night reveals knowledge. There is no speech, nor are there words. (Ps. 19:1–3)

TONIGHT I'M PRAYING THIS FOR _____

20

TONIGHT we pray for the dad who remembers that many of his successes have come from struggles. Life has been hard at times, and sometimes he still wonders if he's ever going to see the good times.

Even a Hall of Fame baseball player succeeds only 30 percent of the time. But it is the steadfastness, the keeping going, the "one foot in front of the other" attitude that puts us in a position to have the success God wants for us. And once we succeed, we remember that the Lord showed us the way. Maybe right now, we're in a position to take the next step for our family. It's a good time to remember that our struggles have made us a better man, a better dad.

Lord, this dad is ready for every trial. He is standing on a mountain of opportunity where he can see the more and the better in the distance. Grant him courage to go forward. In Jesus's name we pray. Amen.

Count it all joy, my brothers, when you meet trials of various kinds, for you know that the testing of your faith produces steadfastness. And let steadfastness have its full effect, that you may be perfect and complete, lacking in nothing. (James 1:2–4)

TONIGHT I'M PRAYING THIS FOR _____

TONIGHT **we pray for the dad who loves his family.** He does all he can for his kids. He understands that he needs to be the core, the rock, the guy who just keeps going. He knows that he and his family are on their own path.

No family's situation is just like another's. No other family has the same mom or children or home or schedule that ours does. We are on our own unique journey as a family. We are traveling together, experiencing the wonders of the Lord every day. And though we don't know every detail of where we are going or how we will get there, God does, and we can trust in Him. We have learned to trust Him through all the seasons of life and through every trial.

Lord, this dad is on a mission to care for his family, and he knows he'll never be relieved from his call. He is uniquely positioned to carry his family down this road because You have prepared him for it. Strengthen his resolve as usual. In Jesus's name we pray. Amen.

He changes the times and seasons; He removes kings and establishes kings. He gives wisdom to the wise and knowledge to those who have understanding. (Dan. 2:21 HCSB)

TONIGHT I'M PRAYING THIS FOR _____

22

TONIGHT we pray for the dad who has courage and is always looking for higher ground. He's worked hard all his life. He asks for no special favors, but he believes in the favor of the Lord for those who love Him and trust Him.

As a dad, we're always ready to take on new challenges. We're prepared to get going the way we always do and to get to the top of every hill we encounter. We have dreams and ambitions, and when we get to the top of whatever mountain we're climbing, we long for more. We don't want to be afraid of a challenge. We know that God's character is one of power and might. And when we trust in the favor of the Lord, we can also raise our children to embrace their challenges, to strive, to achieve, to excel.

Lord, this dad has followed You for a long time and knows where You lead. He's ready for the steep climb if necessary, because he knows that You will make the path upward smooth and straight for tomorrow's journey. In Jesus's name we pray. Amen.

The LORD God is my strength [my source of courage . . .]; He has made my feet [steady and sure] . . . and makes me walk [forward with spiritual confidence] on my high places [of challenge and responsibility]. (Hab. 3:19 AMP)

TONIGHT I'M PRAYING THIS FOR _____

TONIGHT we pray for the dad who understands that his family needs him. He doesn't often speak of it, but meeting those needs is his life's work.

Our "life's work" requires a life that is healthy. But God does not require hard work for us to be accepted or loved. He values us for our own sake, no matter how much we sacrifice our life for others. It is easy to believe that we are alone in our endeavors, rather than trusting God to help us bring about the peace and prosperity our family needs. And if we're not careful, every need becomes our call, every single success and happiness of our children becomes our sole responsibility. God alone is God. Only He can supply all our needs. Without Him, we have nothing and we can provide nothing.

Lord, this dad knows that he cannot do everything by himself. Remind him of Your plan for his family, and grant him a good night's sleep because he has given everything. In Jesus's name we pray. Amen.

I will both lay me down in peace, and sleep: for thou, LORD, only makest me dwell in safety. (Ps. 4:8 KJV)

TONIGHT I'M PRAYING THIS FOR _____

TONIGHT we pray for the dad who starts each day with prayer. Jesus is his role model for keeping a balanced schedule. This dad submits his plans to God daily from the very beginning. He is grateful for what he has and how God strengthens him for his responsibilities. He knows that his family is counting on him, and he looks forward to the challenges.

Instead of asking God to bless our plans, let's ask God what He wants us to do. Only then can we know that our goals are worth pursuing. Conversing with God and getting our goals from Him require patience, but it is always worth it. When we start our plans with God, we are better able to count the cost, and we can expect to be a winner at the day's end because of how the day began.

Lord, this dad takes advantage of every opportunity You give him. Prepare him for another victory tomorrow. In Jesus's name we pray. Amen.

Don't worry about anything; instead, pray about everything. Tell God what you need, and thank him for all he has done. Then you will experience God's peace, which exceeds anything we can understand. (Phil. 4:6–7 NLT)

TONIGHT I'M PRAYING THIS FOR _____

TONIGHT we pray for the dad who takes care of his family. He looks out for his family even if they don't notice every day.

There are days we may feel discouraged. We might be faithful and flexible and still wind up without appreciation. But we can hold firm to the knowledge that whether we hear what a good dad we are or not, our goal doesn't change. We still do the hard work of raising a family that needs us. So in those days, weeks, and perhaps months when our children don't see or appreciate our sacrifice, when other family members disregard us, we know that God chose us to lead, guide, and direct our particular family. Think about it! He has big plans to use us to accomplish great things. If God chose us and He chose the family, we can certainly trust in His wisdom.

Lord, stand with this dad so that he has Your strength in the tough times. Clear away thoughts and feelings of discouragement. Help him to see and know daily what he needs to be doing, even while he is accomplishing all his responsibilities. In Jesus's name we pray. Amen.

I know the thoughts that I think toward you, saith the LORD, thoughts of peace, and not of evil, to give you an expected end. (Jer. 29:11 KJV)

TONIGHT I'M PRAYING THIS FOR _____

TONIGHT we pray for the dad who is working through some difficulties. Maybe he has to work two jobs to provide for his family. Maybe the stresses of a stepfamily are affecting the relationships in the home. Maybe an illness has kept a child in the hospital. Things are far from perfect.

Whatever the circumstances, good or bad, we can stay standing. We can still put one foot in front of the other because God has chosen us for these very qualities of our character. The Lord knows that our best stuff comes from the greatest challenges. He has chosen us to be the best dad to fulfill His call, and He strengthens us when conditions seem overwhelming and we're not sure we can go forward as we have before.

> *Lord, it seems that there is so much more to do. Sometimes it seems as though this dad is the only one who can get the job done. Show him what greatness awaits him when he gets to the other side of these difficult times. In Jesus's name we pray. Amen.*

The righteous man who walks in integrity and lives life in accord with his [godly] beliefs—how blessed [happy and spiritually secure] are his children after him [who have his example to follow]. (Prov. 20:7 AMP)

TONIGHT I'M PRAYING THIS FOR _____

TONIGHT we pray for the dad who puts his family first. He always focuses on his responsibilities to them. He makes sure that their needs are met financially, spiritually, and emotionally.

Although it is not often spoken of, being a dad is hard work. Sometimes it can be difficult to provide for our family's physical needs. But our role is to make sure they have all the basic necessities such as a place to live and food to eat. We also know we must look to the future and create a safety plan for all the just-in-case scenarios of life. To be ready for the extra medical bill when someone falls off their bicycle or catches the latest virus at daycare. To be ready when the car breaks down or simply needs a tune-up. We must lead and be an example of what it takes through hard work and planning so our children can follow in our footsteps. Today and tomorrow, we are capable of the challenge.

> *Lord, give this dad peace in his heart so that he will be an even better dad tomorrow. In Jesus's name we pray. Amen.*

The very God of peace sanctify you wholly; and I pray God your whole spirit and soul and body be preserved blameless unto the coming of our Lord Jesus Christ. (1 Thess. 5:23 KJV)

TONIGHT I'M PRAYING THIS FOR _____

TONIGHT we pray for the dad who makes it his mission to know what his family needs. He sees and hears what is required.

Our family's needs might consist of day-to-day problems—nothing new, different, or exciting. But those needs are important to them. They can't be minimized or ignored. Sometimes our family needs our physical strength and abilities. Sometimes they need our presence and encouragement. But whatever they need, we are designed to provide for and protect our family. As a dad, we have an opportunity to make a lasting difference in our children's lives. The more we achieve as a dad, the more successful we'll feel. The more we prepare, the better the outcome. God is all about progress for all His children and certainly for our family.

Lord, bless this dad who gives it all up for his family. He needs You to prepare his heart and mind, even as he has prepared for tomorrow. Remind him there will always be enough for him and for his family as well. In Jesus's name we pray. Amen.

All the ways of a man are pure in his own eyes, but the Lord weighs the spirit. Commit your work to the Lord, and your plans will be established. (Prov. 16:2–3)

TONIGHT I'M PRAYING THIS FOR _____

TONIGHT we pray for the dad who protects his family. When he comes home from work, he is able to have peace, even though sometimes his day is filled with stress.

There will always be stress at our job because it is the nature of our work, which emphasizes hustle. There will be disagreements at work that could, if we let them, carry over into the time we spend with our family in the evenings. Instead, we learn to leave those at the door when we head home and focus on the love and peace that come from knowing the Lord. Yes, challenges come, but we can stand strong and take the familiar path toward peace.

Lord, this dad is becoming a true hero, and Your strength keeps him going every day. He does not doubt or panic, and he knows that with You, he is going to come out on top at the end of the day. In the face of every obstacle, he plans to prevail. Remind him that he is never alone. In Jesus's name we pray. Amen.

These things I have spoken unto you, that in me ye might have peace. (John 16:33 KJV)

TONIGHT I'M PRAYING THIS FOR _____

TONIGHT we pray for the dad who is working to become a better dad. He works hard to overcome his circumstances, and he has overcome a few setbacks. But every day, his character shows through any difficulties that arise. His family knows him for who he is and not just for what he does.

As a dad, we keep going. Not because of duty or obligation, even though those attitudes creep into our soul sometimes, but because we love our children. The seasons of our life are affected by so many responsibilities that we take on willingly out of our love for our kids. And those duties usually take more time than we have. No matter what we think we might accomplish, time is the enemy of what we have planned. In those seasons, when supper is leftover pizza or cereal and milk because we just couldn't bring home dinner on time, we love our kids that much fiercer, knowing that if we put one foot in front of the other, we will get to where we need to be for them. It's easy to think that what dads do is not particularly special. After all, dads work hard, right? But right this very minute, we are giving up our life, all the things we might want or need, for those we love.

Lord, bless this dad for his perseverance. Remind him of who he really is in You and what he can accomplish with You. Give him peace in knowing that he has been successful as he prepares for tomorrow. In Jesus's name we pray. Amen.

Let all that you do be done in love. (1 Cor. 16:14)

TONIGHT I'M PRAYING THIS FOR _____

TONIGHT we pray for the dad who is grateful. When this dad considers all his blessings, he cannot help but express what he feels. He is grateful for a stressful job because it's preferable to the unemployment line. He spruces up his modest home to give glory to the Lord because it is more spacious than a pup tent. He praises his children publicly because they are an answer to prayer that some families have yet to receive.

When we speak of gratitude, we should do so in every way, every day. When we express our love to the Lord for what He has given us, we acknowledge it out of an abundant heart. Our hearts are abundant because they are so full of excitement, joy, and peace that we literally *must* speak how we feel.

Lord, Your goodness overflows to this dad and his family. Remind them that You watch over them and keep them safe. In Jesus's name we pray. Amen.

Be filled by the Spirit: speaking to one another . . . from your heart to the Lord, giving thanks always for everything to God the Father in the name of our Lord Jesus Christ. (Eph. 5:18–20 HCSB)

TONIGHT I'M PRAYING THIS FOR _____

TONIGHT we pray for the dad who keeps first things first. His children and his family come first every day in every way.

Our heavenly Father is not just *a* father, as a parent is to a child. He *is* Father. And because He is Father, He understands our relational role to our children as well and wants us to take this role seriously. As a dad, we have no greater place than this. Once a father, always a father. But we also have a transactional role as a parent, which we must know that God instilled in us. Just like our heavenly Father, we spend time with our children so we can know what they know. We listen to their hearts, and we hear their words. We're not particularly concerned about how others might feel about how we do our job. Our job is to raise our children in the way that God requires and allows.

Lord, this dad often wonders if he's doing it right. Strengthen his heart to remember Your promises for his life. In Jesus's name we pray. Amen.

I will teach all your children, and they will enjoy great peace. (Isa. 54:13 NLT)

TONIGHT I'M PRAYING THIS FOR _____

33

TONIGHT we pray for the dad who remembers that he's the dad in the family. He coaches, but he's not the coach. He makes decisions, but he's not the CEO. This dad doesn't simply solve problems. He believes in his family, and he believes in his ability and his capacity as a dad to address the needs of each child every day.

In addition to their physical needs like provision and protection, our children have needs that we have a responsibility to meet. We must listen to know those needs. As in all things, we need to take the lead in providing comfort and peace not just in the midst of family storms, when headship seems appropriate, but even in relative peace and tranquility. And when we can't provide and protect, we trust the Lord will step in. Our family is a gift to be cherished and nurtured and cared for, and the Lord looks after His creation. He put our family together, and He will bring them home to Himself.

Lord, this dad has an awesome responsibility to follow Your lead. Give him courage to fully step into his destiny. In Jesus's name we pray. Amen.

Let all bitterness and wrath and anger and clamor and slander be put away from you, along with all malice. Be kind to one another, tenderhearted, forgiving one another, as God in Christ forgave you. (Eph. 4:31–32)

TONIGHT I'M PRAYING THIS FOR _____

TONIGHT **we pray for the dad who gives his life away every day.** He gives up what he wants so his family can have what they need or want.

Taking care of business is important, both at home and away. But our family responsibilities aren't burdens; they are opportunities to work harder at being a good dad than we did the day before, even though we probably spend more than we earn on them, commit more time than we have, and lose more sleep worrying about the day-to-day problems than we can afford. In each instance, we're making a choice to sacrifice our lives in exchange for the true riches that come from our relationships and the development of our character.

Lord, this dad loves his family unconditionally. Nobody makes him do the things he does. He lives his life doing what he's been called to. Strengthen him as always for tomorrow's opportunities. In Jesus's name we pray. Amen.

Therefore I urge you, brothers and sisters, by the mercies of God, to present your bodies [dedicating all of yourselves, set apart] as a living sacrifice, holy and well-pleasing to God, which is your rational (logical, intelligent) act of worship. (Rom. 12:1 AMP)

TONIGHT I'M PRAYING THIS FOR _____

TONIGHT we pray for the dad who is single, with full responsibility for the children in his life. It hasn't always been this way. There was a significant other in his life who made being a parent so much easier, but now they're gone. He is not looking to alleviate his singleness right now but just to raise his children. And this dad feels so alone in his life and responsibilities.

It is important to remember that just as the Lord has a specific plan for our lives, He also has a plan for each of our children and He still expects us to raise them in a godly manner. Since we know that the Lord tells us to forgive one another as He has forgiven us, we can harbor absolutely no resentment toward the person or persons responsible for the separation that exists between this dad and the children's mother. We cannot raise our children to have a pure heart if our heart is impure.

> *Lord, this dad makes all the decisions for his children now. His skill sets must adapt for him to succeed. But he is ready, willing, and able to be his best for his kids. Prepare his heart for a new day tomorrow. In Jesus's name we pray. Amen.*

When they hurled their insults at him, he did not retaliate; when he suffered, he made no threats. Instead, he entrusted himself to him who judges justly. (1 Pet. 2:23 NIV)

TONIGHT I'M PRAYING THIS FOR _____

TONIGHT we pray for the dad who is struggling with a life change. A longtime employment may have ended and he's still unemployed. The fear that life has irrevocably changed and it's always going to be this way rushes into his soul and takes up residence. The desire to provide for and protect his family wrestles with that fear, and there is no peace. When he wakes up, that fear is there, and when he closes his eyes at night, it's there.

We must be honest and admit that joy is probably not the first response we have when we are suffering. The Lord understands how the severe storms of life can affect us the way they do. He weeps with us over our trials, and He casts no blame for the circumstances. We are safe in Him. And because we are safe, *we will get through this.*

Lord, when he begins to get his feet back under himself, when he truly sees You and the peace You provide and he's ready to move forward, show this dad exactly the right next step to take tomorrow. In Jesus's name we pray. Amen.

Forget all that—it is nothing compared to what I am going to do. For I am about to do something new. See, I have already begun! Do you not see it? I will make a pathway through the wilderness. I will create rivers in the dry wasteland. (Isa. 43:18–19 NLT)

TONIGHT I'M PRAYING THIS FOR _____

TONIGHT **we pray for the dad who remembers to dream big.** There've been some setbacks in these recent months, and life hasn't seemed fair. Honestly, he hasn't felt particularly close to God these days, but because he continues to trust Him, he watches and waits with full expectation that the Lord will fulfill His promises. He knows that if he and his family are going to succeed at life, if they are going to experience the types of blessings that God intends, he will have to walk a little bit closer to the Lord.

We all want to have a better understanding of the truth, don't we? And we all want to believe that God is always with us, despite our circumstances. So we are watching to see how our family is going to break through to the light with us at the helm. That's. What. Dads. Do. We watch and we're always ready to move with God.

Lord, this dad and this family have come so far. They've overcome so much. Keep leading them forward into the dreams of the future, following Your voice. In Jesus's name we pray. Amen.

This is the [remarkable degree of] confidence which we [as believers are entitled to] have before Him: that if we ask anything according to His will, [that is, consistent with His plan and purpose] He hears us. (1 John 5:14 AMP)

TONIGHT I'M PRAYING THIS FOR _____

38

TONIGHT we pray for the dad who doesn't let the past limit how he takes care of his family. The struggles of daily life have often caused him to doubt his own abilities.

Think about how our lives can be disrupted because of our past experiences. The challenges we are experiencing are greater because the past is still in the present. But we don't have to be a slave to yesterday, preoccupied with past rewards and accomplishments. We can just do what needs to be done with whatever we have right now. We can adjust our wants and needs to fit what God has in store for us. We know that we need to trust the Lord to really experience the success He has for us. Our true peace comes from accepting the Lord's provision in whatever form and in whatever manner He provides. God has our best interests at heart and has given us everything we need. He is changing us into a dad He can use. And because of that, we have no need to doubt our ability. When we realize what we have, we can fully focus on how our family can prosper, intimidated no longer!

Lord, this dad has no need to fear. Strengthen him even more for the daily trials that arise. In Jesus's name we pray. Amen.

Therefore if anyone is in Christ . . . , he is a new creature . . . ; the old things [the previous moral and spiritual condition] have passed away. Behold, new things have come [because spiritual awakening brings a new life]. (2 Cor. 5:17 AMP)

TONIGHT I'M PRAYING THIS FOR _____

TONIGHT we pray for the dad who lives a life bigger than just his family. He sees things that others don't always see. He's a giver. He knows that everything he has or ever will have comes from God. He imitates what God has done for him by making sure that others have enough. Everybody knows his name, and he's a hero to more than just a few.

Generosity is the very nature of our heavenly Father. When other families are hurting, we can make it a point to be involved when it is needed. We can mow the lawn of the elderly couple across the street. We can fix a car for the young family barely making ends meet. We can buy garage sale items even when we don't need or want anything, because our generosity strengthens relationships with our neighbors. When we are generous to others, God will be generous to us. When our family sees us being generous, they emulate us and know that they can count on God themselves.

Lord, this dad gets tired just like the other heroes he knows. Give him the good sleep of peace and accomplishment. In Jesus's name we pray. Amen.

"God loves a person who gives cheerfully." And God will generously provide all you need. Then you will always have everything you need and plenty left over to share with others. (2 Cor. 9:7–8 NLT)

TONIGHT I'M PRAYING THIS FOR _____

40

TONIGHT we pray for the dad who is making it through this life one day at a time. While he knows that he is doing his best to provide for others, he wonders if his life matters day by day.

We all know that discipline is required to run a cross-country race. Some high-endurance trials are run with the sole purpose of finishing. Sometimes the hardships involved are immense. There are few simple, easy, flat paths to traverse in these races. And in reality, most of our time is spent *walking* on the path that leads to our family's wholeness and prosperity. There often is very little running. Yet we feel as though we have had success because our family is healthy and safe thanks to the small steps and simple decisions we've made.

Lord, remind this dad that only those who have walked this path can understand what was endured and what was gained. Remind him that You have all the resources necessary to meet his family's needs with him at the helm. In Jesus's name we pray. Amen.

Wherefore seeing we also are compassed about with so great a cloud of witnesses, let us lay aside every weight . . . and let us run with patience the race that is set before us, looking unto Jesus the author and finisher of our faith. (Heb. 12:1–2 KJV)

TONIGHT I'M PRAYING THIS FOR _____

TONIGHT we pray for the dad who just feels alone. This dad is all about success, but it seems to come at a cost. The circumstances of his occupation can be exhausting in body and mind. His work feels solitary and he's struggling. He does not feel he has the support of his boss or his coworkers. This dad tries not to think about that because he believes he's too strong. He sometimes feels as though he is taking on the entire world by himself.

Success never really comes easy, even though we're confident that the Lord is on our side. When we start our day, before we even arrive at work, we expect to find the Lord already there. But sometimes He seemingly is nowhere to be found. The expectations and the responsibilities rush in so quickly that we just can't hear His voice. Talk about feeling truly alone. But God is still with us. He is working out His plan in His timing.

Lord, just before he goes to sleep tonight, tell this dad that You are still with him. Help him to be patient as he waits for Your calling to become even more clear. Remind him of his prayers from long ago that You are still answering, and that no matter what his struggles might have been today, better days are still ahead for tomorrow. In Jesus's name we pray. Amen.

Have I not commanded you? Be strong and courageous. Do not be frightened, and do not be dismayed, for the LORD your God is with you wherever you go. (Josh. 1:9)

TONIGHT I'M PRAYING THIS FOR _____

TONIGHT we pray for the dad who gets it done. He remembers that God is his source of joy and strength. Even when he doesn't see his prayers answered right away, this dad trusts that the Lord will be present with him. And as long as he keeps going, keeps moving forward with the Lord as his guide, he will lead his family well.

When we trust in God, we can experience flowing wells of peace and sanctification. As long as we focus on the promises of the Lord and declare His goodness, our family will also know God as the source of excellent things. Not that we remember this every day, of course. We sometimes allow the cares of the world, the distractions of worldly pleasures, and the false security of wealth to blind us to what we know—that He alone is God. The Lord alone sets a path to prosperity. His strength begets strength.

Lord, this dad walks with You and has a safe place to stand in times of trouble. Strengthen him to walk worthy, getting it done for You. In Jesus's name we pray. Amen.

If you abide in My word [continually obeying My teachings and living in accordance with them, then] you are truly My disciples. (John 8:31 AMP)

TONIGHT I'M PRAYING THIS FOR _____

TONIGHT we pray for the dad who saves lives every day. He is that dad who runs toward the fires, who helps those in danger, and who arrives first at an accident scene. He is the one who responds to a phone call at any time of night with a promise to "be right there."

We honor and respect those who run toward danger and keep entire communities safe. They walk the rough roads and have seen and experienced the crisis of living. Sometimes there is only one person who can protect someone from the dangers that arise without warning. Because one person helped first, we now have the inner fortitude to endure our own tests while looking out for those whose lives may be at risk. It is the character of a dad to love the one in trouble because that's what dads do.

Lord, protect the dad who often risks his own safety and security. Give him courage to do the hard things when comfort would be easier. In Jesus's name we pray. Amen.

We can rejoice, too, when we run into problems and trials, for we know that they help us develop endurance. And endurance develops strength of character, and character strengthens our confident hope of salvation. (Rom. 5:3–4 NLT)

TONIGHT I'M PRAYING THIS FOR _____

TONIGHT we pray for the dad who gives his all in everything he does. He gives himself totally to the heart of God. He gives his thoughts, words, and deeds and all his everyday affairs into the waiting arms of the Lord.

God desires more than just raw obedience, where we feel as though we must prove something to Him, or that He will punish us if we don't take just the right steps. No, the Lord is looking for the heart of a servant who wants only to make his master proud, to uplift and glorify the One he serves. God holds nothing back, and neither should we. He brings all of heaven's goodness into our life when we acknowledge who He is. God wants to reward those who seek Him. When we diligently and committedly live for the Lord, our actions reflect who He is and what we believe.

Lord, this dad has a heart for You, just as You keep him in Your heart. Strengthen him in all ways tonight as he prepares for tomorrow. In Jesus's name we pray. Amen.

Now without faith it is impossible to please God, for the one who draws near to Him must believe that He exists and rewards those who seek Him. (Heb. 11:6 HCSB)

TONIGHT I'M PRAYING THIS FOR _____

TONIGHT we pray for the dad who has had some bad news. It's heart-stopping, soul-crushing, "how will I breathe" news that he doesn't know how he'll share with anyone.

We've all had our share of news like that. Someone calls to let us know that there was an accident on Route 5, and wasn't that one of our cars at the scene? Or we've been out of town and we find out that a tornado hit close to our neighborhood. Truth be told, we're doers. We solve problems. And yet in these situations, there's absolutely no solving to be done. It's either in God's control or it's not. And we've learned in our wisdom that it's better to pray before we tackle the trial than after. We want to be prepared for every circumstance when those we love are involved because the information we've been given is never just all there is.

> *Lord, tonight this dad has not yet taken that breath to find the calm place in his life. He doesn't know what to do. He needs You really close right now. He needs that special mercy as he suffers in silence. Comfort him and remind him he is never truly alone in You. In Jesus's name we pray. Amen.*

The enemy has pursued my soul; he has crushed my life to the ground; he has made me sit in darkness like those long dead. (Ps. 143:3)

TONIGHT I'M PRAYING THIS FOR _____

TONIGHT **we pray for the dad who is trying to live his best life.** He's young enough and strong enough, and right now these are his best days. The days aren't perfect and there are some hardships, but everyone in the family is making it and looking out for each other. He's a dad who wants so much for his family.

Granted, youth and strength help keep us going. But at the end of the day, how we approach God's opportunities and promises will determine the good, better, and best aspects of our circumstances. It's a trust thing. Do we trust the Lord or don't we? As long as we can keep moving forward, with the Lord providing direction as He always does, we will prosper in all aspects of our lives. It starts with a healthy fear of the Lord and a willingness to acknowledge that God is God and there is no other.

Lord, this dad has a strong back to carry his family and the determination to lead them to the best life. Make his path straight as he keeps his eyes on You, looking forward to tomorrow. In Jesus's name we pray. Amen.

Those who trust in the Lord will renew their strength; they will soar on wings like eagles; they will run and not grow weary; they will walk and not faint. (Isa. 40:31 HCSB)

TONIGHT I'M PRAYING THIS FOR _____

TONIGHT we pray for the dad who sometimes feels he's still learning about praying, that it's just a conversation between God and His children. So when this dad prays, he prays hard. He knows that his family counts on him to meet the Lord on their behalf, to be their advocate, and he looks forward to this challenge as well.

In order to live in peace with God and to live in His presence daily, we absolutely must believe that He can answer any particular prayer. God wants to be important in our lives. And He can be, but we have to let Him. He's not going to override our choices, for good or ill. He wants to have a relationship with us even more than we want that. And He's willing to wait to hear our words to Him. More importantly, He wants to answer our prayers.

Lord, this dad loves his family, and he knows You do too. Keep him close and hear his prayers. In Jesus's name we pray. Amen.

Keep on asking, and you will receive what you ask for. Keep on seeking, and you will find. Keep on knocking, and the door will be opened to you. For everyone who asks, receives. Everyone who seeks, finds. And to everyone who knocks, the door will be opened. (Matt. 7:7–8 NLT)

TONIGHT I'M PRAYING THIS FOR _____

TONIGHT we pray for the dad who tries to do it all right. He tries to think right, feel right, eat right, spend right, and speak right. The world places heavy responsibilities on him to be all he can be. You know, perfect—that wonderful prison of perfection. Yet at the same time, the world tells him that he can be and do exactly what he wants as long as the kids turn out all right.

We don't have to try so hard; we can be slightly less than perfect, right? At the end of the day, our choice comes down to whether we're in this for ourselves—for what is easier—or whether we're in this for what we can be. The Lord wants us to look for the better, not the perfect. We have children looking up to us to be the guy they can count on and believe in, to set the example for their lives. Only God knows perfectly what is best for us and our happiness. He wants us to be the best dad to *our* children. And just knowing how to do the right things is a good place to start.

Lord, this dad is ready for every challenge, and he's determined to succeed. Strengthen his heart as always. In Jesus's name we pray. Amen.

God has chosen you for salvation through sanctification by the Spirit and through belief in the truth . . . so that you might obtain the glory of our Lord Jesus Christ. (2 Thess. 2:13–14 HCSB)

TONIGHT I'M PRAYING THIS FOR _____

TONIGHT we pray for the dad who has children who are not his flesh and blood. While fathers may face loyalty issues from different children, this dad knows he must show love, trust, and mutual respect for them to thrive.

We sometimes enter godly relationships where children from another relationship are involved. Taking on the responsibility of raising children who have been fathered by someone else creates an even greater obligation to live a Christlike life. Children raised in different families, with different fathers, need us to be a godly influence to center their lives on.

Lord, this dad wants to show his children what it means to provide for and protect them and raise them in a godly environment, where they will relish Your love, mercy, and goodness. Help him remain diligent to provide that. He loves his new family. It is another chance to be the dad You have designed him to be. His children are a sacred trust that he is investing his life in. Help him see the importance and value of all his children, no matter where they are. In Jesus's name we pray. Amen.

If anyone does not provide for his relatives, and especially for members of his household, he has denied the faith and is worse than an unbeliever. (1 Tim. 5:8)

TONIGHT I'M PRAYING THIS FOR _____

TONIGHT we pray for the dad who is what he chooses to become. He does what he has been called to do. He's faithful despite the hardships and setbacks in stressful times. This dad does his best, and through his choices he is becoming more like the Lord every day.

We are all a product of our choices. The life we live today is based upon the decisions we made yesterday. And truth be told, our happiness is based upon those decisions. Our desire is to become a picture of who the Lord would have us to be. Each choice, each decision we make can help us to look a little more like the Lord. If we want to come close to the Lord, to be more like Him, to "do" more like Him, we must decide that the choices we make are not going to be bound by worldly authorities.

Lord, this dad has plans for tomorrow. Give him peace as he sleeps tonight. In Jesus's name we pray. Amen.

Therefore, whether you eat or drink, or whatever you do, do everything for God's glory. (1 Cor. 10:31 HCSB)

TONIGHT I'M PRAYING THIS FOR _____

TONIGHT we pray for the dad who has recently experienced changes in his family circumstances.

Although it is part of our nature to resist change, it happens. We tend to shy away from the hard things until we are sure we can succeed at them. Some of us feel as though we can succeed best and accomplish more by only doing the things we are good at. Wash, rinse, and repeat. But when we're committed to becoming an even better dad, we see more clearly that changes are often God's corrections, and the Lord is to be trusted in all things. The hardest changes are those that alter our thoughts, beliefs, and feelings. We've had them for most of our lives. The things we believe we truly know are heart and soul aspects of our lives. God must touch our heart deeply to make those changes—which also always work for our whole family's good.

Lord, bless this dad's dedication to his family. Reward his trust in You. In Jesus's name we pray. Amen.

Do not be conformed to this world, but be transformed by the renewal of your mind, that by testing you may discern what is the will of God, what is good and acceptable and perfect. (Rom. 12:2)

TONIGHT I'M PRAYING THIS FOR _____

TONIGHT we pray for the dad who wants to make a difference. He knows that his hard work keeps his family going. He also knows that his family looks to him for guidance in the hard decisions.

To truly make a difference, we have to understand that such difference-making power comes from God. Our power, authority, and peace come from our constant reliance on God. Knowing and experiencing God's presence changes us to become the better dad we know we can be. Just as God shows His love and compassion for all His children, so also do we when we make our children a priority in our life. By carrying the hopes and fears and plans and struggles and successes of our children, we show them that we care and are not merely present at home.

Lord, help this dad be a difference-maker. Remind him how he once wanted to be one and still wants to be. In Jesus's name we pray. Amen.

The LORD your God is in your midst, a mighty one who will save; he will rejoice over you with gladness; he will quiet you by his love; he will exult over you with loud singing. (Zeph. 3:17)

TONIGHT I'M PRAYING THIS FOR _____

TONIGHT we pray for the dad who lives life to the full. He knows that everything, everything, everything he has came from the hand of God. Although he was down at times, he didn't stay down. There is no quit to this dad. Everyone knows him for his courage and his determination because he believes that God has ordained and established his success.

Success in life is measured to a great extent by how grateful we are with what we have received from God. The biblical story of Job, with all his wealth and power, reflects how he always acknowledged the provision of God and only God. Likewise, we know that God is the Provider, so we can be dedicated to our family and generous to our friends and neighbors. And we will continue to succeed in every endeavor because we extend our hands toward others with the love of God.

Lord, bless and keep this dad. You have picked him up and he has experienced Your grace. Smile upon him so he may know that the Spirit will help him through any and all of his struggles. In Jesus's name we pray. Amen.

In everything you were [exceedingly] enriched in Him, in all speech [empowered by the spiritual gifts] and in all knowledge [with insight into the faith]. (1 Cor. 1:5 AMP)

TONIGHT I'M PRAYING THIS FOR _____

TONIGHT we pray for the dad who thinks about being a better dad. He's got a good job, he works hard, he makes it home from the road as often as possible, and he loves his family. But sometimes he thinks he ought to do even more. It's easy to think that maybe if he had more faith, more confidence, if he trusted the Lord just a little bit more, everything would fall into place. And pretty soon, in his heart, he's not the hero anymore and he sure can't conquer the world alone.

Sometimes God allows us to experience adversity so we can overcome the trials with His help. He wants us to come to Him so that He can show us He was there all along. With His help, we can take hold of our responsibilities with courage and assurance that we will succeed tomorrow.

Lord, bless this dad who worries. Remind him that You know all his strengths and weaknesses and You can still use him to lead his family. In Jesus's name we pray. Amen.

I know that you can do anything, and no one can stop you. . . . I had only heard about you before, but now I have seen you with my own eyes. I take back everything I said. (Job 42:2, 5–6 NLT)

TONIGHT I'M PRAYING THIS FOR _____

TONIGHT we pray for the dad who loves his life. He's learning a lot about himself, and he's discovered he's a pretty good dad. He's a dad who believes he's living in the open hand of God. He has overcome some adversity, and he deals with changes as they arise. He has done the hard work and made the hard decisions so his family could have opportunities.

The adversity and the changes that we experience can serve as reminders that God intends for us to live with joy. But we don't have joy just because we have overcome adversity or because we have worked hard. Our joy comes from the knowledge that we are going to succeed. Prosperity is around every corner, even if we can't see it immediately. The Lord would have us know that we live in the open hand of God, depending on Him for everything, and that we should want to and expect to be prosperous. It's not so much that we *will* live that way, but that we *can* when we trust Him. Our confidence, our faith in God and His goodness, can grow every day.

> *Lord, this dad still counts on You for all his continued blessings. Remind him that You walk with him daily. In Jesus's name we pray. Amen.*

> You make known to me the path of life; in your presence there is fullness of joy; at your right hand are pleasures forevermore. (Ps. 16:11)

TONIGHT I'M PRAYING THIS FOR _____

TONIGHT we pray for the dad who has confidence in his ability to lead his family. He is hoping to achieve the goals and dreams he's had for so long. He also believes he has become a better dad because of the family the Lord gave him. He knows he has not accomplished what he has in his own strength, because God is on his side. And it's not that he hasn't made a mistake or two. He just keeps going on the path God has set out for him. As he dedicates his life to bringing prosperity to his family, he thanks God for all His blessings.

Confidence is knowing we are fully equipped to accomplish what we've been called to. It is knowing we have faced enough circumstances of lack and of plenty that we see the difference and can walk peacefully between them. It is knowing God wants us to be bold in our actions and that we are capable of rising to the level of success.

Lord, this dad is grateful, and he keeps moving toward Your promises. Keep him safe so he can protect and provide for his family. In Jesus's name we pray. Amen.

The work of righteousness shall be peace; and the effect of righteousness quietness and assurance for ever. (Isa. 32:17 KJV)

TONIGHT I'M PRAYING THIS FOR _____

TONIGHT **we pray for the dad who has done just about all he can do today.** If one more person says, "It'll only take this much longer" or "It'll only cost a little bit more," his front porch light may get turned off and the welcome mat will be turned over.

We want to please the Lord, but often the list of "do this" and "be that" from others has gotten way too long. We feel resentful sometimes when we've given every single thing we have in terms of time and money. But in those moments, we must resolve to put aside our creature comforts and follow the Holy Spirit, who truly resides in our heart.

Lord, this hardworking dad is generous beyond belief. He knows that others have needs, and he does care. There is a balancing act for him as he provides his energies for his family as well. Grant this dad a moment with his family before he rests tonight so he can be charged up for Your service to others tomorrow. In Jesus's name we pray. Amen.

Give, and it will be given to you. Good measure, pressed down, shaken together, running over, will be put into your lap. For with the measure you use it will be measured back to you. (Luke 6:38)

TONIGHT I'M PRAYING THIS FOR _____

TONIGHT we pray for the dad who does his job. It might not be a spectacular job, but he earns his pay every day. He takes the challenges as they come. Likewise, being a dad has its own challenges every day. He doesn't get paid except in hugs and respect and gratitude, and that makes his life about endurance. Throughout his life, the hard and the easy, he has trusted the Lord to help him across the finish line. Even now he is leaning on God for strength to accomplish all his responsibilities in all his circumstances.

A dad who endures is a dad with a strong faith in God and a strong heart for God. A dad who endures exalts the Lord in all he says and does. We do what we do for those we love because it's in our job description. Not because it's expected of us but because we feel the Lord's pleasure in our dedication. At the end of the day, there is a certain reward for the good and faithful dad who rests in his relationship with God.

> *Lord, being a dad requires hard work and even greater dedication. Give him daily confidence and assurance that he can keep doing what You've called him to do. In Jesus's name we pray. Amen.*

> Faith shows the reality of what we hope for; it is the evidence of things we cannot see. Through their faith, the people in days of old earned a good reputation. (Heb. 11:1–2 NLT)

TONIGHT I'M PRAYING THIS FOR _____

TONIGHT we pray for the dad who is separated from his family by a divorce that was not of his choosing. Not only does this affect his day-to-day activities, but it feels like an emotional separation from the rest of his family. He cares deeply for his children, and it breaks his heart when he is not with them.

No matter what the circumstances were leading up to the separation, the world would have us believe there was always something else we could have done to prevent it. We are not bad people just because someone does not love us anymore. Certainly God designed marriage to last a lifetime. Wedding vows include "till death do us part." Despite all this, divorce happens, and in its wake is profound loneliness. This is when we must remember to guard our heart. We know that God will never leave us nor forsake us, and now He wants each of us to prove Him and experience His faithfulness and love.

Lord, You have experienced separation Yourself, and You weep over divorce and separation from family. Bring this dad through this difficult season. In Jesus's name we pray. Amen.

You, O Lord, reign forever; your throne endures to all generations. . . . Restore us to yourself, O Lord, that we may be restored! Renew our days as of old. (Lam. 5:19, 21)

TONIGHT I'M PRAYING THIS FOR _____

TONIGHT we pray for the dad who believes that tomorrow will be better. He wants to live to honor God as well as to influence those around him. That's what makes tomorrow better. Most importantly, he doesn't just resolve to do something or think good thoughts or wish for good luck. He plans. This dad knows that life is too short to just let it happen, because circumstances will rise up and derail his best intentions.

We all remember past moments and incorporate them into our future plans. We remember times when we were successful and knew we were going to make it, and we make plans for success again. And we want to lead our family's conversations so they can have a better tomorrow. We're the ones who speak and act in faith, hope, and love at all times. We're the ones who set the example for our family to follow.

Lord, this dad always wants to take his family to higher places. Bless his mind, his heart, and his strength. In Jesus's name we pray. Amen.

The one who wants to love life and to see good days must keep his tongue from evil . . . and do what is good. He must seek peace and pursue it. (1 Pet. 3:10–11 HCSB)

TONIGHT I'M PRAYING THIS FOR _____

TONIGHT we pray for the dad who has lost a child. The loss of this child disrupts his own spiritual well-being, and it often requires supernatural faith to feel our heavenly Father's presence.

When a mother experiences the loss of a child, God is with her. When a father experiences the loss of a child, God is with him as well. The tragedy of miscarriage and stillbirth is far too common, and the pain that we feel as a father, while different from the mother's, prevents us from being the strength that our partner needs to recover from the loss. The restoration needed to endure this type of suffering must come from the heavenly realm, where hope is present. Just as God knows each of us and the baby before he or she was formed in the womb, He prepared a way for us to get through the possibility of a tragedy such as this.

> *Lord, You lost a Son, and You are not far off from this dad's suffering. Strengthen him as he tries to grieve with faith in You. In Jesus's name we pray. Amen.*

> In the same way, it is not my heavenly Father's will that even one of these little ones should perish. (Matt. 18:14 NLT)

TONIGHT I'M PRAYING THIS FOR _____

TONIGHT we pray for the dad who is mentally and emotionally exhausted. Things are just not as they should be. He has been faithful to pray and plan and prepare and provide all the things his family needs. He is doing all he can, and yet he doesn't see a lot of good news coming to his address. It seems like the world has figured out a way to kick him while he's down.

God does not change. He is for us, and He is always listening for our prayers. We must trust that what was true when we prayed and planned is still true. Even when what we are experiencing right now doesn't make sense, we can keep trusting God for ourselves and our family. We believe that God has given us a family to protect, and we will fulfill that role.

Lord, provision and peace are in Your hands. Give this dad rest in his preparations and confidence that he will be successful tomorrow no matter what unfolds. In Jesus's name we pray. Amen.

I am leaving you with a gift—peace of mind and heart. And the peace I give is a gift the world cannot give. So don't be troubled or afraid. (John 14:27 NLT)

TONIGHT I'M PRAYING THIS FOR _____

TONIGHT we pray for the dad who worries that he's not doing enough as a dad.

When we don't feel like we're enough, we immediately start working harder to prove that we are. Soon we are confronted with our own shortcomings, and we start a never-ending cycle of trying to prove to the Lord that we can be who He has called us to be. These thoughts of insufficiency are deadly. We forget that He is the One who has called us and He knew who He was calling. He's already on our side, waiting to hear from us about what we need.

> *Lord, this dad works an awful lot of hours, and it doesn't seem like he's home very much. He wants to be a fun dad, but work, chores, and providing for the family keep him busy most of the time. Remind this dad that his most important role for his family is as a provider. Help him to know that he's doing all he can. Remind him that in You he will find his sufficiency. In Jesus's name we pray. Amen.*

Not that we are sufficiently qualified in ourselves to claim anything as coming from us, but our sufficiency and qualifications come from God. (2 Cor. 3:5 AMP)

TONIGHT I'M PRAYING THIS FOR _____

TONIGHT **we pray for the dad who is trying to keep his family safe.** He feels like just a regular dad in a regular job, trying to make the very best of these difficult economic times. He's seen other families struggle, and he's been blessed not to have to experience struggles so close to home until now. He's trying to keep the lid on the outflow of finances for as long as he can.

When finances are tight, we can get a little worried—that our children may ultimately have to understand the difficulties the family is facing, that a financial turnaround might not happen soon. But when our lives changed unexpectedly in the past, God was faithful to help us weather the storm—and our children saw His goodness as well. If we stay faithful, we can be ready for even the deepest challenges.

Lord, this dad needs a great God to do great things. Help him to see the good things You're doing and have already done for him. Always remind him that You will be with him tomorrow as well. Help him and his family as they weather this storm. In Jesus's name we pray. Amen.

As a father has compassion on his children, so the LORD has compassion on those who fear Him. (Ps. 103:13 HCSB)

TONIGHT I'M PRAYING THIS FOR _____

TONIGHT **we pray for the dad who is desperate.** The last dollar is in the bank, and there are way too many days left before payday. Or maybe he's taken the last of his medication and the doctor holds out little hope. *Desperate.*

There are times we can be so overwhelmed that we have absolutely no idea which way to turn or what to do. We've done all the things we've always done in the past, and they didn't work this time. All we can do is pray and rely solely, wholly, and completely on the goodness of God.

> *Lord, this dad just needs a shot at success. He's gone through days like this before, but they're still so, so hard. He knows You're there, but sometimes it seems so quiet. He knows You never slumber or sleep and You always answer the prayers of Your children. Break through to this dad who feels like his prayers always stop at the ceiling. Send a miracle for a desperate dad tonight. In Jesus's name we pray. Amen.*

As for me, I trust [confidently] in You and Your greatness, O Lord; I said, "You are my God." My times are in Your hands; rescue me from the hand of my enemies and from those who pursue and persecute me. (Ps. 31:14–15 AMP)

TONIGHT I'M PRAYING THIS FOR _____

TONIGHT we pray for the dad who has stresses in his life. Stresses like "How much will my paycheck be this week?" or "How long must I be gone?" or "How long will it take to get that done?"

Stresses come when life circumstances change abruptly. When everything was peaceful and calm, we could rest in the knowledge that things were moving along as they should. But now that they are not, we want to be able to reassure our children, because children always ask the questions we are asking ourselves anyway. We want to have answers at the ready, to tell them they have nothing to fear because their dad has nothing to fear. We want to be the dad who knows what to do and how to make it happen. Sometimes it may feel as though the world is chasing us down a blind path, but we still must shoulder our responsibility to plot a true course for our family. And when we cry out to God for answers and help in times of stress, we will once again experience the goodness of God.

Lord, this dad trusts Your promises, but he still needs Your wisdom to see the best outcome. Give him the courage to implement Your vision. In Jesus's name we pray. Amen.

I waited patiently and expectantly for the LORD; and He inclined to me and heard my cry. (Ps. 40:1 AMP)

TONIGHT I'M PRAYING THIS FOR _____

TONIGHT we pray for the dad who believes that words matter. He's a man of uncommon respect, and people listen to him. He's a man who uses his words to move mountains. His family trusts him to say and do the right things, even if they are hard.

We know words have creative power. We remember that God created the heavens and the earth by the simple act of speaking them into existence. So we have to be careful to support and encourage and promote the actions our family is taking. Their hopes and dreams, not to mention their simple happiness, can be fulfilled or shaken by our conversation.

Lord, this dad has to strike the perfect balance between hope and discouragement. Watch over his words and give them the power they deserve. Give this dad a good night's rest so he can see tomorrow as You do—a perfect opportunity for something wonderful. In Jesus's name we pray. Amen.

Do not let unwholesome [foul, profane, worthless, vulgar] words ever come out of your mouth, but only such speech as is good for building up others, according to the need and the occasion, so that it will be a blessing to those who hear [you speak]. (Eph. 4:29 AMP)

TONIGHT I'M PRAYING THIS FOR _____

TONIGHT **we pray for the dad who knows that the Lord loves His children.** He knows God has a plan for his life and for his children's lives. He works hard because he knows that's where his opportunities come from. He wants his children to have even more opportunities than he had. He's willing to do all the difficult things because that's what dads do. Yet he knows that God's love is even greater than his own.

As God's children, we do what we do in our own strength, but God, who is greater, is able to do more than we ask or think. He is God and there is no other, and His joy restores complete wholeness to us with grace and mercy. Never forget that power to achieve comes from Him, and we have been created to excel. When we look to and understand the power He has and how He wants to bestow it to us, we can expect that the roads we walk will be smoother and straighter than they might be without His guidance.

Lord, make this dad's road a little easier tomorrow. In Jesus's name we pray. Amen.

Beware lest you say in your heart, "My power and the might of my hand have gotten me this wealth." You shall remember the LORD your God, for it is he who gives you power to get wealth. (Deut. 8:17–18)

TONIGHT I'M PRAYING THIS FOR _____

TONIGHT **we pray for the dad who has to be ready for a new challenge.** Perhaps it is a situation so all-encompassing to his family that their whole way of life is under assault. He's accustomed to living within his means. He is used to the daily trials. He also does okay in a crisis. But tonight this dad is facing an emergency that changes everything. So many plans on hold, so many expectations postponed or, worse, unfulfilled. And he's not sure he's up to it.

Here's where we must see ourselves differently. We must see ourselves the way God sees us. Each of us is more than just a dad who gets things done. God sees all those times we took care of business. No matter what the circumstances are right now, because of who we are in God, He knows that we are more than capable of not just managing the challenges but rising up to heavenly heights of success.

Lord, this dad has no one to turn to but You. He's ready like never before to believe in Your goodness and to trust in Your promises. Give him the strength to lead in hope so his family can have peace. In Jesus's name we pray. Amen.

Though a mighty army surrounds me, my heart will not be afraid. (Ps. 27:3 NLT)

TONIGHT I'M PRAYING THIS FOR _____

TONIGHT we pray for the dad who is carrying the burden for his family's well-being.

We cause ourselves all sorts of grief when we begin to rely on our own singular importance, when we believe that we are alone in our efforts to keep our family afloat. The moment we start relying only on ourselves is the moment we step out of God's kingdom of light and into a kingdom of darkness. The enemy of our soul would like nothing better than to separate us from the love of God and for us to believe that we are alone in the world. We have to keep our mind and our heart in tune with the Lord at all times.

Lord, this dad knows that his job is hard and that life is not always fair. He works to keep the lights on and makes sure everyone is safe, and he doesn't rest until the troubles are gone. Remind him tonight that no matter how hard he works, whether he believes it or not, You watch with him at night and walk with him in the day to give him peace. In Jesus's name we pray. Amen.

If you warn righteous people not to sin and they listen to you and do not sin, they will live, and you will have saved yourself, too. (Ezek. 3:21 NLT)

TONIGHT I'M PRAYING THIS FOR _____

TONIGHT **we pray for the dad who puts his life on the line.** To him, a crisis is a way of life and an emergency is a daily event. He is truly strong and of good courage. Yet, unlike fear, courage does not come naturally. This dad must believe in the rightness of his actions in spite of the threats to his own well-being. This courageous dad has been trained to put his own fears aside and to act in faith immediately.

What is that faith, exactly? The belief that our actions are God-inspired. EMTs, law enforcement, firefighters, and those who transport the gravely injured know about the importance of immediacy in their actions, that time is precious. They also deal with the hard truth that sometimes it's too late. For dads who struggle in the midst of disaster, disease, and often death, there must be angels who comfort and protect them as they try to restore life from tragedy.

Lord, there is no greater gift than sacrificing a life for a friend. Whenever tonight's shift ends, bring the peace that only You can provide and the assurance that this dad did his best. In Jesus's name we pray. Amen.

No one has greater love [nor stronger commitment] than to lay down his own life for his friends. (John 15:13 AMP)

TONIGHT I'M PRAYING THIS FOR _____

TONIGHT we pray for the dad who solves problems one at a time. There's just too much to tackle all at once. This is a strong dad, and with the Lord's help, he will overcome everything that has caused him to stumble.

There are many problems in life, but we have probably dealt with circumstances similar to what we're going through right now and we managed. We overcame them. Clearly, the Lord is with us right now, in this very moment that we are sharing this prayer with Him. He knows every need we have, and we can trust Him to meet those needs. He sees the secrets of every heart, and there is nothing we cannot ask Him, nothing we can bring to the throne of grace that He will not answer. He searches minds and hearts, and He gives to each one according to their own heart, their own plans, their own deeds. God has been and continues to be the One who picks us up and prepares us for the next steps on our path.

Lord, strengthen this dad as he seeks answers to each problem, one at a time. In Jesus's name we pray. Amen.

Seek first the kingdom of God and His righteousness, and all these things will be provided for you. (Matt. 6:33 HCSB)

TONIGHT I'M PRAYING THIS FOR _____

TONIGHT we pray for the dad who doesn't let fear rule his life.

So many thoughts of fear try to enter our hearts each day. Some enter through the words of others, and some we have when we are alone. Maybe we've been given only months to live and we're still battling the disease. Sudden downturns in the economy might cause our business to tank. Or maybe tonight's family argument escalated to separation or divorce. But we do not need to fear. Both our confidence and prudence come from God. We can invest in our health so we will be able to provide for our family as long as we can. We can invest in our business by making prayerful adjustments to our finances. We can invest in our marriage because it affects our entire family. When we rely on the Lord to keep us and our family safe, we can be confident in our plans and have peace in our life.

Lord, You know this dad's name and every step he's taken. Ease what fears he might have so that he can continue to lead his family in strength. In Jesus's name we pray. Amen.

Now who is there to harm you if you are zealous for what is good? But even if you should suffer for righteousness' sake, you will be blessed. Have no fear of them, nor be troubled. (1 Pet. 3:13–14)

TONIGHT I'M PRAYING THIS FOR _____

TONIGHT we pray for the dad who finishes well.

How many of us have started endeavors with great intentions? We had time, resources, and experts to tell us exactly what to do and when to do it. We were young enough and strong enough that there was no way we could fail, right? But then failure crept in, and suddenly we wondered if we were working way too hard for the return. What happens to us? At that moment, we must keep going. We can never lose momentum in our walk with the Lord. As He is moving, so must we move as well. We must be intentional and passionate about our relationship with the Lord, especially when doubt appears in our minds. We also must remember that there are other dads supporting us, and we can give them hope, hold them up, and encourage them to keep going too.

Lord, this dad knows that finishing well means maintaining his focus from beginning to end. He wants to fight the good fight, persevere, and have the spiritual success that comes from meeting You at the beginning of every day. Give him grace and meet him exactly where he is. In Jesus's name we pray. Amen.

Therefore, my dear brothers and sisters, stand firm. Let nothing move you. Always give yourselves fully to the work of the Lord, because you know that your labor in the Lord is not in vain. (1 Cor. 15:58 NIV)

TONIGHT I'M PRAYING THIS FOR _____

TONIGHT we pray for the dad who never backs down from a challenge. And the greatest challenge he faces on a day-to-day basis is being a successful father.

There will be a million small and seemingly insignificant moments through which we might show ourselves to be a dad God has called. And each of these important moments will also show that we're clearly not a perfect dad. But we want to bring our children to a place of courage and conviction so they can succeed in their own lives. Our children need to be able to adapt like we have and to work past their fears. They are watching us win the daily battles that arise, which shows them they don't have to be afraid even when the big struggles come.

> *Lord, this dad wants to teach his children how to always do what's right. Strengthen his heart as he looks after and protects his kids while they grow in grace. In Jesus's name we pray. Amen.*

You yourselves are our letter of recommendation, written on our hearts, to be known and read by all. And you show that you are a letter from Christ delivered by us, . . . not on tablets of stone but on tablets of human hearts. (2 Cor. 3:2–3)

TONIGHT I'M PRAYING THIS FOR _____

TONIGHT we pray for the dad who believes that he's exactly who he's supposed to be. This is a dad who has the character of a warrior. He's been tempered through the fires of adversity.

When we go through a battle, God burns some of the impurities out of us and strengthens us at the same time. Each one of those victories and defeats prepares us for the next battle, so we'll know when to step out in faith and when to be still and listen for instruction from the Lord. Tough times may come, but when we plan ahead where we can, our family is as prepared as possible. With the Lord's help, we are strong enough to endure any trial and come out stronger. Most importantly, we don't need to panic. Our faith and trust are in the provision and plan of God.

> *Lord, strengthen this dad for tomorrow's battles. Give him the confidence that he is ready and the courage to engage in any challenge. In Jesus's name we pray. Amen.*

> I know also, my God, that You test the heart and delight in uprightness and integrity. In the uprightness of my heart I have willingly offered all these things. (1 Chron. 29:17 AMP)

TONIGHT I'M PRAYING THIS FOR _____

TONIGHT we pray for the dad who finds himself away from the kids far too often. His absences are based upon a desire to provide their sustenance and protection. Yet his desire is to also provide for their emotional health, which is difficult to do in those absences.

There's no doubt God wants us to have our own spiritual health. If we are not whole spiritually, we aren't going to be able to see to the needs of our children and our families. If we are healthy spiritually, we are better prepared to help them with their own physical and emotional lives. There is no doubt that our children deal with emotional issues just as we do. As much as we focus on whether or not there is food on the table, our children think about whether Dad is around or not. Do our children feel safe? It's up to us to make sure.

Lord, help this dad to remember that being fully present can often overcome days of separation. Open his eyes to see new avenues of support so that he might be the spiritual and emotional presence in his children's lives that You have equipped him to be. In Jesus's name we pray. Amen.

Now may the Lord of peace himself give you his peace at all times and in every situation. (2 Thess. 3:16 NLT)

TONIGHT I'M PRAYING THIS FOR _____

78

TONIGHT we pray for the dad who believes he has what it takes to be a dad. His children watch him humble himself and see that he always takes responsibility for his decisions, good or bad. He wasn't born with humility. He had to acquire it from the Lord. He knows the difference between seeking God in the choices he makes for his life and automatically humbling himself to accept God's plan, even if that plan doesn't accord with what he might choose.

God promotes His children who rely on His grace to receive His blessings. When we are humble before the Lord, we can teach our children how to prosper and have joy in their lives. Every single day is a chance to make our children better. We believe in them, encourage them, and promote them because that's what dads do. And through us, our children also learn what it is to be humble before the Lord. When we follow the Lord's leading, we set an example for our children that He can be trusted.

> *Lord, this dad remembers Your promises and that You always keep Your children in Your heart. You make it possible for them to prosper. Bless this dad's dedication to always being the best dad he can be. In Jesus's name we pray. Amen.*

Humble yourselves, therefore, under the mighty hand of God so that at the proper time he may exalt you. (1 Pet. 5:6)

TONIGHT I'M PRAYING THIS FOR _____

TONIGHT we pray for the dad who is ready for a breakthrough.

It's really hard to ascribe to the Lord those things that are really challenging in our lives. Sometimes we call them "tests," as we are finding out just how committed we are to the course of action set before us. We may remember from our youth that the Lord will give us the desires of our heart as long as we trust Him. It is also often true that the Lord will place a test in our path just as our heartfelt desires are about to come to pass. He wants us to remain committed through the challenges when they appear.

Lord, this dad has trusted You. He has prayed. He has held on to hope. And now he is ready to see change come. He feels like he is on the edge of everything coming together for his good and for the good of his family. Step into his situation with Your change. In Jesus's name we pray. Amen.

It is [not your strength, but it is] God who is effectively at work in you, both to will and to work [that is, strengthening, energizing, and creating in you the longing and the ability to fulfill your purpose] for His good pleasure. (Phil. 2:13 AMP)

TONIGHT I'M PRAYING THIS FOR _____

TONIGHT we pray for the dad who wants to be a part of a brotherhood of winners.

When we have to make decisions in our lives, we know that unless we are particularly close to the Lord and His wisdom, we can miss the opportunity to have real success. Consequently, we usually seek wise counsel from other dads in our same life circumstances who have that close relationship. So it's to our advantage to surround ourselves with dads we can learn from and trust. The Lord set us up to be a brotherhood of believers, of those who would call upon the name of the Lord. We do life together. We have a responsibility for each other. We can become the mentors of others seeking after the Lord and His goodness. The Lord has it in His mind to take care of our brothers. When winning is where we all want to be, we must realize that in the grand scheme of things, in our community of brothers and trustworthy friends, when one wins we all win. That is our promise to each other, to lay down our lives for each other.

Lord, this dad believes in the power of trustworthy friends. Provide those for him, and strengthen him to be a friend to others. In Jesus's name we pray. Amen.

This is how we know what love is: Jesus Christ laid down his life for us. And we ought to lay down our lives for our brothers and sisters. (1 John 3:16 NIV)

TONIGHT I'M PRAYING THIS FOR _____

81

TONIGHT we pray for the dad who was once told he'd never be a success. Some said he would crash and burn or he would never be able to stay on track.

Even when others don't believe in us, we don't give up on ourselves, instead believing in God's plan for us. Maybe we worked hard to overcome difficulties and challenges while growing up. Maybe we didn't start with much and haven't seen much more. However, with the Lord's help, we can still best the uncertain economies when others around us wilt under the pressure. We may have to change jobs, but we keep going and we're able to say that we're persevering. Things are probably not perfect, but we can believe in a big God who always believes in us.

Lord, this dad knows his responsibility is to the family You gave him. Remind him that this race is a long-distance run, and give him extra steps for tomorrow's race. In Jesus's name we pray. Amen.

I do not account my life of any value nor as precious to myself, if only I may finish my course and the ministry that I received from the Lord Jesus, to testify to the gospel of the grace of God. (Acts 20:24)

TONIGHT I'M PRAYING THIS FOR _____

TONIGHT we pray for the dad who leads out in hope. He lives in a world of purpose and destiny. He doesn't even consider the possibility that he might fail. He begins each day with hope and conviction.

When it seems like the whole world is falling apart, we can still keep our wits about us. We can remember other times when, with God's help, we overcame emergencies. As a dad believing in our purpose, we know that even in trying times, dreams can still come true and prayers can still be answered. And we can lead our children and family to have the same hope and believe in the wonderful truth of the gospel. There are always people who don't have as much faith and always doubt. We can be the hopeful dad who is an encouragement to those who give up too soon.

Lord, this dad keeps going, knowing that You have everything under control. Reward his determination and conviction to see his crisis through. In Jesus's name we pray. Amen.

I sought the LORD, and he heard me, and delivered me from all my fears. They looked unto him, and were lightened: and their faces were not ashamed. This poor man cried, and the LORD heard him, and saved him out of all his troubles. . . . O taste and see that the LORD is good: blessed is the man that trusteth in him. (Ps. 34:4–6, 8 KJV)

TONIGHT I'M PRAYING THIS FOR _____

TONIGHT we pray for the dad who dreams big dreams. For himself, he dreams of patience. He prays that he can be the dad who calmly depends on the Lord during chaos and disorder and in the midst of calamity and trials. That he can be the one who does all he's able to and then waits on the Lord. And that he can find gentleness and be the dad his family needs.

We all want to be the dad who knows relationships matter and the struggles of the world can be dealt with one by one. For our family, while we place our earthly achievements in God's hands, we dream of the spiritual rewards of peace and security, laughter and joy. A family where our children always have peace and their mom and dad are the team they were meant to be.

Lord, listen to this dad's dreams tonight as he prays for what seems like a miracle, just like the ones You have granted before. He's praying hard and seeking Your plan for his family for as long as it takes. Bring his dreams to pass. In Jesus's name we pray. Amen.

As for you, O man of God, flee from these things; aim at and pursue righteousness [true goodness, moral conformity to the character of God], godliness [the fear of God], faith, love, steadfastness, and gentleness. (1 Tim. 6:11 AMP)

TONIGHT I'M PRAYING THIS FOR _____

TONIGHT we pray for the dad who has a burning desire to overcome the current economic downturn. He's dedicated to his family, and he's determined to keep the wolves at bay every day. There have been few easy answers these days, but the circumstances suggest that there will still be struggles.

The world and those in authority usually take no responsibility for the difficulties they present to families. Their power and influence can wreak havoc on those who choose to keep a modest lifestyle. But the needs of our family are like a fire in our heart that we continually tend to and keep watch over by stirring up the gifts that God has placed in us. It is a forever process that we must remain committed to, no matter what trials come our way.

Lord, hard times come to many of us, especially in a troubled season for our nation. Strengthen this dad to maintain his focus. Protect his family and prepare them for a better tomorrow. In Jesus's name we pray. Amen.

Then I said, I will not make mention of him, nor speak any more in his name. But his word was in mine heart as a burning fire shut up in my bones, and I was weary with forbearing, and I could not stay. (Jer. 20:9 KJV)

TONIGHT I'M PRAYING THIS FOR _____

TONIGHT we pray for the dad who finds he must be the strong one. Not the perfect dad, but the strong dad.

Our lives are often a series of disappointments. It's not because we enjoy making the wrong decisions or because we don't know how to make the right ones. It's because when we discover we are on the wrong path, we don't move off of it. We've all done it. We choose our plan B and make God's plan A unavailable, sometimes forever. Once we are on the wrong path, all the subsequent decisions available to us merely further our distance from the path we should have chosen.

> *Lord, it takes a strong dad to admit that sometimes he has not listened to Your voice. He knows his family trusts him to lead them out of their difficulties. He reassures them that You will deliver them from harm. He wants them to know that he's been here before and, together with You, he's got this. But he needs a strong heart. Make his even stronger. In Jesus's name we pray. Amen.*

With my voice I cry out to the Lord; with my voice I plead for mercy to the Lord. I pour out my complaint before him; I tell my trouble before him. (Ps. 142:1–2)

TONIGHT I'M PRAYING THIS FOR _____

86

TONIGHT we pray for the dad who believes that tomorrow is going to be great. He knows that every moment is an opportunity to do something or be someone he never has before. This dad sets aside time so those opportunities will have space to breathe in his world.

God is always at work preparing a path for us that will lead to new and different possibilities. Are we willing to see something differently, to find just the right life for our family? God is always inviting us to join Him in His adventures. Sure, change can be hard, and sometimes we have to assure our family that they're going to be all right. But we can bring them through because that's what a dad does. We go boldly before our family, and they follow because they can see our joy in the Lord.

Lord, this dad deals with problems every day, but he always looks to You for the new things. He doesn't dwell on what might have been. Keep his eyes on his changing horizons so that he doesn't miss the next opportunity. In Jesus's name we pray. Amen.

You know the saying, "Four months between planting and harvest." But I say, wake up and look around. The fields are already ripe for harvest. (John 4:35 NLT)

TONIGHT I'M PRAYING THIS FOR _____

TONIGHT we pray for the dad who wants to be the very best he can be. He wants all the i's dotted and the t's crossed. He believes that if he uses all his God-given abilities, God will help him complete his responsibilities and bring him success. But sometimes the world just gets in the way. Sometimes this dad is exhausted or incapacitated and some things get left undone.

We cannot run someone else's race. When we are done with ours, we are done. And God sees the desires of our heart to do our best for Him. He doesn't expect us to do what we legitimately cannot do. He does say, however, that He will bless the work of our hands. And when we see our faithful God faithfully bless us, there is joy!

Lord, this dad needs a word of encouragement for his efforts. A good word to spare his heart when he closes his eyes tonight so he can start over tomorrow. Remind him just how much You love him as a good and faithful servant. In Jesus's name we pray. Amen.

Do you not know that in a race all the runners run, but only one receives the prize? So run that you may obtain it. (1 Cor. 9:24)

TONIGHT I'M PRAYING THIS FOR _____

TONIGHT we pray for the dad who does his best to protect his family. He knows that without him, they could easily be overwhelmed by circumstances.

There have been dozens of times when the Lord protected us and our family from dangers. As a warrior, we have seen some of them ahead of time since we are called to stand guard for our family. We are always ready to protect their reputation and peace. We trust that God is on our side, ready to vanquish those dangers as He stands behind us, waiting for our call. There have also been times that the Lord saved us from perils we were completely unaware of. He is guarding our spirit, our soul, and our body in advance, strengthening us to fight the battles for our family.

Lord, help this dad to see that he is a true warrior, one whose heart is strong and whose shoulders are strong enough to carry his family through any turmoil that arises. Instill in him the confidence to overcome these and any future challenges. In Jesus's name we pray. Amen.

The LORD shall go forth as a mighty man, he shall stir up jealousy like a man of war: he shall cry, yea, roar; he shall prevail against his enemies. (Isa. 42:13 KJV)

TONIGHT I'M PRAYING THIS FOR _____

TONIGHT we pray for the dad who is struggling with illness. He has good days and not-so-good days. His mind, his body, and his spirit are completely exhausted. This is a strong dad, a great dad, who is not accustomed to having to manage his health.

When we're sick, there's nothing we want more than to pull all the pieces of our life back together the way they were—where things might have been hard, but we still succeeded. Now is when we need to remember that this sickness is not forever, but our constant prayer is "Lord, won't You please make it stop?" We worry that when we feel better we won't be able to do all and be all we need to be. We know better, don't we? We've seen this movie before, where the good guy vanquishes death, hell, and the grave. That's us. There's not one of us who doesn't have a story about surviving the dead of night. Because the Lord did, in fact, make the sickness stop. He doesn't just revive us; He restores us to life. Our job is to recover with the strength He gives us.

Lord, You are near to this dad even as he fears that he is struggling alone. Your hands are full of mercy and peace. Pour those out on this dad and his family tonight, and make tomorrow a miracle. In Jesus's name we pray. Amen.

He Himself existed and is before all things, and in Him all things hold together. [His is the controlling, cohesive force of the universe.] (Col. 1:17 AMP)

TONIGHT I'M PRAYING THIS FOR _____

TONIGHT we pray for the dad who is struggling with a big decision. He's always tried to live God's way in the past because it is true and it works, even if he didn't know exactly how or why.

We can trust in a good God because we know that the plans the Lord has for us are all good. When we think back, we can see how living in the open hand of the Lord brings peace. We have received the Lord's blessings in so many ways, but maybe tonight we are struggling. Maybe it's a big decision that will affect our family on so many levels. We need wisdom to continue to walk the path that has been set before us. As we weigh the pros and cons of this matter, the choices that hang in the balance, we know only the Lord can carry us to victory. Because the Lord loves us, He will provide the answer.

Lord, there is none like You, and there is none like this dad. He needs You like never before. He walks worthy in Your sight as he seeks You. Remind him that joy always comes in the morning. In Jesus's name we pray. Amen.

We walk by faith, not by sight [living our lives in a manner consistent with our confident belief in God's promises]. (2 Cor. 5:7 AMP)

TONIGHT I'M PRAYING THIS FOR _____

TONIGHT we pray for the dad who believes in prayer that covers his family. He's keeping the prayer walls up and he's not letting down his guard. He is like a watchman on the walls of the city of Jerusalem during the time of Nehemiah, keeping guard over his household with prayer.

When we pray, it is as though we stand in front of the doorway of our home and shield our family. There is power in prayer because it puts every situation into the hands of the Lord. Even better, we don't pray alone. We can invite our wife, children, and even extended family to join in this circle of prayer of faith. That way, our family comes to understand that God often uses our community to strengthen one another, with families praying for each other. God's plan is to always bless His children, in all places, for His glory and their good.

Lord, this dad trusts You in all things and believes You for all things, and he knows that You have his family in the palm of Your hand. Carry them as only You can. In Jesus's name we pray. Amen.

Therefore I tell you, whatever you ask in prayer, believe that you have received it, and it will be yours. (Mark 11:24)

TONIGHT I'M PRAYING THIS FOR _____

TONIGHT we pray for the dad who understands what's important. He's aware of the culture that says as long as he does the right things in the right order and for the right reasons, the Lord will bless all his endeavors.

That's never been God's plan. We cannot rely on the self-help ideas that the world is fond of. When we're at our best, God is first. Period, end of story. He is *the important One*. There shouldn't even be a competition. God's plans are so much greater than what we can read in a book. When we try to balance our lives to *include* God, we always discover stress creeping into our situations. Instead, He should always be first in our family. In the Bible, God emphasized our roles as a parent. He knew that the priority of taking care of our children would be the hardest thing we'd ever do.

Lord, because this dad's fatherly priority is for his children and their needs, he doesn't worry about what others might think. His only real job is to raise the children You gave him in the way that You provide. Strengthen this dad's heart to remember Your promise for his life. In Jesus's name we pray. Amen.

The conclusion of the matter is: fear God and keep His commands, because this is for all humanity. (Eccles. 12:13 HCSB)

TONIGHT I'M PRAYING THIS FOR _____

TONIGHT we pray for the dad who always fights through the storms of life. This present storm has taxed this dad like no other. But he keeps going, and when things get complicated, he figures out a way. He knows that life happens and complaining about it slows down the solution.

There are opportunities for whining about the difficulties of our situations and opportunities for praising God in them. Never forget that the Lord knows everything. In the story of Jesus stilling the storm that impeded His journey across the Sea of Galilee, He knew such a storm was possible, if not probable. He knew those transporting Him across the lake were not as proficient in such circumstances. And we have to believe that the Lord knows everything or it will be impossible to trust Him for the outcome. We can trust Him to see us to the other side.

Lord, this dad has been putting one foot in front of the other for weeks now. He would love a smooth and straight path. Clear a new way for him tomorrow. In Jesus's name we pray. Amen.

I have called you back from the ends of the earth, saying, "You are my servant." For I have chosen you and will not throw you away. (Isa. 41:9 NLT)

TONIGHT I'M PRAYING THIS FOR _____

TONIGHT we pray for the dad who needs to forgive.

One of the hardest things to remember about following the Lord is that it is a continuing action. He is continually providing, continually protecting. And He is continually forgiving. The Lord tells us if we want to be forgiven, we must also forgive. We are supposed to be in a continual state of forgiveness. Yes, continual. It's a heart thing. The Lord warned us that offenses will come, and come they do. Since there is no crime that will prevent Him from forgiving us, so also it must be that there is no offense we cannot forgive. The one who offends us often has no idea of the pain they've caused. The Lord told us that vengeance is His and He will repay the wrongdoer. And He will heal us of the hurt we've experienced when we forgive that person. Forgiveness is the key that releases us from the pain of another's offensive words or actions.

> *Lord, this dad's been hurt or betrayed by someone he trusted. The hurt remains to this day, and he suffers with that pain. Show him that his best response is to forgive even as You forgave him. In Jesus's name we pray. Amen.*

> If you forgive those who sin against you, your heavenly Father will forgive you. (Matt. 6:14 NLT)

TONIGHT I'M PRAYING THIS FOR _____

TONIGHT we pray for the dad who remembers a simpler time.

It's been about thirty-five years since the introduction of the internet. In that time, there have been four cultural generations—Generations Y, Z, Alpha, and Beta. Children born in these generations have experienced an increase in information that has quadrupled in that time. Meanwhile, our knowledge of truth has not kept up with our understanding of God's role in our lives. And to a great degree, God's presence in our lives has diminished because we think we know everything apart from Him. So as this dad remembers a time of God's presence, he carries on as he always has. He believes his primary role and responsibility is to keep his family safe from harm. And he very much believes that those simpler times of prosperity, provision, and safety are a part of God's plan for him and his family.

Lord, this dad longs for the peace that only You can provide. Help him see all Your blessings, and show him that simpler life. In Jesus's name we pray. Amen.

We encourage you, brothers, to do so even more, to seek to lead a quiet life, to mind your own business, and to work with your own hands, as we commanded you. (1 Thess. 4:10–11 HCSB)

TONIGHT I'M PRAYING THIS FOR _____

TONIGHT we pray for the dad who waits upon the Lord. He is one of those dads who is the envy of all his friends. He never seems to get rattled, even when it seems that the whole world is crashing down upon him.

We can trust the Lord in all things, even when it appears that He is busy attending to the other side of the world. Even then, we can become stronger. We can take care of the tasks we have been charged with, all the while expecting the Lord to be present. We can declare that the Lord has a plan and will accomplish it in due time. Let's not let our faith waver, because the Lord has always been faithful. And at the end of the day, if He has seemingly not answered our prayers, we can still complete the day and sleep the sleep of the contented, confident that tomorrow will be even better than today.

Lord, even when life seems uncertain, it is clear to You. This dad has met every challenge as it came because You have always been on his side. Give him rest in the preparation of his day and the promise of a successful tomorrow. In Jesus's name we pray. Amen.

God is not a God of disorder but of peace. (1 Cor. 14:33 NLT)

TONIGHT I'M PRAYING THIS FOR _____

TONIGHT we pray for the dad who keeps going. He gets up early in the morning to start his day at work. And make no mistake, he's on his knees consulting with the Lord to make sure his plans are not only approved but also approvable.

We shouldn't ever be committed to a plan until the Lord has heard it. We should always expect some editing to what we have designed. So we carry out our responsibilities with gratitude because the Lord has shown us favor. Not because He has completed our tasks for us but because we have sought Him in the night and He has heard us in the morning.

Lord, this dad's accomplishments aren't well known outside of his family. He doesn't desire to live in the limelight because You are his light. But he carries on because that's what dads do. He has dreams of peace and security. He's an inspiration to his family because he's always striving, looking for that next best opportunity. Strengthen his mind, body, and spirit. In Jesus's name we pray. Amen.

Weeping may tarry for the night, but joy comes with the morning. As for me, I said in my prosperity, "I shall never be moved." By your favor, O LORD, you made my mountain stand strong. (Ps. 30:5–7)

TONIGHT I'M PRAYING THIS FOR _____

TONIGHT we pray for the dad who needs hope. He's a good man, a good son, and most importantly, a good dad. He is feeling pretty overwhelmed right now. He has been relying on his own mental and physical toughness, but today he needs to find a seed of hope.

We want to believe that we can have a brighter future tomorrow even when our circumstances look pretty bleak today. Failure can seem so close, and we feel like everyone is expecting everything from us, even as they wonder if we're going to make it. But when failure gets close, the Lord gets closer. We can look for that glimmer of hope that comes from an unexpected place. We know that hope in the Lord does not disappoint.

> *Lord, plant a seed of hope in this dad's heart that tomorrow things will begin to get easier for his family. As he places his hope in You, he will praise You forever. In Jesus's name we pray. Amen.*

From the end of the earth I call to You, when my heart is overwhelmed and weak; lead me to the rock that is higher than I [a rock that is too high to reach without Your help]. For You have been a shelter and a refuge for me, a strong tower against the enemy. (Ps. 61:2–3 AMP)

TONIGHT I'M PRAYING THIS FOR _____

TONIGHT we pray for the dad who made it through another day. As he sits at his kitchen table, with a hard day behind him and one just like it coming up tomorrow, he feels a little bit alone. He'd just like to feel the Lord more present than he does today. This dad sometimes works so hard that he doesn't seem to have the time to hear the Lord's voice or even feel Him near.

Whether we know it or not, the Lord is always present, especially when we least expect Him. God provided miracles for people who already believed in Him, and sometimes they were surprised by His presence. Rest assured that the Lord is present, especially on those days He seems the most distant. So we shouldn't be discouraged, because we've done our best every day. And we can legitimately, expectantly wonder what He's going to do next.

Lord, remind this dad that there are some good surprises waiting. Remind him also to look up and see Your blessings on his journey. In Jesus's name we pray. Amen.

What eye did not see and ear did not hear, and what never entered the human mind—God prepared this for those who love Him. (1 Cor. 2:9 HCSB)

TONIGHT I'M PRAYING THIS FOR _____

100

TONIGHT we pray for the dad who does the hard jobs. Not just the work and labor that some find unpleasant, but also the jobs where no one seems to know or care about how hard they actually are.

Sure, there's payment for work done and a job completed. But we all know that cash goes only so far to compensate us. If we're honest, even if we had a billion dollars, we'd still like to know that our time was well spent. When we keep going even after our full day has finished, when we just want to get out of our car and sit and think about nothing at all, we still pick ourselves up and complete all the chores that didn't get finished. It's not about who completes the tasks at home or who has worked the hardest in the family. We see what needs to be done and we do it. That's who we are. Even though we are not always appreciated, we are still called to give our best for our family, to help fulfill the responsibilities that other family members might have.

Lord, there are blessings in giving everything we have—our money and our time. Multiply each in this dad's life. In Jesus's name we pray. Amen.

God is not unjust so as to overlook your work and the love that you have shown for his name in serving the saints, as you still do. (Heb. 6:10)

TONIGHT I'M PRAYING THIS FOR _____

TONIGHT we pray for the dad who can't sleep. He has so much on his mind that he tosses and turns half the night. The rest of the time, he gets up and tries to figure out the next step for the next day.

There are so many reasons that we might not sleep at night. It might be medical and we need help with a physical issue. Sometimes the reason is stress and worry and we need the peace of God to flood our heart and calm every fear. Dads worry just like moms do when their children are sick or sad or in pain. When the kids are struggling, we try to help as best we can—but sometimes there is nothing we can do, so we just toss and turn and pray. Still, we know that we can hand our worries over to the Lord, just as He wants us to do.

Lord, help this dad to get much-needed rest so he can face his challenges with strength and a clear mind. And when he calls Your name tonight, remind him that he and his family will be safe tomorrow. In Jesus's name we pray. Amen.

I lay down and slept [safely]; I awakened, for the LORD sustains me. (Ps. 3:5 AMP)

TONIGHT I'M PRAYING THIS FOR _____

TONIGHT we pray for the dad who is the best dad we know. But he doesn't always feel like the best dad. The difficulties he faces every day are enough to bring him to his knees. And that's where he stays, listening to what the Lord is telling him.

When the world seems to bring its worst, we can still give our all every day, doing everything we can. Because God is always with us, we know we can conquer any foe and overcome any difficulty and be confident that we will be standing and praying at the end of the day. Since the Lord has provided all our needs, He will help us take care of our family, and we do not need to fear or feel overwhelmed. The Lord provides everything we need to thrive.

Lord, this is the dad You called to fulfill Your plan at this time. He's still the best at what he does, and he's looking forward to being his best self every day. He's determined to see the tough days through. Strengthen his resolve as always. In Jesus's name we pray. Amen.

Finally, be strong in the Lord and in the strength of his might. (Eph. 6:10)

TONIGHT I'M PRAYING THIS FOR _____

TONIGHT we pray for the dad who has a satisfied life—safe, secure, everyone's happy at home. What could be better? He loves easy, as we all do, but the great dad doesn't just remain content with where he is.

Simply put, sometimes the Lord has more in store for us if we're willing to look around the next corner. And isn't that what we are about as a dad? We look for new beginnings and explore opportunities to do more than we ever have. If we are true to ourselves, when things get too easy, we should ask, "What's next?" The Lord is eager to hear those words. He has plans for us that we don't consider when our situation is safe. Yet the Lord is out there, waiting for us to ask Him for what is possible or, better still, what might be a little bit impossible. When we really turn our eyes heavenward, it will make us a better dad.

Lord, remind this dad that as he looks over the landscape, his journey with his family is always just beginning with new and different adventures. Strengthen him for tomorrow. In Jesus's name we pray. Amen.

The plans of the diligent lead surely to abundance, but everyone who is hasty comes only to poverty. (Prov. 21:5)

TONIGHT I'M PRAYING THIS FOR _____

TONIGHT we pray for the dad who hopes for a wonderful tomorrow. He does his best, he has a plan, and he has everything he needs to complete the assignment. At the end of the day, he always wants to know he has done what God has called him to do. That there was nothing left undone. That he has finished well.

As a dad, we hold our family close and try to protect them from the worst of the world. We know there will be sacrifices, as there always are when we have to stand between our family and the troubles of this world. But when we place our faith in the One who made heaven and earth, we can know with certainty that a wonderful tomorrow is on its way. We can trust that the Lord has given us abilities and worth, and we can lead our family to safety.

Lord, it takes a great dad to portray confidence and strength when times are tough. You've picked a great dad for this family. Renew his determination and his dedication as he prepares for tomorrow. In Jesus's name we pray. Amen.

His master said to him, "Well done, good and faithful servant. You have been faithful over a little; I will set you over much. Enter into the joy of your master." (Matt. 25:23)

TONIGHT I'M PRAYING THIS FOR _____

TONIGHT we pray for the dad who cares very, very deeply for other families. Some of his greatest satisfactions have come during those times when he has mowed the lawn of an elderly neighbor or fixed the car of a disabled friend.

During natural disasters, most of the time we're confident that our family is going to be fine. In those circumstances, once we've come into our own security, we take a breather, we chill, we give ourselves grace to rest in our good fortune. But it is within us to look out for others who may be near or far away. Can we be ready to help some other family while they struggle? We know we can come through our own emergencies only with the Lord. And God's strength, assurance, and peace will boost the spirits of families just like ours.

Lord, this dad is taking Your favor across the street, across town, or on the road. Bless him for his faithfulness as he serves others. In Jesus's name we pray. Amen.

For you, my brothers, were called to freedom; only do not let your freedom become an opportunity for the sinful nature (worldliness, selfishness), but through love serve and seek the best for one another. (Gal. 5:13 AMP)

TONIGHT I'M PRAYING THIS FOR _____

TONIGHT we pray for the dad who leads from the front of the line. He takes an active role in determining the needs of his family. As their provider and protector, he also provides the tools and the supplies necessary for them to thrive. Most importantly, this dad has done everything he asks anyone else to do. He makes sure that everyone knows what needs to be done and the steps necessary to accomplish the tasks.

When God asked Abraham to take his own son Isaac to a mountain in order to sacrifice him, God had already provided a ram as a substitute. He knew what was needed and provided it. That's us. We make sure that needs are met before they are desperate. And if everything has been provided, then we have peace and are the first to laugh, the first to make fun times, and the first to hug when hugs are called for. That's peace in the family.

Lord, grant this dad strength to be a leader even when his day seems at an end. In Jesus's name we pray. Amen.

Let each of you look not only to his own interests, but also to the interests of others. (Phil. 2:4)

TONIGHT I'M PRAYING THIS FOR _____

TONIGHT we pray for the dad who is hanging on for dear life. Things are far from perfect in his community. The natural disasters that have been so close to home have stretched his capacity to provide for his friends and neighbors.

As a dad, we usually have a lot of faith and know that we're able to make good decisions for our family. But when a disaster strikes, we wonder what might happen if it touches our family, whether they live nearby or far away. How can we protect them from where we are? But the Lord is not surprised by these situations, and they will never overcome His plans and His provision.

Lord, this dad believes that You are the Maker of heaven and earth and nothing is new to You. Remind him of everything he can accomplish with Your help. In Jesus's name we pray. Amen.

Though the LORD give you the bread of adversity and the water of affliction, yet your Teacher will not hide himself anymore, but your eyes shall see your Teacher. And your ears shall hear a word behind you, saying, "This is the way, walk in it," when you turn to the right or when you turn to the left. (Isa. 30:20–21)

TONIGHT I'M PRAYING THIS FOR _____

TONIGHT we pray for the dad who is struggling with issues he has no control over. It's not surprising that life feels like a chaotic game at times. When he understands the rules of the game, he plays to win, and usually he does. He also adjusts as the rules change.

We like being ahead, to know what play the world is calling. That's one way we become and stay successful. However, when things get to be unpredictable, we fear that losing the game of success will make us appear as less in our family's eyes. On days when we think we are getting ahead, some new circumstances create more stresses for us and our family. But if we continue to persevere throughout, our trials will come to an end sooner and we will reap the rewards of our efforts.

Lord, remind this dad that trusting in You leads to better outcomes. Help him not to be afraid and to keep going. In Jesus's name we pray. Amen.

Whoever is slow to anger is better than the mighty, and he who rules his spirit than he who takes a city. (Prov. 16:32)

TONIGHT I'M PRAYING THIS FOR _____

TONIGHT we pray for the dad who is just in total and complete love with his children. They are funny, smart, kind, rambunctious, trying, growing, and patient with their dad, and not necessarily in that order.

Since they are children, we can still be frustrated with and because of them. Our children love us because they don't know anything else. Hopefully they realize that our frustration is not anywhere near a true picture of our feelings for them. When we consider who we are and who the dad they see is, we realize we must work on our own patience, with them and everyone else. We know that our impatience does not derive from their actions. We are the grown-up, and the Lord expects us to show love to the world through our patience.

> *Lord, this dad's children make his day better and brighter, and every day is a challenge to maximize his time to see them more. He would do anything and everything for them. Extend the hours of his day so he can be the dad he wants to be with his kids for even a few minutes longer. In Jesus's name we pray. Amen.*

With all humility [forsaking self-righteousness], and gentleness [maintaining self-control], with patience, bearing with one another in [unselfish] love. (Eph. 4:2 AMP)

TONIGHT I'M PRAYING THIS FOR _____

TONIGHT we pray for the dad who is running out of explanations for his family. This dad believes he has what it takes to get them out of struggles. Yet the circumstances just aren't letting up.

When we have times like this, sometimes we do not put prayer first. We ask anyone and everyone about how to get out of the trials we're in—maybe a lawyer, maybe a doctor, maybe a friend. Strangely, we ask Jesus last. Yet Jesus has all the answers we need. We simply need to ask Him. When we've been rowing in a storm for days and days, maybe it's time to stop using our own strength.

Lord, there is a story in Scripture about You walking to Your friends when the wind and waves were high. You walked a long way until they could see You. And then one of them recognized You. This dad is looking for You to help in his storm. Guide him through it as only You can. In Jesus's name we pray. Amen.

While they were talking and discussing it, Jesus Himself came up and began walking with them. . . . Then their eyes were [suddenly] opened [by God] and they [clearly] recognized Him. (Luke 24:15, 31 AMP)

TONIGHT I'M PRAYING THIS FOR _____

TONIGHT we pray for the dad who is hooked on God. He knows the Lord, and they are on a first-name basis. He knows that the Lord has his happiness in mind at all times. And the way he taps into it is to search for the Lord and find Him. He doesn't let anything get in the way of the assurance of power, provision, peace, and protection found in the Spirit of Messiah that is in him.

In the beginning, Adam and Eve relied on God for everything. God provided their sustenance and their protection. Only when they chose independence and the desire to discover what it meant to take care of themselves did they become separated from God. The Lord would have us be entirely dependent upon Him. To refuse to be separated from the Word of God. To have our soul so enthralled with the Word that we can't imagine being deprived of it. It is so necessary to see the supremacy of the Word of God as opposed to anything else we can feel, see, touch, or smell.

> *Lord, this dad longs for You. Open his eyes that he can know— really know—what You have in store for him. Bless him as he continues to live for You and Your Word. In Jesus's name we pray. Amen.*

> Remember [thoughtfully] also your Creator in the days of your youth [for you are not your own, but His]. (Eccles. 12:1 AMP)

TONIGHT I'M PRAYING THIS FOR _____

TONIGHT we pray for the dad who laughs. This dad knows that the Lord has a plan for him.

The enemy of our souls rages at any plan of God because he only has a bit part in it at the end. The enemy would have us focus only on our surroundings here on earth rather than our true home in heaven. Yet we dwell with the Lord in heavenly places even while still living on earth. If we let this spiritual truth sink in, it will change the way we think and live. So we can join the hosts of heaven in laughing at evil plans. But only if we continue to fully embrace God's plan. We are not always in a position to understand God's work and workings, but we know that they are so much higher than those of a fallen angel. The accuser of our faith cannot fulfill anything on his own. He rages at that reality while we hold him in derision.

Lord, You have a plan of creation and success for this dad. Bring that plan to pass for him. In Jesus's name we pray. Amen.

He who sits [enthroned] in the heavens laughs [at their rebellion]; the [Sovereign] Lord scoffs at them [and in supreme contempt He mocks them]. (Ps. 2:4 AMP)

TONIGHT I'M PRAYING THIS FOR _____

TONIGHT we pray for the dad who suffers in this world. He hasn't made it through the wilderness unscathed too many times recently. He knows that some days are just harder than others, and he's been known to complain a bit to the Lord for those setbacks and stumbles.

The Lord has a big heart, and He's willing to hear our criticisms about the plan for us and how it's working out for us. We are destined to have many great spiritual victories while also surviving the hard and seemingly continuous attacks of the enemy. Our flesh also wants to participate in those victories, but Jesus warns us that times will often be hard. We are ambassadors of the Most High God and we must persevere, even when our earthly trials seem to overshadow our heavenly responsibilities.

Lord, bless this dad with heavenly ammunition while he walks this road with You, and remind him that the sufferings are not the only outcomes to Your plan. In Jesus's name we pray. Amen.

From that time on Jesus began to show His disciples [clearly] that He must go to Jerusalem, and endure many things at the hands of the elders and the chief priests and scribes . . . and be killed, and be raised [from death to life] on the third day. (Matt. 16:21 AMP)

TONIGHT I'M PRAYING THIS FOR _____

TONIGHT we pray for the dad who knows the Lord is gracious.

Some people have the notion that if they have received a great gift or been relieved of some great responsibility, they are somehow honor bound to repay the value of what was given. But when God made covenants with His people, they were made with no expectation of return. God understands that His gifts are so great that they can never be repaid. His choice to show mercy to someone is based upon His goodness and not on the merit of any of us. We need to stop trying to earn God's favor and start believing that He knew what He was doing when He sent a Messiah to manifest God's favor in our lives.

> *Lord, You have set this dad apart. He understands that You make promises just because You can. You have blessed him even though he has nothing in himself—past, present, or future— that can compare with what he has received. And he knows that what he has received can never be repaid. Remind him of Your goodness every day. In Jesus's name we pray. Amen.*

After these things the word of the LORD came to Abram in a vision: "Fear not, Abram, I am your shield; your reward shall be very great." (Gen. 15:1)

TONIGHT I'M PRAYING THIS FOR _____

TONIGHT we pray for the dad who has a job to do. He works hard, and he pays the bills. He holds himself to a high standard when he is with his family. But his God-given responsibility, his job, is to make sure that the family he's been given has everything they should ever need.

There is no relief from the duty of a dad; there is no break in the action. At the end of the day, we know that we don't just work for an employer. We don't complete a task or a job or a contract for someone just because someone intends to pay us. We are stewards of the Most High God, in whose employ we are entrusted and expected to do our best. When God sent us into the game, He expected results. He trained us, He prepared us, and He called us into service. A good dad watches and says, "I can do that." A great dad says, "Hang on, I've got this."

Lord, Your words are "Yes" and "Amen" when this dad prays. Make him into the dad he was called to be. As he stewards Your gifts, supply him with more. In Jesus's name we pray. Amen.

To everyone who has [and values his blessings and gifts from God, and has used them wisely], more will be given, and [he will be richly supplied so that] he will have an abundance. (Matt. 25:29 AMP)

TONIGHT I'M PRAYING THIS FOR _____

TONIGHT we pray for the dad who still wants to win. He feels like he's already gone twelve rounds with the whole world and he just wants the bell to ring.

Life is a prizefight. Each of us is just in the early rounds and there are more to come. As we all know, the prize is not necessarily in the here and now, in the today and tomorrow, which is what makes the fight so daunting. We want our rewards immediately, and those rewards seem to keep us going. But when we looked to the Lord for eternal life, we signed up for a lifetime appointment in the army of God. And the reward is the reputation of a good and faithful servant who serves the King of Kings.

Lord, You have made a way for this dad where there has been no way. This wise dad must keep his eyes and ears open to see the path and hear Your voice. Give him grace to serve You, and keep his eyes on your eternal prize. Shine a light for him and speak Your Word for him to win. In Jesus's name we pray. Amen.

Soldiers don't get tied up in the affairs of civilian life, for then they cannot please the officer who enlisted them. And athletes cannot win the prize unless they follow the rules. (2 Tim. 2:4–5 NLT)

TONIGHT I'M PRAYING THIS FOR _____

TONIGHT we pray for the dad who sometimes needs to be reminded that he is a good dad. He loves his children and his family. He does his best day in and day out. When this dad wakes up in the morning, his family is on his mind, and when he goes to sleep at night, his family is better because he spent the day working hard for their benefit.

To be a great dad starts with loving God. We want to always keep His Word and His promises tucked away in our heart. We want to lean on the Lord when this world doesn't seem to make sense. God is more than able to sustain us despite what we see. We can trust in His Word, which says that all things will work out for our good.

Lord, help this dad to remember that he is right where You want him to be. He is the provider and the caretaker of his home. He is a good dad who makes this world a better place. Bless him tonight. In Jesus's name we pray. Amen.

"You will not need to fight in this battle. Stand firm, hold your position, and see the salvation of the Lord on your behalf, O Judah and Jerusalem." Do not be afraid and do not be dismayed. Tomorrow go out against them, and the Lord will be with you. (2 Chron. 20:17)

TONIGHT I'M PRAYING THIS FOR _____

TONIGHT we pray for the dad who has a dream. A simple dream, really.

There are big dreams, of course. A new luxury car, a swimming pool—you know, the good life. The world equates material possessions with success and happiness. And sure, we want to live life to the fullest and enjoy every moment. Yet when the things we held dear in the fullest life are gone, what is left? Instead, we can be happy with the simple dream of enough. We all know what that means, right? To find joy in experiences and prioritize the relationships with our family. These are the things that bring us real happiness. When the door locks, the appliances work, the car starts, and we can go to the store and get ice cream for our children, this is enough. When we go to sleep, there will be enough for tomorrow as well. That's peace, and the Lord wants us to know that it's real and possible.

> *Lord, bless this dad with Your peace as a heavily laden wagon of provision rolling downhill. In Jesus's name we pray. Amen.*

His divine power has bestowed on us [absolutely] everything necessary for [a dynamic spiritual] life and godliness, through true and personal knowledge of Him who called us by His own glory and excellence. (2 Pet. 1:3 AMP)

TONIGHT I'M PRAYING THIS FOR _____

TONIGHT we pray for the dad who is steady. He's working as hard as he can, paying the bills as best he can, fixing the car, and doing pretty much anything that needs to be done. He finds time to spend with the kids because he can and because they're everything to him.

Our godly behavior as a dad is a result of godly thinking. While we aren't consistent all the time, we need to realize that real success comes from being stable and steadfast in the Lord. Trusting in Him will keep us anchored securely in the harbor of His love. We know what God's will is for us: to walk and talk and act in a way that is pleasing to Him. Tomorrow we can start fresh, providing for our family, because we promised we would.

Lord, this dad is beloved and puts his trust in You. Give him strength for each day. In Jesus's name we pray. Amen.

We all, with unveiled face, continually seeing as in a mirror the glory of the Lord, are progressively being transformed into His image from [one degree of] glory to [even more] glory, which comes from the Lord, [who is] the Spirit. (2 Cor. 3:18 AMP)

TONIGHT I'M PRAYING THIS FOR _____

TONIGHT we pray for the dad whose job requires him to live in the moment. This dad doesn't always get to think long and hard about his decisions, so he moves ahead and relies on his God-given ability to choose the wise course of action. But in all this moving and choosing and recovering, he never gets to fully appreciate the space and time of God's moments.

It's been said that we have two lives: the one we learn with and the one we live after that. So much of what we do is, in fact, a learning process. We do what we think we need to do, without stopping to consider the peace available to us when we rest in the Lord and let Him refresh us in the decision-making. We live either in the past, with the what-ifs, or in the future, with the never-ending what-could-be's. We rarely, if ever, live here and now in the peaceful presence of the Lord. So let's begin living in the now, learning as we go.

Lord, this dad is always maturing, always ready to hear Your voice, but sometimes the world overwhelms him with the constant decisions he must make. You are the keeper of time. Redeem his time so he can see how to accomplish even more. In Jesus's name we pray. Amen.

Don't worry about tomorrow, for tomorrow will bring its own worries. Today's trouble is enough for today. (Matt. 6:34 NLT)

TONIGHT I'M PRAYING THIS FOR _____

TONIGHT we pray for the dad who knows that some of the most important successes happen in ten-minute intervals.

We all have a limited lifespan on this planet. We only have so many years, so many months, so many minutes. Once our time is spent, it can't be recovered. Without a doubt, we are willing to spend ten minutes finalizing the details of tomorrow's delivery route or verifying the presentation for the company vice president. But what about eating a bite at breakfast with the kids or calling our daughter to catch up on her day? Do we have time for those? When we turn to God for help with our endeavors, He can redeem our time and help us make more of it than we thought possible. God's presence makes anything He touches—and certainly our time—better.

Lord, this dad knows that those ten-minute intervals combine to create ten-year increments—decades—which add up to a lifetime of success. Bless him and redeem his time and his daily efforts tonight. In Jesus's name we pray. Amen.

We know we love God's children if we love God and obey his commandments. Loving God means keeping his commandments, and his commandments are not burdensome. (1 John 5:2–3 NLT)

TONIGHT I'M PRAYING THIS FOR _____

TONIGHT we pray for the dad who had some wins this year, then some losses. The wins came with hard work and everyone saw the blessings, and the financial opportunities changed his family for the better. But when the losses came, this dad realized he had to abandon the world's economy and focus on God's economy.

We need to remember our financial opportunities are provided by the Lord in order to carry out His plan. He uses us as a trusted agent of His resources. And we can be confident the Lord will always use His trusted overseers to accomplish His purpose. We may think that what we've been given is ours alone and we know exactly how to use it to the best advantage. However, God's ways are not always our ways.

Lord, You have shown this dad promise, and You have also given him hope. He knows how to prosper and how to rest in Your quiet reflection. Give him wisdom and knowledge tonight so that he might be generous with Your resources tomorrow. In Jesus's name we pray. Amen.

Instruct those who are rich in the present age not to . . . set their hope on the uncertainty of wealth, but on God. . . . Instruct them to do what is good, to be rich in good works, to be generous, willing to share. (1 Tim. 6:17–18 HCSB)

TONIGHT I'M PRAYING THIS FOR _____

TONIGHT we pray for the dad who, despite all his best efforts, is tired. The dad who got up before dawn, and the only way he makes it back to the house is by the lights on the tractor. Or he struggles to keep alert as the lines on the highway fade together while he drives his tractor trailer. Or his newborn has been on hourly feeding schedules these last several nights and his supervisor says the project deadlines are coming up no matter what.

We know these kinds of days and nights, when we kept up, did what was asked of us. We met all the expectations the world laid on us. And we succeeded on so many levels. We ought to be thriving. But some days we're just beat. Not beaten, because we never give up—just beat. This is when we can lean on the Lord, resting in His care, trusting in His strength to carry us.

Lord, this dad is doing his best—it's what he does, and he will do it tomorrow as well. There's always been a reward in Your providence for the dad who gives his all. You have always strengthened him in those times when he wondered if he'd done enough. Remind him that he can rest in You, and make the promise of peace come to pass in his life. In Jesus's name we pray. Amen.

Those who live to please the Spirit will harvest everlasting life from the Spirit. So let's not get tired of doing what is good. At just the right time we will reap a harvest of blessing if we don't give up. (Gal. 6:8–9 NLT)

TONIGHT I'M PRAYING THIS FOR _____

TONIGHT we pray for the dad who still has a goal or two he'd like to achieve. He was working on a few things when everything just seemed to change. God knows his heart and his journey, and He knows that this dad put everything down to take care of those he loves.

All of us have experienced trials that we would like to forget. Of course, there are likely a few we're proud we've overcome (and probably take too much credit for). But that's why we can trust God to fulfill His promises. God loves us so much that we can count on Him to bring us closer to Him. He's always been faithful to protect us and our family. And He never slumbers or sleeps from helping us reach our goals and dreams. It's not just the things He provides or the blessings He bestows. It's about making us into the dad we can be. And none of us has the same journey.

Lord, honor this dad's choices to serve his family first. Open his eyes to see a future for his goals. In Jesus's name we pray. Amen.

Grow in the grace and knowledge of our Lord and Savior Jesus Christ. To him be the glory both now and to the day of eternity. Amen. (2 Pet. 3:18)

TONIGHT I'M PRAYING THIS FOR _____

TONIGHT we pray for the dad who is humble. He knows that everything he has and everything he ever will have are a direct result of how great God is.

God is God and we are not. Worshiping Him puts us into a position of receiving all He has to offer us. To worship means to bend a knee. Our first responsibility in the morning should be to take a knee and remind ourselves that any and all success we are about to have will come from the One who made heaven and earth. We know there will be victories and defeats, and hopefully more wins than losses.

Lord, there will be days when the world will get the better of this dad. But he keeps going because, while challenges may come, his will is not defeated. His dreams are still in front of him. His life is not just a series of tasks but a dedication to a dream—a dream of family. And because he knows that even his dreams are already in Your mind and heart for him, he takes a knee every day. Bless this dad with peace and assurance for tomorrow. In Jesus's name we pray. Amen.

O people, the Lord has told you what is good, and this is what he requires of you: to do what is right, to love mercy, and to walk humbly with your God. (Mic. 6:8 NLT)

TONIGHT I'M PRAYING THIS FOR _____

TONIGHT we pray for the dad who sometimes feels empty. He's supposed to bring the new, the different, and the exciting, but there's just nothing there. These are the times when he feels far away from God. So far away, in fact, that he can't remember the last time he felt God's presence.

This can happen when we put all our earthly desires ahead of the Lord, when all we think about is how we're going to be richer or more prosperous. We're more concerned with our things than with the One who made it possible for us to have them. We're more aware of how hard we've worked than we are of the One who rewards us for working for Him. It's a pride thing and it happens. We think we're the most important person in the room because we haven't given the Lord any place in our lives.

Lord, this dad needs a wake-up call from his heavenly Father. Remind him that You are better than all his earthly treasures. Remind him that You are the good One even on bad days. Help him to always have a healthy supply of joy to share so that those who count on him will see You in him. In Jesus's name we pray. Amen.

You have given me greater joy than those who have abundant harvests of grain and new wine. (Ps. 4:7 NLT)

TONIGHT I'M PRAYING THIS FOR _____

TONIGHT we pray for the dad who sometimes feels like he could lose everything he's worked so hard to build. He might not have had much to say a blessing over, but he always knew that there was enough for one more day. Now this dad thinks he might be just one person in a sea of humanity, all trying to keep the wheels on in their own homes.

Life is life and it can be so unfair. Yet we are God's chosen. He knows us, He loves us, and we are His. Not only have we been set apart for His service, purchased with the blood of Jesus Christ, but He sees us as exceptional in our own right. We may not be particularly artistic or athletic, but the Lord knows exactly who we are. He will not let you lose everything He has provided for you in order to succeed.

Lord, this dad has done the right things, he's made the right choices, and he's still standing. You said You would hear from heaven those who call Your name. Lord, this faithful dad is calling right now. Show mercy and favor in his life. In Jesus's name we pray. Amen.

You are a chosen race, a royal priesthood, a holy nation, a people for his own possession, that you may proclaim the excellencies of him who called you out of darkness into his marvelous light. (1 Pet. 2:9)

TONIGHT I'M PRAYING THIS FOR _____

128

TONIGHT we pray for the dad who knows how to make important decisions. Because, for a dad, just about every decision is important.

We have to be willing to trust in the Lord if He is leading us to make a choice. He doesn't make decisions for us. While He gave us the gift of free will so we could choose to love Him and receive His peace, earthly decisions are still subject to His oversight. Whether to fix the car or find some other transportation. Whether to have health insurance or make sure there's food in the fridge. Or, in the bigger picture, whether to keep the safe job or venture out for something greater. In times of trouble, dads like us are faced with these decisions all too often. As it's been said, "If it was easy, anybody could do it."

Lord, hearing Your wisdom may take practice, and yet it's always available to us. Speak Your truth loudly in the ear of this faithful dad as he leads his family. In Jesus's name we pray. Amen.

The LORD was not in the wind: and after the wind an earthquake; but the LORD was not in the earthquake: and after the earthquake a fire; but the LORD was not in the fire: and after the fire a still small voice. (1 Kings 19:11–12 KJV)

TONIGHT I'M PRAYING THIS FOR _____

TONIGHT we pray for the dad who believes he can do better.

From time to time, all of us have been engaged in circumstances that we were, to put it mildly, surprised to find ourselves in. And we're often surprised to see how far we've come down the road to dis-ease in our bodies and minds. When we accept the Lord's death and resurrection as our own, He makes our old nature dead. However, we all have an ongoing responsibility to actually consider it dead. It's only when we are successful with that responsibility that we can change our lives for the better. So many of our real troubles consist of our inability to see ourselves as God sees us. He loves us, and He knows our hearts and what we can accomplish given the right set of circumstances. The Lord happens upon each of us on our best days and our worst days with mercy first, and judgment only if we refuse His offer of mercy.

> *Lord, this dad has engaged in a lifestyle that he is ashamed of. He knows those choices have not been his best. But he also knows he is capable of changing his situation. Help him to stop living his worst life and start living the life You have in store for him. In Jesus's name we pray. Amen.*

Through faith in the name of Jesus, this man was healed—and you know how crippled he was before. Faith in Jesus' name has healed him before your very eyes. (Acts 3:16 NLT)

TONIGHT I'M PRAYING THIS FOR _____

TONIGHT we pray for the dad who knows God's hard words. He knows all about how he has sinned and is worthy of God's punishment.

We are all well aware of those words, and unfortunately, we take them to heart. We believe we're not worthy of God's love or His forgiveness—period, end of story. So we walk around condemned in our souls and broken in our bodies because we believe that we are eternally separated from Him. We lost our ability to wholeheartedly trust God after the fall in the garden of Eden. Sin keeps us from seeing God as He truly is, a loving Father who prepares a straight path for us but doesn't force us to walk on it. That's up to us. He never stopped loving us, He never stopped forgiving us, and He is prepared right now to show that love and forgiveness to His very worthy children whenever we decide to reunite ourselves with Him by turning to His Son. But sometimes the hard part is believing that God wants us to experience the love He has for us right now.

Lord, You have told this dad, "Come this way and it's so much easier," and "Hang on, the best provision is coming." Remind him of the redemption available in Your Son. In Jesus's name we pray. Amen.

All this is from God, who reconciled us to himself through Christ and gave us the ministry of reconciliation. (2 Cor. 5:18 NIV)

TONIGHT I'M PRAYING THIS FOR _____

TONIGHT we pray for the dad who is accustomed to making good decisions.

Wouldn't it be great if we always knew exactly what to do in every circumstance? Turn right or left? Get a tattoo? Beef or chicken? These are easy choices with easy answers. Well, if all our choices were as easy as these, we would be tempted to put our trust in ourselves. We want to be self-reliant, to know that we have the answers and are beholden to no one. But the Lord places way too many unusual choices in front of us for us to think that we know everything. And there have been more than just a few times we have taken the wrong path. We may not want to have to ask the Lord which is better—beef or chicken, left or right. But if we have the mindset to ask Him what to do in the easy choices, we will be in the habit of asking when the choices are more critical.

Lord, this dad has been faithful to seek Your face in many things. Remind him that You still listen to his voice, and to listen for Yours. In Jesus's name we pray. Amen.

Now the mind of the flesh is death [both now and forever—because it pursues sin]; but the mind of the Spirit is life and peace [the spiritual well-being that comes from walking with God—both now and forever]. (Rom. 8:6 AMP)

TONIGHT I'M PRAYING THIS FOR _____

TONIGHT we pray for the dad who wants to walk worthy. It's a tough call, and this dad knows it. He realizes that he should conduct himself in a way that honors the Lord.

We want the opportunity to please the Lord, knowing that pleasing Him is also walking by faith and staying faithful to His Word. Walking worthy is a lifetime achievement. It's a long path and easy to stumble off of. Scripture relates the story of a prodigal son who found life hard and felt as though he would never have what he was entitled to. He returned after realizing the best life was actually in his father's house (Luke 15:11–32).

Lord, this dad is returning to You, perhaps from far away. Place the robe or uniform of Your army on his shoulders, place a ring on his finger or a sword of power in his hands, and put on the shoes or boots that take him where he needs to go with no lack of provision. Let him walk with the authority of who he is as a son of the King, knowing that his attire was placed on him by the One he serves. Looking good, standing tall, let him be the one who gets the call to walk worthy. In Jesus's name we pray. Amen.

Everything created by God is good, and nothing is to be rejected if it is received with thanksgiving. (1 Tim. 4:4)

TONIGHT I'M PRAYING THIS FOR _____

TONIGHT we pray for the dad who prays always. This dad knows the difference between praying in times of distress, need, or want, and praying just because he desires to be close to God.

As hard as it might be to pray when it seems like the Lord is absent, it can be categorically harder to pray "just because" when our needs aren't being met. But the Lord tells us that praying brings us closer to Him. And the more we come close to God, the more we are changed to become like Him. It's not just about getting our finances improved or our bodies healed, or even changing the person who daily offends us. It's about changing us to be like Him. If we had the chance, wouldn't we like to be in the garden of Eden before the fall, when God would walk with us in the cool of the day?

Lord, this dad wants to have an audience with the One who made heaven and earth. Receive him into Your presence every day in every way. In Jesus's name we pray. Amen.

Watch ye therefore, and pray always, that ye may be accounted worthy to escape all these things that shall come to pass, and to stand before the Son of man. (Luke 21:36 KJV)

TONIGHT I'M PRAYING THIS FOR _____

TONIGHT we pray for the dad who makes plans to accomplish his goals. He knows that everything has to be completed if he expects to win. He is accustomed to crossing the finish line. He's committed to his family and he works hard every single day.

Our days are not just about how hard we work or our performance. The Lord loves us and strengthens us and keeps us going by His grace. We can also encourage our family to push forward as they count on us to press on through good times as well as tough times. They know that if we can make it, we will show the way to the good life that's coming. And that's really what the Lord wants for us and our family—to have abundant life, a more-than-enough life, an everlasting life. So we've got this.

Lord, this dad gets weary at times. Sometimes he wonders if he'll have what it takes tomorrow. But You are in tomorrow just like You were in today. Refresh his heart and mind tonight. In Jesus's name we pray. Amen.

I am certain that God, who began the good work within you, will continue his work until it is finally finished on the day when Christ Jesus returns. (Phil. 1:6 NLT)

TONIGHT I'M PRAYING THIS FOR _____

TONIGHT we pray for the dad who is learning how to stretch.

Any of us who have had joint surgery know that the muscles and ligaments surrounding the joint have to be routinely and carefully stretched after surgery or they will atrophy. And once atrophied, they will be of little or no use. Their strength and function can be lost, potentially forever. However, it is also true that if those ligaments and muscles are stretched appropriately, they grow and become stronger. It's the same with our spirituality. The Lord is always searching for those who are searching for Him. It takes a good deal of stretching to leave our comfort zone and look for Him. But when we find Him, we can find wisdom and understanding to help us go about our lives from day to day. So do we stretch and find Him or coast into our lives and remain lost in our circumstances?

Lord, there have been so many things already that this dad has had to reach for. Sometimes his arms just don't seem long enough. Every day, he gets up and realizes that there will probably be a few more changes today. So he keeps reaching to You for the successes that he believes You have in store for his family. Open his eyes to seek you in everything tomorrow. In Jesus's name we pray. Amen.

You have given me the shield of Your salvation; Your right hand upholds me, and Your humility exalts me. (Ps. 18:35 HCSB)

TONIGHT I'M PRAYING THIS FOR _____

TONIGHT we pray for the dad who is trying to make up for lost time with his family. He wonders if the decisions he made in the past have really turned out the way he hoped they would. He wasted time on fruitless work when he thought just working hard was enough. Now he wonders if God is disappointed in him for his massive effort and no results—or the wrong results.

God doesn't work that way. The closer we get to the heart of God, the more we will realize His love covers even wasted time. The past is the past and it should remain there. Of course, we plan to the best of our ability with the information we have. We listen to God, do our best, and trust Him for the results.

Lord, this dad needs assurance and a sign of support. He trusts that You are still in his plans. Remind him that You know exactly where he is, even when he feels lost. In Jesus's name we pray. Amen.

Don't live like fools, but like those who are wise. Make the most of every opportunity in these evil days . . . but understand what the Lord wants you to do. (Eph. 5:15–17 NLT)

TONIGHT I'M PRAYING THIS FOR _____

TONIGHT we pray for the dad who has "discovered" he's a dad and everything that word means. He is not merely a father but one who has a special relationship with a child.

This fatherhood business can be something of a mystery to us. Not that we don't know we are a father, but often we don't realize just how important our role is. We've done all the dad things, like making a living and providing a roof over our kids' heads. But maybe it's starting to dawn on us that we hold a very special place in God's heart and there is more to this role than just walking, talking, and breathing as the male parent in the house. Let's keep that special place and remember that our children really do not and cannot grow up well on their own. We need to reconfigure our thinking and doing to fulfill the responsibility of sharing our life with our children and encourage them to share their lives with us.

Lord, remind this dad that fatherhood is a lifetime appointment and bless him in his successes. In Jesus's name we pray. Amen.

We have all had human fathers who disciplined us and we respected them for it. How much more should we submit to the Father of spirits and live! (Heb. 12:9 NIV)

TONIGHT I'M PRAYING THIS FOR _____

138

TONIGHT we pray for the dad who believes he's becoming a better dad. He's able to focus more on the tomorrows and leave the yesterdays behind. Most of all, he doesn't live his life in fear. No matter what, he doesn't let words of fear into his home. This "better" dad keeps everybody grounded.

It can be hard to have a cheery outlook when emotional trials or financial tribulations take center stage in our family's life. It's understandable to be anxious or afraid because of sudden changes in our family's circumstances. And isn't it true that the suddenness is what really gives us pause? Changes that come at us over time can be managed, but there are some circumstances we fear more than others because of our history. Yet we know that as long as the Lord is present in our lives and in our homes, we never need to fear, and we can have confidence that our words and our actions will reflect His goodness to our family.

Lord, You and You alone can heal this dad's mind and heart so he can go forward in peace. Keep him safe from all fears. In Jesus's name we pray. Amen.

God is our refuge and strength, always ready to help in times of trouble. So we will not fear when earthquakes come and the mountains crumble into the sea. Let the oceans roar and foam. Let the mountains tremble as the waters surge! (Ps. 46:1–3 NLT)

TONIGHT I'M PRAYING THIS FOR _____

TONIGHT we pray for the dad who is proud to be a dad. He considers this his best work. It is hard, it can be taxing, but he loves every second of it. He has a sense of delight and satisfaction with what his child is able to accomplish.

Something happens when a father first holds his child. There is a sense of joy and responsibility that can be quite overwhelming. It is as though we know instantly what will be required of us in the future. Things like teaching our child how to ride a bike, tie their shoes, or cook a meal. Having a child changes everything. The day we became a dad was one of our finest moments, and we will always be that dad. Being a dad changes our heart and makes us willing to give up conveniences and comforts. As a father, we are willing and able to make even greater sacrifices for our children and family.

> *Lord, renew this dad's faith and dedication to make every day just like this one and to never forget what he feels like right now. Help this dad to express his pride to his children so they can grow in their own faith daily. In Jesus's name we pray. Amen.*

You are My Son, My Beloved, in You I am well-pleased and delighted! (Luke 3:22 AMP)

TONIGHT I'M PRAYING THIS FOR _____

140

TONIGHT we pray for the dad who is a peace officer. This dad often encounters violence in unexpected situations and circumstances. He does what he does because he loves his profession. He wants to protect those around him as well as the people and families he knows and loves. But he also wants to stand up for the good that his children see in him.

Until our children reach an age of accountability and reason, they probably think of us as superheroes. They know in their hearts that there are such things as good and evil. Even in the relative safety of home, they've probably called out "Daddy!" when they were afraid of things that went bump in the night. To them, we are the good guys and we can protect them from any evil threat. They probably don't understand the world as it is or can be, but when we are asked to defend those our children love, we are protecting them as only we can.

Lord, this dad stands in Your favor and power. Strengthen his resolve to always be ready to take this responsibility. In Jesus's name we pray. Amen.

Be strong and courageous; don't be terrified or afraid of them. For it is the LORD your God who goes with you; He will not leave you or forsake you. (Deut. 31:6 HCSB)

TONIGHT I'M PRAYING THIS FOR _____

TONIGHT we pray for the dad who remembers that God always answers his prayers. He knows prayer works, and the wise dad counts on it for himself and his family.

Because God Himself commands us to pray, we can be certain that our prayers do not fall on deaf ears. We pray because we believe praying works. And because we believe that, our prayers are extremely powerful. Prayers we prayed decades ago for success, God is still answering. Prayers we prayed yesterday for a sick child, God is still answering. And prayers we're praying *right now* for that big decision, God is answering. God didn't forget those long-ago prayers or those yesterday prayers. He also hasn't forgotten the prayers of a faithful wife to make us even better. Even if the specific answer to a specific prayer for a specific need has not yet arrived, God is working to fulfill each request and to meet every need. If we're not careful, it would be so easy to say about God, "Whatever will be, will be."

Lord, this dad wants so much for his family. The more and the better. Help him see all Your answers. In Jesus's name we pray. Amen.

The earnest prayer of a righteous person has great power and produces wonderful results. (James 5:16 NLT)

TONIGHT I'M PRAYING THIS FOR _____

TONIGHT we pray for the dad who has been a good dad. He's been doing dad things so long that he can't think of anything he would be doing otherwise. He provides for and takes care of his family 24/7, 365, and yet sometimes he feels as though his own life gets lost in the mix.

It's easy to forget that Jesus was a man just like each of us before He came into His own as our Messiah. He was a carpenter's son from Nazareth. He took care of his mother Mary after his father Joseph died. He had a strenuous lifestyle just like most of us. Even He had to deal with the day-to-day responsibilities of a loving son that were not necessarily associated with His ministry. But He was adored by people not because of His physical stature or His hard work but because He pointed them to the Father who loved them. And pointing others to the Father is our responsibility as well.

> *Lord, this dad doesn't need a miracle right now. He really needs to know that he's important just for who and what he is—a hardworking guy making the best choices he can for his family and pointing them to You. Strengthen his heart and renew his dedication to his family. In Jesus's name we pray. Amen.*

Him we proclaim, . . . that we may present everyone mature in Christ. For this I toil, struggling with all his energy that he powerfully works within me. (Col. 1:28–29)

TONIGHT I'M PRAYING THIS FOR _____

TONIGHT we pray for the dad who is rich in the best way. For much of his life, he has been committed to a simple lifestyle. He has learned to be content in the understanding that he has been made in the image of God and everything he has is meant to reflect the glory of God. This lifestyle has allowed him to see the value of faith and family.

We know that we cannot stand before God and say that we deserve anything. What we have and how we use it are acts of worship. We might not have the fattest wallet, but we have everything we need. Our goals may be in the future, but we still have successes today. Our home may not be the swankiest, but our family is happy within it. More than anything, our greatest treasure will always be the family we've been given. And that great treasure is worth everything. The long days. The hard work. The sleepless nights.

> *Lord, there's a special peace for the dad who knows he's done his best for his children. Grant him the assurance tonight and the bright hope for tomorrow that they will have an inheritance of that same peace and security. In Jesus's name we pray. Amen.*

Keep your life free from love of money, and be content with what you have, for he has said, "I will never leave you nor forsake you." (Heb. 13:5)

TONIGHT I'M PRAYING THIS FOR _____

TONIGHT we pray for the dad who has had enough disappointments. Maybe he's divorced instead of married. Maybe he's been laid off instead of promoted. Maybe he's been separated from his children until further notice. All these events and circumstances have changed this dad in such a way that he can barely move forward. He sees the disappointments in his mind constantly, and they make him believe he is a failure in all he does. He hasn't been able to achieve the potential of the future because of his focus on the past.

It's hard to look at what is available to us when we are hoping and praying that the promotion and the reconciliations come to pass. How can we be content when we are so discontented? By never losing our faith that the Lord is for us in all things.

Lord, this dad needs a fresh outlook on his life. Show him that the hill of disappointments he's hiking around is actually a mountain of opportunities he can climb. Open his eyes to see new paths to the blessings You have already prepared for him. Strengthen his heart to believe, to try again. In Jesus's name we pray. Amen.

Do not, therefore, fling away your [fearless] confidence, for it has a glorious and great reward. (Heb. 10:35 AMP)

TONIGHT I'M PRAYING THIS FOR _____

TONIGHT we pray for the dad who is a steadfast rock in storms. The storms of life have tested his mettle. But he knows that the good, better, and best of his life are not just related to what his kids can brag about. He understands that his life is not just about earthly rewards.

A new car or a bigger house might sound nice. We can work for those things, and they are wonderful to have. And it's a whole lot easier to be steadfast when there's something tangible in the front yard. But persevering is all about finishing well. If it was easy, anyone could do it. In financial hard times, we work harder. In family troubles, we stand taller. When something absolutely, positively must get done, we take charge because we know we can and must.

Lord, this dad believes that Your reward will come as he remains steadfast in his trust in You. And he has to be able to see farther ahead to guide his family. Give him the vision to succeed tomorrow. In Jesus's name we pray. Amen.

You will keep in perfect peace those whose minds are steadfast, because they trust in you. Trust in the LORD forever, for the LORD, the LORD himself, is the Rock eternal. (Isa. 26:3–4 NIV)

TONIGHT I'M PRAYING THIS FOR _____

TONIGHT we pray for the dad who keeps digging in when it's hard. He's trying to get a foothold in the game of life, and sometimes he feels like he's walking in cleats on concrete. It's been difficult recently to make plans or know that his family is truly safe. But he keeps going, believing that tomorrow will be better. He's accustomed to making all the decisions until he notices that the game is getting out of hand. And that's when he realizes he hasn't been in charge as much as he thought.

The Lord of heaven and earth is the One who decides the outcome of our endeavors. We can work as hard as we want, but it is the Lord who is in charge of the results. Our family is important to us, and we want to be the one they look up to for wisdom and guidance. To accomplish that, we need to put our trust in the Lord and turn over the play calling to Him.

Lord, this dad is determined to make the right decisions. Open his eyes to see the clear path forward and Your divine plan. In Jesus's name we pray. Amen.

Look, I have laid a stone in Zion, a tested stone, a precious cornerstone, a sure foundation; the one who believes will be unshakable. (Isa. 28:16 HCSB)

TONIGHT I'M PRAYING THIS FOR _____

TONIGHT we pray for the dad who is fighting for his child's future. This is a fight that he intends to win. When his kids are involved, he is all in.

Our children are a gift from God. They are more than just extensions of their parents. They are not just small adults with traits and personalities to be treated as problems to be managed. They have life, and they are entitled to the abundant life that the Lord intends for them to have. They are a divine blessing with a promise, a legacy, and an inheritance in them and for them. And their lives require our greatest devotion and energy. From the time they are infants, we must hold them close because the Lord sees their spirits and wants them protected. As a dad, we often see their maturity in physical stature, but we should still see them as vulnerable and in need of our protection.

Lord, we pray for this dad in this spiritual battle. Help him to have Your wisdom, Your patience, and Your understanding. Help him to fight to make his children's future bright. In Jesus's name we pray. Amen.

Praise the Lord! How joyful are those who fear the Lord and delight in obeying his commands. Their children will be successful everywhere; an entire generation of godly people will be blessed. (Ps. 112:1–2 NLT)

TONIGHT I'M PRAYING THIS FOR _____

TONIGHT we pray for the dad who is working to overcome a great setback in his life. He thought he had done everything he could to wipe that unfortunate incident out of his life. He remembers it like it was yesterday, even though he was so, so young when it all went down. The judge had seemed fair-minded and had promised that the record would be expunged if this dad kept his nose clean. But he just recently found out that there was no expungement, and all the truth of his life has come to light.

All our missteps are like this, in a way. But the Lord wants to release us from the fear of forever judgment in our daily lives, regardless of how those stumbles might appear to others.

Lord, this dad has been diligently striving to improve his life with his family in spite of his dilemma. He has been intentional, and it hasn't been easy. But he knows he has to keep going if he ever wants to have the peaceful life he believes You have in store for him. Remind him You are with him at every single step. Give him supernatural strength. In Jesus's name we pray. Amen.

Bring me out of prison, that I may give thanks to your name! The righteous will surround me, for you will deal bountifully with me. (Ps. 142:7)

TONIGHT I'M PRAYING THIS FOR _____

TONIGHT we pray for the dad who is free. Truly free. He is daily realizing God wants him to be who God has made him to be and to do what God has made him to do. He is finding out that he does not have to be bound by the attitudes the world holds for him.

We are free to make our own decisions with and for our family. We do not have to be bound by the past in any of its forms—bad job, bad relationships, bad memories. Instead, we can take the strength and abundance of the Lord that He has promised and wear them as a cloak to remind us of His authority. We know the world won't provide for all our needs, and we are not beholden to whatever material or emotional control someone wants to have over us. We have been through the fire of trials, and our blessings have come from the Lord. Tonight we can rest in the promise of God that the truth will make us free.

> *Lord, thank You that this dad has all the tools, skills, and abilities he needs to succeed. Free him on his journey. In Jesus's name we pray. Amen.*

In my distress I prayed to the LORD, and the LORD answered me and set me free. (Ps. 118:5 NLT)

TONIGHT I'M PRAYING THIS FOR _____

150

TONIGHT we pray for the dad who stays and competes. His plan every day is to succeed and accomplish his goals.

Our plan might be compared to hiking the entire Appalachian Trail. We must gather supplies for each day's journey. We must map out our course and what we can accomplish for that day . . . every day. Others are on the trail with us, with different goals and different supplies and different plans of attack, and we go forth to reach the end of our unique journey. We have daily successes throughout the course of it, but completing the journey itself is the goal. Every day, we remember that we're a dad, and those daily accomplishments keep us going to the next ones. Things aren't always easy, and we have to make hard decisions and pray they are the best ones for our family, because somebody else will have a different idea, a different goal. And because we know our circumstances will change tomorrow, we can prepare for those changes.

Lord, this dad counts on You for everything. Remind him that You have his back. In Jesus's name we pray. Amen.

Each one should test their own actions. Then they can take pride in themselves alone, without comparing themselves to someone else. (Gal. 6:4 NIV)

TONIGHT I'M PRAYING THIS FOR _____

TONIGHT we pray for the dad who lives with diligence every day. On the best days, he rejoices. On the difficult days, he remembers the best ones.

It is so easy to put off tasks that look hard to our natural eyes. We dread tasks that we have not been successful at in the past because we are ashamed of failure. But that attitude ensures our failure. We can never accomplish the tasks we do not start. We must use our spiritual eyes to see the possibilities of success. No matter what, let's commit to making the day all we can make of it. Whether it's good or bad, we keep our eyes forward and continue one step at a time. The best opportunities are just that next step ahead.

Lord, this dad is dreaming of a place of rest and peace, not so he can stand still but so he can rejoice in Your promises. Bless him mightily in his coming and going. In Jesus's name we pray. Amen.

The soul (appetite) of the lazy person craves and gets nothing [for lethargy overcomes ambition], but the soul (appetite) of the diligent [who works willingly] is rich and abundantly supplied. (Prov. 13:4 AMP)

TONIGHT I'M PRAYING THIS FOR _____

TONIGHT we pray for the dad who survived his own childhood. A childhood where nothing was taken for granted. Where growing up was a preparation for a life that was rarely fair, but it was good. This dad was and still is a blessing from the Lord. God intended for him to be a source of joy and a reward as a son to his parents, and as a dad in the future.

Many of us had a dad who loved us, who made us better, who showed us how to be the dad we were supposed to be when we finally grew up. A dad who showed us that work matters and hard work matters more. A dad who gave us no quarter and expected none in return, but who was always fair. A dad who believed in Someone bigger than himself and made sure that we did too. God's plan has always been for parents to produce children who would glorify Him.

Lord, this dad is trying to make all the right choices for his children. He's remembering all the lessons he learned and hoping he can pass them on to those who really count. Give him grace for his continuing journey. In Jesus's name we pray. Amen.

I made Your name known to them and will make it known, so the love You have loved Me with may be in them and I may be in them. (John 17:26 HCSB)

TONIGHT I'M PRAYING THIS FOR _____

TONIGHT we pray for the dad who is praying for a specific healing.

We've all wondered where God was when our children were really sick, times when daily care was required. We can remember that the Lord is well aware of our circumstances and is expecting us to call, so to speak. We should also admit that we tend to specify the Lord's intervention within a particular time, and that's where our predicament lies. The Lord wants us to trust Him with our deepest hopes so that we can experience the greater joy when He answers.

Lord, this dad goes to work and puts in a full day, but his day is way too long. His work responsibilities plus care at home plus the emotional support he gives is using just about all he has, and sleep is definitely at a premium. This dad is praying for his child even though he feels discouraged about how long the sickness has continued. Give him rest and strength tonight, and remind him that as You hear his prayers, You are always in his tomorrow. In Jesus's name we pray. Amen.

Aren't five sparrows sold for two pennies? Yet not one of them is forgotten in God's sight. Indeed, the hairs of your head are all counted. (Luke 12:6–7 HCSB)

TONIGHT I'M PRAYING THIS FOR _____

TONIGHT we pray for the dad who is busy collecting all the threads of his life. He feels unraveled, and he's trying to tie all the loose ends into a coat he recognizes. He really liked how that coat used to fit. Not so long ago, it was a pretty tight weave. He could accomplish all he set his hands to. He knew everything he needed to know—where to go, how to get there, and who was going to pay for it. He loved the idea of power and confidence. And he believed the Lord loved him even more for his continued trust in Him.

But when we realize that we do not have to accomplish great things for the Lord to love us, we can begin to live and move and have our being in that love for what it is—a promise of His peace. We can take the desires of our heart to great heights, and all men will marvel at what we have been able to accomplish because of the Lord's involvement in our lives.

Lord, as a master weaver, You can take what this dad has and put him back together again. Show him what he looks like in Your eyes, and give him peace as he goes. In Jesus's name we pray. Amen.

We know [with great confidence] that God [who is deeply concerned about us] causes all things to work together [as a plan] for good for those who love God, to those who are called according to His plan and purpose. (Rom. 8:28 AMP)

TONIGHT I'M PRAYING THIS FOR _____

TONIGHT we pray for the dad who is searching for answers. He knows not all questions have immediate answers but feels if the Lord only knew just how urgent his circumstances were, surely He would restore his life to what it was before. Before the divorce, before the diagnosis, before the termination notice or the eviction notice. Aren't there words he can pray to bring God into his situation now?

A dad might ask, "Lord, why did this happen right now?" And if he is honest, he knows that the answer to his question might be "Because." It is a hard word, but the truth is that the Lord knows where we are right now. All our searching will lead us to the Lord, the very best destination. That's where all the solutions and answers are.

Lord, You are not One who can be moved by our expressions of how important we are or how much we've given or how sincere we are. You hate the struggles and the fears that hold this dad back. Strengthen him on his journey to find the answers he desperately desires. In Jesus's name we pray. Amen.

If you remain in Me and My words remain in you [that is, if we are vitally united and My message lives in your heart], ask whatever you wish and it will be done for you. (John 15:7 AMP)

TONIGHT I'M PRAYING THIS FOR _____

TONIGHT we pray for the dad who has big, big plans.

Many of us have heard "He who fails to plan has a plan to fail." Most of us also know that big goals and big dreams start with small successes. Yet we often stop at the smaller achievements. Why is that? It's usually because we have a set point in our thinking. "When I have that truck" or "When we have that house in *that* part of town" or "When the kids are all settled" are often the set points for our goals. We tend to think that when we have reached that goal, we can stop and coast. But the Lord's plans are often far bigger than we can imagine. We don't realize that He is making arrangements behind the scenes for us to move beyond those first goals. Sometimes He's calling us into a life of responsibility for more than just our own families.

> *Lord, this dad wants to do his best to fulfill Your plans. He knows that there are even greater expectations for him than he might have realized in Your kingdom. He's the dad who wants to honor You in all things. Bless him as he prepares for the future You have for him. In Jesus's name we pray. Amen.*

> Then the Lord said to me, "You have seen well, for I am [actively] watching over My word to fulfill it." (Jer. 1:12 AMP)

TONIGHT I'M PRAYING THIS FOR _____

TONIGHT **we pray for the dad who travels extensively for his work.** He's worked long enough to recognize stressful situations and frustrations. And because this dad is often at the whim of the weather and road conditions, he lives a life of uncertainty.

Life is a journey, and God cares about all the work we do. There are going to be good days and nights and not-so-good days and nights. Sometimes there will be weeks on end where the job means the same yellow lines and the same diner food. Many of us have traveled long roads, and none of us are the first to feel discouraged. But we can trust God to complete His plan and bring relief and finances in uncertain times. He chose us because He knew that He could count on us to complete the journey. And because each of us has been chosen, He will supply what we need to succeed.

Lord, this dad has so little peace in his life. He needs assurance that You have a plan for him and his family. Remind him of Your promises in all his circumstances. In Jesus's name we pray. Amen.

I had fainted, unless I had believed to see the goodness of the LORD in the land of the living. (Ps. 27:13 KJV)

TONIGHT I'M PRAYING THIS FOR _____

158

TONIGHT we pray for the dad who is wondering if he can take that next step. Success came easy in the past, but now he has doubts about tomorrow.

Sometimes change is hard, and we all handle it differently. It's easy to avoid the changes that present themselves to us if we aren't absolutely certain that they are for the better. When we're younger, we tend not to think about the consequences of our actions. But once we become dads and an entire family is counting on us, well, if the next step isn't right, it's wrong. So when we sit at the kitchen table, or in the cab of our truck, or maybe in our chair after the kids are asleep, we often lay out some plans that we're not sure we can finish. We feel the pressure to have all the things coming together be *just right*.

Lord, pull up a chair or open that door and show this dad exactly which plans are the right ones and which ones can wait. Give him wisdom in his planning and courage to follow through. In Jesus's name we pray. Amen.

If we know that he hears us in whatever we ask, we know that we have the requests that we have asked of him. (1 John 5:15)

TONIGHT I'M PRAYING THIS FOR _____

TONIGHT we pray for the dad who cares for a chronically ill family member.

The normal, everyday responsibilities of being a dad are usually doable. But additional tasks of care can make each day seem endless, especially when the infirmity doesn't subside. One of the hardest things we face in our care for our family is that not every trial is fixable. Sin entered the world, death became an issue, and we are all dying in some form or fashion, each in our own way. We grieve with the infirm person as well as the caregiver, neither of whom can fully understand God's plan in the suffering. Sometimes the best we can hope for in the moment is that the spiritual part of us, the heart of God within us, is being refined to be more like Him. Even if we never learn what the Lord intends for our refining.

> *Lord, the stress of thinking that tomorrow will probably be just like today can be overwhelming. And while this dad's hopes and dreams appear to be on hold, You still have a plan. Strengthen him to commit his energies to providing the best care he can for everyone as he trusts in You. Remind him that You will always make up the difference. In Jesus's name we pray. Amen.*

Nevertheless, I will bring health and healing to it; I will heal my people and will let them enjoy abundant peace and security. (Jer. 33:6 NIV)

TONIGHT I'M PRAYING THIS FOR _____

TONIGHT we pray for the dad who has reasons to rejoice. Maybe it's because that new job takes effect. Maybe it's because he's coming home sooner than expected. Maybe it's because his family is getting ready to grow. For every event, this dad remembers God in all His blessings. He knows God has intervened in his life, and he has trusted Him in all things.

God wants us to experience joy in everything we do and everything we have. We have a tendency to think we should rejoice at great occasions. But we can celebrate the wonderful, unexpected answers to prayers, and we can celebrate the seemingly mundane blessings of a cool rain on a hot day or a hug from one of our children. We can always rejoice, even when there are obstacles.

> *Lord, we know that You have everything under control and You have prepared this dad to overcome obstacles. Now You are sending blessings his way and his destiny is taking shape. Rejoicing is in order as he trusts in You. In Jesus's name we pray. Amen.*

Rejoice in the Lord always [delight, take pleasure in Him]; again I will say, rejoice! (Phil. 4:4 AMP)

TONIGHT I'M PRAYING THIS FOR _____

TONIGHT we pray for the dad who is struggling right now. Not so much with immediate losses like jobs, relationships, or physical health, but with lost opportunities. You know, not measuring up.

Sometimes our greatest burden is our great potential. When everybody says we're going to make it big, we want to know we're going to survive our mistakes, free from fear, free from worry. When we believe in ourselves and our ability to make things happen and they just don't happen, what do we do? We can still hold on to the promises we've been given. We can still live a life of honor and experience all the blessings of God.

> *Lord, You know that his reward hasn't come . . . yet. That his joy hasn't come . . . yet. That his wholeness hasn't come . . . yet. That if he quits today, it will be one day too soon. Remind him that You are the source of all his blessings and he has the choice to receive them. Give him another day to go forward. In Jesus's name we pray. Amen.*

The LORD doesn't see things the way you see them. People judge by outward appearance, but the LORD looks at the heart. (1 Sam. 16:7 NLT)

TONIGHT I'M PRAYING THIS FOR _____

162

TONIGHT we pray for the dad who knows that what he is going through is real. Unfortunately, he has a tendency to magnify those trials in his mind. He is often wondering, "What if . . . ?" before he's even had a chance to address the issues that are troubling him. And that anxiety weighs him down with unnecessary burdens. To him, his fears are real, his sleeplessness is real, and his worries are real.

Fear is often a function of past experiences, and we make decisions based on how we responded in the past. So when we can calm our mind and refuse to consider the prison of the past, we can focus on possible solutions to our problems. We can also weep with those who weep in their own trials, and help them look ahead to what is possible when they overcome their fears.

Lord, there are miracles in Your hands and promises in Your voice. Bring total healing to this dad's mind tonight. In Jesus's name we pray. Amen.

Cast your burden on the LORD, and He will sustain you; He will never allow the righteous to be shaken. (Ps. 55:22 HCSB)

TONIGHT I'M PRAYING THIS FOR _____

TONIGHT **we pray for the dad who gets up every morning and does what he needs to do.** Driving a truck, working in a shop, moving information from place to place. Or maybe his responsibilities keep him at home for homeschooling. And while he's committed, he knows there is an enemy of our souls.

The enemy has different names and characters. At the very least, that enemy can be characterized as the personification of a worldview that is against the authority of God. The enemy can also be described as a culture that wars against who we are and what we believe. When we're enlisted in the army of God and believe in the leadership of Jesus Christ, we need to be ready to go wherever that leads us. Our ultimate claim to fame is that we never quit. We choose our challenges, we're good at what we do, and we plan to win every day. We suit up because our family counts on our determination.

Lord, You have this dad on speed dial for a reason. Bless his dedication tonight and give him peace for tomorrow. In Jesus's name we pray. Amen.

We can make our plans, but the LORD determines our steps. (Prov. 16:9 NLT)

TONIGHT I'M PRAYING THIS FOR _____

TONIGHT we pray for the dad who remembers how much good there is in his life and in his family. He doesn't expect the worst to happen, and he doesn't dump his bad news on his family as soon as he comes home.

We know that our responsibility is to bring home the bacon, so to speak. And that's not just the food, shelter, and clothing our family needs on a daily basis. We have to be the guy who calms fears, solves problems, and is strong, especially when our family needs us. We can do these things when we are willing to release control in our life and follow the Lord wherever He leads.

Lord, this dad doesn't always know how You're going to work out the solutions, but he's willing to trust You in every situation. You continue to give him direction and show him the best way to fulfill Your purpose in his family's life. Ease his heart and bring the good things and good times more into focus. In Jesus's name we pray. Amen.

Oh, how abundant is your goodness, which you have stored up for those who fear you and worked for those who take refuge in you, in the sight of the children of mankind! (Ps. 31:19)

TONIGHT I'M PRAYING THIS FOR _____

TONIGHT we pray for the dad who seeks stability after a long day.

God calls His people to all things for His glory. It doesn't matter what other responsibilities we may have set aside to accomplish it; His calling is right and true. Unfortunately, our best plans settled on His calendar can be and often are changed at a moment's notice. These changes surprise us, but there are no surprises to God. He ordains and establishes what His divine will should be. So we start the day with God in preparation. Let's call on Him while it is today. Because some days the Lord's plan comes after a hard day has already passed and we're ready for a rest, not a change.

Lord, this was a tough day for this dad, and there might be another one just like it tomorrow. Give him grace to see Your plans in advance, as he only wants to serve You. And for those responsibilities placed before him that he just wasn't able to get to, prepare his tomorrow in advance. In Jesus's name we pray. Amen.

The Lord is good, a stronghold in a day of distress; He cares for those who take refuge in Him. (Nah. 1:7 HCSB)

TONIGHT I'M PRAYING THIS FOR _____

TONIGHT we pray for the dad who knows he can't be afraid if he is to succeed.

One of the things we can never forget is that God is in absolute control of everything. We may not like the results of our own actions or the actions of others, but at the end of the day, God knows what is about to happen. And because He's in charge of the future, He can say, "Do not be afraid." If we are always looking around for what bad things might happen, we will never be able to grasp what is before us to succeed in our choices. There are times when we'll worry about how things will work out. There are times when we'll feel like the circumstances will never change for the better. But even when things look bleak and the struggles are real, we have to be strong and face them today instead of tomorrow.

Lord, remind this dad of his victories and erase his fears, small and large. Remind him he can be standing tomorrow in Your strength with a clear heart and mind. In Jesus's name we pray. Amen.

God has not given us a spirit of fearfulness, but one of power, love, and sound judgment. (2 Tim. 1:7 HCSB)

TONIGHT I'M PRAYING THIS FOR _____

TONIGHT we pray for the dad who is up for a challenge. It seems like he's always ready to accomplish some yet-to-be-determined test. It could be something that he's never done before. Or maybe it's something he used to be able to do and now wonders if he's still "got it."

Challenges help us become who we are supposed to be. The greatest challenge we will ever face is becoming a father. We are promising to help at least one human being grow from birth to adulthood. God expects us to provide for that child and protect them from themselves and the world until He releases us from the physical responsibility. But God never absolves us of the spiritual and emotional responsibility of always looking out for that child. So when we struggle with this challenge, it is only because we are destined to be a great dad. That is why dads don't quit. They know, really know, how very much is riding on the outcome.

Lord, this dad needs Your strength and assurance that he is ready for his own challenge. Grant it, Lord. In Jesus's name we pray. Amen.

When he was yet a great way off, his father saw him, and had compassion, and ran, and fell on his neck, and kissed him. (Luke 15:20 KJV)

TONIGHT I'M PRAYING THIS FOR _____

TONIGHT we pray for the dad who has always had aspirations for himself and his family. He has always wanted what's best for them, even if his job was hard or his goals took some time to achieve. He's always been willing to go the extra mile, take the long road, and try hard, especially for those things that are of great value.

Life isn't always easy, so we need to be ready to pick ourselves up after a struggle and keep going. But there's more to our lives than just our work and aspirations. We're not just doers, making sure that we dot every "i" and cross every "t." Our days should not be consumed with how well we have overcome the struggles in our lives. Sure, we do overcome and we want to start the next day fresh. But the Lord is the real prize, right? His peace, His presence—these are the aspects of our lives that give us the most joy. The struggles fade when He appears. And so, with God's help, we find out that we can have a richer, more peaceful understanding of the world and our place in it with our family.

Lord, give this dad fresh eyes to see the true prize and the determination to reach it tomorrow. In Jesus's name we pray. Amen.

May you have the power to understand, as all God's people should, how wide, how long, how high, and how deep his love is. May you experience the love of Christ. . . . Then you will be made complete with all the fullness of life and power that comes from God. (Eph. 3:18–19 NLT)

TONIGHT I'M PRAYING THIS FOR _____

TONIGHT we pray for the dad who tries to be his best, to be strong and wise every time. He chooses every day to be exactly what his family needs.

Being a dad is hard work, but each time we choose to do our best, we become better at providing for our family. At the end of the day, in order to make the right choice, we must give our most earnest attention to the Lord. We're free to pick our own path, for sure, but we want to obey God. Not out of any duty or obligation, but because we know there will be peace in our heart when the decision we've made honors the Lord.

Lord, this dad always wants to make the right decisions. Remind him that You are strong, You are wise, and You have a good path for him as well. Make the way plain so that each step gets him to where You want him to be. In Jesus's name we pray. Amen.

If any of you lacks wisdom, let him ask God, who gives generously to all without reproach, and it will be given him. But let him ask in faith, with no doubting. (James 1:5–6)

TONIGHT I'M PRAYING THIS FOR _____

TONIGHT we pray for the dad who is going for it. There's an opportunity out there that has eluded him for some time, and he's decided it's worth making the additional effort.

We live in a culture where people who give quite a bit less than their all are excused because they have been passed by or not rewarded for what they have actually achieved. Those people disdain hard work because they believe they're entitled to choose the remuneration for their endeavors. But God instills in us a sense of fulfillment for the work we do because He intends it to be productive on our behalf. He wants us to count the cost beforehand and consider whether the work can be completed. And when we decide that whatever it takes, the work will get done, we need to start and not stop until it's finished. No more "But this" or "But that." No more "If only I'd . . ." It's time to give our all so we can reach our goals.

Lord, this dad has asked You many times for the resolve to make a difference. Grant him that request again. In Jesus's name we pray. Amen.

You shall eat the fruit of [the labor of] your hands, you will be happy and blessed and it will be well with you. (Ps. 128:2 AMP)

TONIGHT I'M PRAYING THIS FOR _____

TONIGHT we pray for the dad who has an idea. Not a hope, not a wish, not a dream. Not a "Gosh, that would be great" or a "Maybe this could happen," but instead, "I believe in my ability to succeed."

The Lord has made us creative. Every one of us has some level of creativity so that we can bless the Lord by our expressions of the gifts He's given us. He saved us to do good things, to step out in faith. Haven't we all thought at one time or another, "Wow, I could have done that"? No, not all ideas make a million dollars. Yet success in small things often proves we are more capable than we might think. So we try again.

> *Lord, this dad knows You give good gifts and, as a good Father, You want him to prosper. Multiply the ideas in his heart and give him the courage to act on them. In Jesus's name we pray. Amen.*

We are His workmanship [His own master work, a work of art], created in Christ Jesus . . . for good works, which God prepared [for us] beforehand, . . . so that we would walk in them [living the good life which He prearranged and made ready for us]. (Eph. 2:10 AMP)

TONIGHT I'M PRAYING THIS FOR _____

TONIGHT we pray for the dad who believes he can overcome the problems he's faced all his life. These problems have kept him from successes in the past, but he never wants to believe that failure is forever. This dad was raised to see the Lord in each and every step and misstep, and that's how he trained his children. He's looking for that fresh outlook on life. He's confident that the Lord has a plan to move him from the valley to the mountaintop.

God does not choose great men to accomplish ordinary things on the earth. He chooses ordinary men to accomplish great things! And ordinary men like us experience failures from time to time. More than likely, those failures prevent us from even greater disappointments later on. When we willingly present those missteps to the Lord, He will shine the light of His mercy on us, and we can begin anew in our endeavors to bring about success in our family.

> *Lord, this dad is determined to make a way where there has been no way. Help him use what he knows as well as what he's learned to be a success for his family. In Jesus's name we pray. Amen.*

> If we confess our sins, he is faithful and just and will forgive us our sins and purify us from all unrighteousness. (1 John 1:9 NIV)

TONIGHT I'M PRAYING THIS FOR _____

TONIGHT we pray for the dad who just isn't making it. He's sure he can succeed. He's been there before. But this night, probably this week, maybe even this month, there hasn't been much to brag about.

We've all felt like we weren't making it at times. We know what that feels like. All sorts of trials and tribulations can make us believe there's just no end in sight to our troubles. Financial issues, health issues, loneliness—the difficulties never seem to let up. When something desperate befalls us, that corner we're backed into just seems so dark and closed. We're ready to step into the light that everyone else talks about, but we just can't see it. At these times, we don't recognize how close the Lord actually is. And hopefully the family we love is standing strong with us.

Lord, this dad is down right now, but he's trusting You for the "up" once again. Lift him to higher heights as he wrestles through difficulties with the help only You can give. In Jesus's name we pray. Amen.

Then the LORD answered Job out of the whirlwind and said, . . . "Since your days began, have you ever commanded the morning, and caused the dawn to know its place, so that light may take hold of the corners of the earth and shake the wickedness out of it?" (Job 38:1, 12–13 AMP)

TONIGHT I'M PRAYING THIS FOR _____

TONIGHT we pray for the dad who is who he is. He's a good dad who accepts how he's made and what he does. He knows there is no purpose in attempting to hide his actions and character from the Lord.

God knows the truth. So we do the very best we can, knowing life can change at any moment. We cannot be concerned about what it will take to make tomorrow successful. We must make tough decisions every day. And it's only when we stop worrying about decisions we've made in the past that we are able to see clearly the choices for today. Today we can try our best to make choices that bring life and health to those we love.

> *Lord, being a dad is hard work. Show this dad how to have an even better tomorrow. In Jesus's name we pray. Amen.*

Moses said to the LORD, "Oh, my Lord, I am not eloquent, either in the past or since you have spoken to your servant, but I am slow of speech and of tongue." . . . Then the LORD said to him . . . "I will be with your mouth and teach you what you shall speak." (Exod. 4:10–12)

TONIGHT I'M PRAYING THIS FOR _____

TONIGHT we pray for the dad who believes he's going to make it through another day. He doesn't often do anything more spectacular than pay the bills and love his family the best way he knows how.

But sometimes there are unexpected crises. Are there any other kinds? If we saw them coming, they wouldn't be crises but trials we could address the way we always have. Take comfort in knowing that there are no crises to God. He is in control. The wind and the waves are subject to His bidding. He is not surprised by anything that might happen to us. Still, it's easy to wonder how today and even tomorrow will play out. But if the bills are paid and the doors are locked and everyone is where they're supposed to be, that's not just making it, that's prospering.

Lord, this dad is making it through sheer determination. Ease his burden from carrying today's heavy load, and reward him with the promise of a better tomorrow. In Jesus's name we pray. Amen.

Beloved, I pray that in every way you may succeed and prosper and be in good health [physically], just as [I know] your soul prospers [spiritually]. (3 John 2 AMP)

TONIGHT I'M PRAYING THIS FOR _____

TONIGHT **we pray for the dad who sometimes feels as though he's still just making his way.** In the beginning of his career as a father, he wasn't sure he would make it. Or, at least, his learning curve was going to be longer and more winding than that of anything he'd ever embarked upon.

There are some things we're really good at as a dad. We make a decent wage and the family has an okay life. We want to be the dad who can look out for them in every way possible, to keep them safe and sound, even though such an expectation seems impossible today and maybe tomorrow as well. That's what we worry about. But we can remember that God is the One who placed our family into our hands and told us to keep them safe. When we do our best, that's always been good enough.

Lord, this dad is seeking understanding. You have a plan specifically for him and he's working it. Show him the full picture as Your purpose comes to pass. Strengthen his heart tonight. In Jesus's name we pray. Amen.

I am the Lord, who opened a way through the waters, making a dry path through the sea. (Isa. 43:16 NLT)

TONIGHT I'M PRAYING THIS FOR _____

TONIGHT we pray for the dad who is committed to overcoming the normal, natural setbacks in his life. He's been a mover and a shaker, and he wants the life where he's on top again. But he never wants his family to fear, and he's confident that by trusting in the Lord he will rise to the challenge just like he always has.

Our lives cycle through different feelings and emotions on an almost daily basis. Sometimes it's a depression mindset that's gotten worse or a deep desire to cast out fears of failure. For most of us, it's not as though these fears just emerged yesterday. We've been there and we're still doing that. We may even have taken on some new bad habits that our family worries about. The toughest part of getting to the place of healing for our mind and our emotions is believing that we can get there from where we are. It requires taking that first step to where the Lord is standing, holding out His hand.

Lord, this dad knows he's an overcomer by Your grace. Strengthen him even more to fulfill his destiny. In Jesus's name we pray. Amen.

Come to Me, all of you who are weary and burdened, and I will give you rest. All of you, take up My yoke and learn from Me, because I am gentle and humble in heart, and you will find rest for yourselves. (Matt. 11:28–29 HCSB)

TONIGHT I'M PRAYING THIS FOR _____

TONIGHT we pray for the dad who leans into his potential.

Each of us has been given gifts by God that are made greater by how we use them. The Lord gives us these gifts so we can do the work of the ministry each of us has. Some gifts involve the use of our hands and feet, our physical bodies, to accomplish God's will on the earth, while some gifts allow for us to administer and direct others in the best use of their own strength. Some of us are better at calculating numbers, teaching our kids, or arguing in a courtroom. Some of us, like doctors and social workers, give our everything to make sure others have what they need. But each of us, in our own way, should be aware of what we have received from the Lord and how we can become a better dad as we grow in our potential.

Lord, this dad is growing stronger in You than ever before. He is learning to walk the path You have laid out before him with greater clarity than he's ever had. He knows that You guide him every day as he diligently seeks Your face. He's grateful for what he's been given, so bless him tonight. In Jesus's name we pray. Amen.

See to it that no one takes you captive through hollow and deceptive philosophy, which depends on human tradition and the elemental spiritual forces of this world rather than on Christ. (Col. 2:8 NIV)

TONIGHT I'M PRAYING THIS FOR _____

TONIGHT we pray for the dad who loves his kids. He works hard so that these gifts from God will see how to succeed in this life. He wants to leave the best part of himself with them. He wants to show them every day what family means and what it takes to keep them safe and strong.

As a dad, as a father, we are responsible for our children forever. Sometimes family circumstances evolve to a point where we are forever dads to children we see only periodically. Conversely, sometimes we inherit, if you will, children we have never known before. Since God wants us to always see ourselves as a parent, as a father, how we come to know these additions to our family is all a part of God's plan for our lives. He has not and will never release us from that awesome responsibility. These children are loved by God, and He ordains and establishes the families that He desires.

Lord, dads who love their kids are, by definition, doing a good job. Remind this dad of that fact tonight, tomorrow, and every day. In Jesus's name we pray. Amen.

I have no greater joy than this: to hear that my children are walking in the truth. (3 John 4 HCSB)

TONIGHT I'M PRAYING THIS FOR _____

TONIGHT we pray for the dad who just wants to be happy. Work's okay, and he's not exhausted from it. It's just that he'd like to look around and be happy with what he has before feeling like he must go out and get "more."

The world is not on our side about what brings us happiness. The Lord instilled the concept in dads about providing for a family almost when we were born. We just knew that it was our role to take care of our family. And when they were provided for, we were content. But then the world stepped in and somehow convinced us that we couldn't be happy if we didn't have "more," and that our family wouldn't be happy unless they had "more" as well. It was like the goalpost moved and enough wasn't enough anymore. The pressure on dads is sometimes too much.

Lord, this dad doesn't have to yearn for something else. He just wants a moment of satisfaction, and he finds that in You. Be present with him as he takes a breather today. In Jesus's name we pray. Amen.

Godliness actually is a source of great gain when accompanied by contentment [that contentment which comes from a sense of inner confidence based on the sufficiency of God]. (1 Tim. 6:6 AMP)

TONIGHT I'M PRAYING THIS FOR _____

TONIGHT we pray for the dad who knows he's a good dad. He leads from strength instead of fear. He remembers how he once held his daughter's hand as she took her first wobbly steps. He remembers when he let go of her hand and she began to walk on her own, ever so gingerly, until she lost her balance and fell down. Sometimes she stepped forward; sometimes she fell and picked herself up. But because dad was there, she knew she would walk someday.

Our children are characteristically humble and teachable. They believe in us. They trust us. It is only as we grow into adults that we forget we had that same level of trust. Now when we encounter God, right away we start asking questions of the One who picks us up when we fall.

Lord, this dad knows where he is going, and he leads confidently because he remembers that You have never let go of his hand. Lead him to continue to trust You and to bring his family safely through any challenge. In Jesus's name we pray. Amen.

I assure you . . . unless you repent [that is, change your inner self—your old way of thinking, live changed lives] and become like children [trusting, humble, and forgiving], you will never enter the kingdom of heaven. (Matt. 18:3 AMP)

TONIGHT I'M PRAYING THIS FOR _____

TONIGHT we pray for the dad who looks forward to tomorrow as an opportunity. Yesterday's expectations may have been tough, today's trials were seemingly minute to minute, but tomorrow always has potential. The responsibilities of fatherhood never go away. He must deal with his own struggles that can hold him back but still chart a course to family security.

It is God who gives us the power to obtain wealth, but it is only with diligent effort that we can say we will see success. God promises blessings, both material and spiritual, to those who acknowledge His presence in their lives. God wants us to have real peace, the kind that allows us to live a secure life, one with provision of adequate resources. So no matter what yesterday and today have been, we keep our head up and eyes forward because tomorrow will be better.

Lord, remind this dad that only You can truly set him on a path to success. Remind him to keep his eyes focused on You. In Jesus's name we pray. Amen.

My God shall supply all your need according to his riches in glory by Christ Jesus. (Phil. 4:19 KJV)

TONIGHT I'M PRAYING THIS FOR _____

TONIGHT we pray for the dad who is a successful business owner. For a long time, this dad worked for others and learned everything he could about how to be in business. He didn't waste one opportunity to gather the knowledge and skills to run his own enterprise someday. When his senses told him that it still wasn't possible, his faith saw it completed. Now that day is here, and he is using every ounce of strength and courage to make a go of it.

There are so many challenges in the business world, and many of them are out of our control. But we can control our own efforts and work hard to be a success for our family.

Lord, bless this dad as he continues to watch over those he loves. He's never been extravagant, just a dad who believes in himself and the voice of the Lord. He knows that each task, each expectation, each responsibility makes him the dad You have called him to be. Remind him tonight that he's got this. In Jesus's name we pray. Amen.

Write down this vision; . . . so one may easily read it. For the vision is yet for the appointed time. . . . Though it delays, wait for it, since it will certainly come and not be late. (Hab. 2:2–3 HCSB)

TONIGHT I'M PRAYING THIS FOR _____

TONIGHT **we pray for the dad who tries to do it all.** He likes to succeed in everything he does—you know, checking all the boxes when it comes to his responsibilities with his family. He's pretty sure there isn't anything he can't do if given enough time, and there isn't anything he won't do for his family.

There's nothing wrong with getting things done. Aren't most of us like that? If given the task—the key word being "given"—don't we move toward completion? But the Lord is not interested in what we can do in our own strength. We're supposed to be rejoicing in what we can and do accomplish *because* of Him and His strength and commitment. It is not our works that save us. Instead we can be focused on our relationship with the Lord.

> *Lord, this dad does what he does by choice and not by obligation. And he gives his whole heart to what he does with his children. You lived Your life just that way, powered by Your Spirit. Remind this dad that You will always strengthen his heart. In Jesus's name we pray. Amen.*

We who serve God by his Spirit, who boast in Christ Jesus, and who put no confidence in the flesh. (Phil. 3:3 NIV)

TONIGHT I'M PRAYING THIS FOR _____

TONIGHT we pray for the dad who needs to see the path before him clearly. He knows better than to settle for the easy path and just take what comes. He also knows that he must often push through the difficulties to thrive. So this dad watches for the path the Lord has set before him.

The path we choose determines our destination. If we wanted to take a trip from Oklahoma City to Alaska, we wouldn't head south to Dallas. No matter how much we wanted to go to Alaska, we just wouldn't get there. So it's important that we let the Lord guide us in our journey, wherever we are going. God wants to walk with us on the path He has chosen for us. And only when we walk together with Him on that path can we fully experience all the joy He has in store for us. Let's never forget that although the path can be rocky, if we keep the Lord close at hand, we can avoid the pitfalls that might cause us to stumble.

Lord, open this dad's eyes to see the best way to lead his family to prosperity. In Jesus's name we pray. Amen.

Ponder the path of your feet; then all your ways will be sure. Do not swerve to the right or to the left; turn your foot away from evil. (Prov. 4:26–27)

TONIGHT I'M PRAYING THIS FOR _____

186

TONIGHT **we pray for the dad who has to work too many shifts at his job.** Sometimes he wonders if he's in over his head because he just cannot seem to get ahead. The extra shifts all seem to pay so much more, but there is always the sacrifice of time with his family. His kids are often in school when he goes off to work, and they're asleep when he returns. But he has to keep the good pay for their sake. He knows that keeping his family safe is his most important responsibility.

For those of us who go to work in the dark and come home in the dark, life can be lonely. The kids might be awake when we leave but are probably asleep when we return. It makes us miss them something awful and wonder when we'll be able to see them more. It's time to trust the Lord with His timing and let Him work out the details for when the job is finished.

Lord, this dad has a tough job to do, and he steps up to fulfill it every day. Give him the tools necessary to finish his daily routine. Strengthen him so he may see all his dreams come to pass. Help him find the joy and peace he needs to make his job bearable again. In Jesus's name we pray. Amen.

The LORD directs our steps, so why try to understand everything along the way? (Prov. 20:24 NLT)

TONIGHT I'M PRAYING THIS FOR _____

TONIGHT we pray for the dad who works hard in keeping up with all his responsibilities.

It seems that no matter which direction we turn, there is always some emergency waiting for us around the bend, and there's not always enough time to regroup and rethink a daily schedule when emergencies arise. There is no doubt that our responsibilities and the pressures of the world make us feel like the urgent often overwhelms the important. However, God is not surprised by our time and talent issues. He is not controlled by time as we are. His will is perfect, His timing is perfect, and His blessings are perfect. God acts and gives us the opportunity to accomplish His plan *exactly* when He wants it to be completed.

Lord, expand this dad's vision so that he can trust in your timeline. Give him wisdom tonight to see all the important things of tomorrow in a new way. In Jesus's name we pray. Amen.

Teach us to number our days carefully so that we may develop wisdom in our hearts. (Ps. 90:12 HCSB)

TONIGHT I'M PRAYING THIS FOR _____

TONIGHT we pray for the dad who remembers the Spirit of God within himself. He works through difficulties knowing that he has the peace, the provision, and the protection of God. This dad wants the pure stuff, the real deal, the "I don't know how I lived without it" confidence that God walks with him daily.

God Himself, in the person of the Holy Spirit, takes up permanent residence in the heart of the believer. And this Spirit assures us that we belong to the Lord, that we can have fellowship with Him. Imagine that! Walking with God as it was in the beginning, when nothing separated us from a perfect life. When we get ahold of that—I mean *really* grab it and wave it like we don't care who knows it—nothing will be able to stop us! And blessings will fall on us that we will not ever want to quench.

Lord, this dad is a child of God, an heir to heavenly fortunes, and tomorrow can be the best day of his life. Make Yourself real in his life right now, and prepare him for tomorrow. In Jesus's name we pray. Amen.

He is the Spirit of truth. . . . But you do know Him, because He remains with you and will be in you. (John 14:17 HCSB)

TONIGHT I'M PRAYING THIS FOR _____

TONIGHT we pray for the dad who is intentional.

We have to be intentional about our relationship with the Lord before any good plan for our lives will come to pass. Most importantly, however, we must allow the Lord to be the ultimate decision-maker for our plans. That means we must decide that we will die to our own wants, needs, and desires and rely on His wisdom and the Holy Spirit to make the call. Only then should we make plans and attempt to follow through. We can be goal driven, but the goals must be His. And once we understand the goals He intends, we can focus on the process by which they are accomplished.

Lord, this dad knows that life happens and things don't always work out just right. But his desire to accomplish what he believes is Your instruction is greater than any setback that arises. So he keeps going, knowing that if he stops, pretty much everything else does too. At the end of the day, he trusts You for the results. Bless him with a little more drive for tomorrow to keep going Your way. In Jesus's name we pray. Amen.

I say, walk by the Spirit, and you will not gratify the desires of the flesh. (Gal. 5:16)

TONIGHT I'M PRAYING THIS FOR _____

TONIGHT we pray for the dad who is confident. He's confident because he knows that when he prays, the God of heaven and earth is actually listening to him. He believes that this same God will do what he is asking of Him. There are ups and downs, but this dad keeps going forward because there is no quit in him. He prepares for each day as though his kids' lives depend on him, because they do.

We can become better dads when we believe in ourselves, sure. But what really opens the well of our souls is when we believe that God is making us better by our praying. The more we pray, the more our confidence grows. We can rest assured that this confidence has absolutely nothing to do with our own feelings or how often we pray. It is the assurance of our relationship with the Lord, being in Him, that empowers us.

Lord, this dad knows where his hope comes from, and he thanks You for it. Keep him in Your strength as well. In Jesus's name we pray. Amen.

In whom we have boldness and confident access through faith in Him [that is, our faith gives us sufficient courage to freely and openly approach God through Christ]. (Eph. 3:12 AMP)

TONIGHT I'M PRAYING THIS FOR _____

TONIGHT we pray for the dad who knows his strength. He recognizes that he can stop feeling vulnerable to enemies and start feeling equipped to contend with them.

Whether we know it or not, the Lord has placed within us the ability to care for and protect others. Most of the time we let someone else do it because, well, we're pretty busy right now. If we only knew the power and the resources we have at our command, we would stop being Clark Kent and start acting like Superman. In prior times of war and conflict, strong leaders have encouraged those under their protection that they can sleep soundly because rough men stand ready to defend them. The whole armor of God is intended to be an offensive weapon to protect those who would be harmed, not just the wearer. King David did not put on the armor God provided him just to protect himself. He used it to protect Israel.

> *Lord, this dad believes he can be a strong man and use Your Word, Your truth, and Your righteousness to protect and save those who would be harmed by the enemy's wiles. Strengthen him today and tomorrow. In Jesus's name we pray. Amen.*

We do not wrestle against flesh and blood, but against the rulers, against the authorities, against the cosmic powers over this present darkness, against the spiritual forces of evil in the heavenly places. (Eph. 6:12)

TONIGHT I'M PRAYING THIS FOR _____

TONIGHT we pray for the dad who is on a one-way journey.

We have a tendency to believe that following the Lord is a life of drudgery. After all, didn't He say that we should deny ourselves, ignore our wants, and carry our cross? Aren't we pretty sure He means no days off? And how about those Christians who don't deny themselves? How should we feel about them? But we've got it all wrong. The Lord is telling us that we should put aside our human frailties, our base wants and desires, while still recognizing that our cross actually represents a spiritual position and presence. We are not supposed to follow ourselves or to elevate our wants and needs over Him. We are to follow Him to the exclusion of everything else. Remember, a cross represented a one-way journey back in the day. This is not a life filled with unmet desires but instead a life of fulfilled relationship with God.

Lord, the whole world was created for Your children. They have been created in Your image. When this dad denies himself and his authority and follows You and Your authority, he will have all the grace, humility, and patience to experience Your kingdom and glory. Bless him as he follows You. In Jesus's name we pray. Amen.

I lift my eyes to you, O God, enthroned in heaven. We keep looking to the LORD our God for his mercy, just as servants keep their eyes on their master. (Ps. 123:1–2 NLT)

TONIGHT I'M PRAYING THIS FOR _____

TONIGHT we pray for the dad who is sometimes uncertain about what he should do.

We have all wondered at times whether we have actually heard the voice of the Lord. We know that we're supposed to pray always, just for the opportunity to be more clear about what the Lord's answers sound like. Many of us have heard or read about how each shepherd calls their own flock in their own unique way. Jesus told His followers that His sheep know His voice. We should know the Lord's voice as well. And most of the time, we are ready to say, "Lord, if it be Your will, bid me to [fill in the blank]." But sometimes when we hear His voice and the answer is different for this time and this circumstance, we just want to say, "Lord, is there anyone else up there with You?" It is as though we are hoping for a second still small voice.

Lord, this dad trusts You in all things. He listens to You for all things. He is successful in his daily walk because he knows Your voice. During this time of promise and promises in his life, when he hears that encouragement to dream bigger and to go faster than yesterday, remind him of exactly what Your voice sounds like. In Jesus's name we pray. Amen.

Ascribe to the LORD, you heavenly beings, ascribe to the LORD glory and strength. . . . The voice of the LORD is powerful; the voice of the LORD is majestic. (Ps. 29:1, 4 NIV)

TONIGHT I'M PRAYING THIS FOR _____

TONIGHT we pray for the dad who knows he has to be the rock. Wherever he is, whatever he's doing, he's living his life knowing that his family needs him. He is always the dad and that never changes. He knows who he is and who the Lord has made him to be, making him strong enough to meet the challenges of the day.

Some of us can remember watching westerns directed by John Ford. The location was set in Monument Valley, which is in southeastern Utah and northern Arizona. As a camera pans the scenery, we see huge rocks, perhaps hundreds of feet high, towering over the landscape. They seemingly have no connection to any of the other rocks. They are unmoving and unchanging. However we might imagine a rock, as a dad, we are a rock when we know God personally and understand who He is. We know that the Lord is worthy of praise, and we will always be the ones who declare His strength on the earth.

Lord, continue to walk with this dad and be ever present with his family. In Jesus's name we pray. Amen.

Come, let us shout joyfully to the L ord, shout triumphantly to the rock of our salvation! (Ps. 95:1 HCSB)

TONIGHT I'M PRAYING THIS FOR _____

195

TONIGHT we pray for the dad who can change.

One of the hardest things for dads to do is change their plans. We like to make our lists, and we like to know what lies in store for us throughout our day. However, it is the essence of humility to recognize that we do not have all the answers. Remember the adage "98 percent of the truth is still a lie"? Well, the same can be said that if we are not absolutely sure we are right, then we are wrong. So when God says, "This is the way you should go," it is somewhat pointless to head somewhere else. While He is God and He does not change, a sudden bend in the road or different signposts than we are accustomed to probably seem unnerving to our mortal understanding and make us doubt what the plans are.

> *Lord, this dad knows You are in control. He doesn't lose his cool when circumstances change. He's confident that these new and different directions will lead to better outcomes than he might have anticipated. Send Your Holy Spirit to ease his heart and mind in the changes. In Jesus's name we pray. Amen.*
>
> The end of a matter is better than its beginning, and patience is better than pride. (Eccles. 7:8 NIV)

TONIGHT I'M PRAYING THIS FOR _____

TONIGHT we pray for the dad who is confident in his ability to raise his children.

Raising children isn't hard. Not really. In the beginning we're told that all we have to do is keep them warm, fed, and dry. Those are the instructions for infants, to keep them from crying and disturbing our slumber. And we continue to do those things for as long as they're part of our household. We keep them warm with a roof over their heads, we keep them fed, and we keep their faces dry when we wipe their tears away. That's what we do, and we're good at it. The hard part is teaching them how to survive away from us in an often godless world. We teach them that they can accomplish their goals because God loves them unconditionally and will stand with them. We show them how to win because God has stood with us as well. But in our heart of hearts, we know there's still more than that. To raise them right, we must share our heart with them. In order to accomplish and win, they must know the God who knows their dad.

Lord, keep this dad's heart strong and his eyes on You so he can show his children what real confidence is. In Jesus's name we pray. Amen.

Where your treasure is, there your heart [your wishes, your desires; that on which your life centers] will be also. (Matt. 6:21 AMP)

TONIGHT I'M PRAYING THIS FOR _____

TONIGHT we pray for the dad who feels as though he has always been a survivor. He's willing to lead his family through the challenges that often accompany these days. He knows there are exciting times coming for this family when they rally together.

There are all sorts of survivors. We all know someone who has survived the worst experience imaginable. And all of us have survived the life we have chosen to live. For better or worse, no one has the right to compare their life with ours. And when struggles are a part of our life, it would be so easy to question why we must endure them, and not some other person who has never faced a day of hardship. Yet if we spend our time trusting God instead of questioning Him, we can believe that the best days are still to come.

Lord, this dad is well prepared to take his family where You lead them. Strengthen his heart in the journey. In Jesus's name we pray. Amen.

Jesus said to him, "If I want him to stay alive until I come [again], what is that to you? You follow Me!" (John 21:22 AMP)

TONIGHT I'M PRAYING THIS FOR _____

TONIGHT we pray for the dad who charges straight ahead into the storms.

Storms are a part of life. No matter how we position ourselves, we're going to experience heavy weather, as it were. No amount of preparation will prevent us from dealing with trials and tribulations. The mere fact that we have survived storms in the past does not mean there won't be more just around the corner. But if we find ourselves in the storm of the century, the Lord tells us to, like any good sailor, steer into the storm, pointing into the waves, always moving forward to keep from capsizing.

> *Lord, You have protected this dad in his storms. He has remained faithful to Your lead even when he felt that things have not always gone well. Give him wisdom to help him overcome poor decisions in the past. Help him as he leads his family and seeks to get them through, all the time saying, "Come on, we can do it." Help him to continue because his family always comes first. In Jesus's name we pray. Amen.*

Let me be delivered . . . from the deep waters. Let not the flood sweep over me, or the deep swallow me up. (Ps. 69:14–15)

TONIGHT I'M PRAYING THIS FOR _____

TONIGHT we pray for the dad who is ready to start a new workweek.

We have a tendency to treat the Sabbath as the end of the week. We're familiar with the notion that God created the world in six days and on the seventh day He rested. We've worked hard for six days, and now it's a day of rest for us as well. But that seventh day was not a "do nuthin'" day like we think. You see, God intended for the day of rest, that seventh day, to be an anticipation for His plan in the coming six days. The first six days of creation were just that—creation days. Everything that was had been completed. But in God's economy, it's on that seventh day that we are to spend time with Him, listening for His instructions and trusting He will provide strength and power to engage in creative activity all over again. We're not creating the sun, the earth, and the seas as He did. But we are re-creating in our own world to accomplish His purpose.

Lord, this dad has indeed worked hard this week. He's done what You have asked him to do, and he has accomplished Your purpose with success and excellence. Tonight he's ready to hear from You about what tomorrow brings. Bless him as he stops and rests with You. In Jesus's name we pray. Amen.

One person considers one day to be above another day. Someone else considers every day to be the same. Each one must be fully convinced in his own mind. Whoever observes the day, observes it for the honor of the Lord. (Rom. 14:5–6 HCSB)

TONIGHT I'M PRAYING THIS FOR _____

200

TONIGHT we pray for the dad who has hope in the Lord. In the everyday walk of his life, he has stayed strong and managed accordingly. He refuses to lose hope no matter what circumstances surround him. Most of all, he keeps his family safe because he remembers that they are still his most important responsibility.

There are many times when we could have given in to temptation. We may have been wrestling with temptations for years, and sometimes we feel surrounded by the things that would call us away from the Lord and our family. But we cannot abandon our faith or the family God has given us. When others turn to addictive behaviors, we turn from temptation and put our faith in God. We take delight in the Lord's presence. And we learn that as we spend time with the Lord, He will help us want what He wants.

Lord, this dad keeps going forward carrying hope with him as his lifeline. Bless his commitment to You and bring his family peace, hope, and joy. In Jesus's name we pray. Amen.

Watch and pray that you may not enter into temptation. The spirit indeed is willing, but the flesh is weak. (Matt. 26:41)

TONIGHT I'M PRAYING THIS FOR _____

TONIGHT we pray for the dad who wants to be a better dad. It's not the same as being a better worker or a better student. Supervisors and professors have goals and responsibilities that the dad might have to adhere to if he wants to succeed. But his children see him for who he is, and he wants to measure up.

We can very easily get caught up in tasks and responsibilities, clocks and calendars, and lose sight of the importance of those around us. We often exchange the important for the urgent, and we fail to connect with the flesh-and-blood people around us. Once we've given our all to our work or educational responsibilities (all with the idea of making money, of course), there's just not that much left for anything or, more importantly, anyone else. Being that better dad is about building relationships with our family, especially our children. It's hard because we can't always measure how we're doing. But the more we portray Christ in our demeanor, attitudes, and words, the more our children will respond to our overtures of a relationship.

Lord, open this dad's eyes to see the path to becoming a better dad. Show him how to love his children better day by day. In Jesus's name we pray. Amen.

The reward for humility and fear of the Lord is riches and honor and life. (Prov. 22:4)

TONIGHT I'M PRAYING THIS FOR _____

TONIGHT we pray for the dad who knows what needs to be done. Not everything gets done right away, but whatever he starts, he finishes. He makes difficult decisions and accomplishes his tasks no matter what resistance he faces. He sets his face like flint toward God's expectations, and he doesn't get distracted or discouraged.

Whatever God has to offer, we want to take. We know that if we give up at any point, we have given up too soon. No matter what the world speaks to us—anxiety, fear, you name it—we can focus on the good things of God. From beginning to end, we want to stay committed to our family and work through whatever life brings with determination and patience. Tonight we can surrender ourselves to the will of our heavenly Father in every way.

Lord, sometimes this dad is weary and wonders if he'll have what it takes tomorrow. He has kept everybody going, and they have counted on him to press on through these very tough times. Remind him that You are in tomorrow just like You were in today. Refresh his heart and mind. In Jesus's name we pray. Amen.

A righteous man falls seven times, and rises again, but the wicked stumble in time of disaster and collapse. (Prov. 24:16 AMP)

TONIGHT I'M PRAYING THIS FOR _____

TONIGHT we pray for the dad who believes he can make a difference.

Not one of us has any idea just how important we are in God's economy, in the kingdom of God. The Lord has given us abilities, opportunities, and a desire to accomplish miracles in His name. He even reminds us that when we have provided blessings to the least of His children, He will be the One who acknowledges our handiwork on His behalf. The Lord doesn't brag about how much we give of our wealth or how hard we work for a church. He brags about our acts of love and our care and concern for those who are in need right now. And when we stand before Him, with our crowns for Him in our hands, He will receive us with honor because we honored Him.

Lord, this dad works hard to provide for all the needs of and be responsible for his family. But he wants to know that he counts for something more than just making his pay. At the end of the day, he knows that as a dad, he will change the life of at least one human being. And that's forever. Remind him that his importance is always measured by his godly influence. In Jesus's name we pray. Amen.

I am the good shepherd. I know My own sheep, and they know Me, as the Father knows Me, and I know the Father. I lay down My life for the sheep. (John 10:14–15 HCSB)

TONIGHT I'M PRAYING THIS FOR _____

TONIGHT we pray for the dad who has a son going off to college. This dad did his best to raise his son up to be a man who is responsible and kind and honest and loyal. He gave him every tool he could to live in this world as a Christian man who loves the Lord.

Sometimes we worry that we didn't do enough as we send our son out to make his way in the world. Did we forget to tell him something important, like how to make his own decisions? But we also know that our son was well-raised in the faith and the Lord will be with him wherever he goes. Though we may have occasional trepidation about our son's safety, we can trust the Word, which says that the Lord is a friend who sticks closer than a brother. We can trust the Lord's promise to watch over our son and walk with him.

Lord, may this dad have peace as he sees his son off and throughout the school year. Be present in his son's life in undeniable ways, and may they both be blessed by this new educational year and experience. In Jesus's name we pray. Amen.

There are "friends" who destroy each other, but a real friend sticks closer than a brother. (Prov. 18:24 NLT)

TONIGHT I'M PRAYING THIS FOR _____

205

TONIGHT we pray for the dad who still has childhood pals.

We may not live in the same community as our friends anymore, as most of us move away as adults. But as we have aged together or apart, with our decidedly different families, we usually look back fondly on the times we spent with our childhood friends, having matured to the point that our lives now make more sense than they did while we were growing up. These friends know all our stories, our strengths, our weaknesses, and—shameless sports analogy to follow—whether we could throw a football spiral. They know *us*. They also may be dads who the Lord still uses, and He multiplies our combined abilities to reach others and do even greater works than we might have thought possible years before.

Lord, this dad is grateful for the relationships that You have used to make him a better dad. He remembers the joys and sorrows that he shared with his friends. Those friends are a gift and he is grateful. Bless their lives. In Jesus's name we pray. Amen.

What about your brother . . . ? I know he can speak well. . . . I will help both of you speak and will teach you what to do. (Exod. 4:14–15 NIV)

TONIGHT I'M PRAYING THIS FOR _____

TONIGHT **we pray for the dad who sometimes feels invisible for his service.** There have been times in his life recently when he felt an urge to be more involved in the life of his local church. He's been faithful to keep the peace and support the church throughout his community.

It's wonderful to watch how dads are changed when they are moved by the Holy Spirit to be engaged in the life of a local church. Many of us have been there, moving from attending a men's Bible study to serving with other dads in community functions. The Spirit moves us from sitting in the back of the boat waiting for the next storm to blow up, to taking care of business when it does. This is work that is appropriate and effective. Soon we realize that our lives are being used to bring honor and glory to the Lord, for whom we are doing the good work in the first place.

> *Lord, this dad goes about his life making sure that he's dotted all the i's and crossed all the t's, confirming all the responsibilities of church life that he's signed up for. Remind him that You are well pleased with him as tomorrow comes. In Jesus's name we pray. Amen.*

As they were ministering to the Lord and fasting, the Holy Spirit said, "Set apart for Me Barnabas and Saul for the work I have called them to." Then after they had fasted, prayed, and laid hands on them, they sent them off. (Acts 13:2–3 HCSB)

TONIGHT I'M PRAYING THIS FOR _____

TONIGHT **we pray for the dad who remembers when things were easier.** Until just recently, he and his whole family were doing well. There were some stumbles but they were getting along just fine. Now it's hard to see many financial blessings. Finances are tight. He can't just buy what his kids want or take that trip. But this dad wants to trust the Lord in every area of his life. He knows that he is more than his job and what he can provide for his family.

God wants us to always focus on Him and not on our daily cares and comforts. We start the day with God, but soon it's filled with all the distractions that clutter our mind, our will, and our emotions. And soon we can't remember how good life actually is.

Lord, remind this dad to take that moment to really get in touch with You. You don't require much in these circumstances—just his presence as he seeks Your presence. Remind him that You are close. And as always, help him keep his family safe. In Jesus's name we pray. Amen.

I will [solemnly] remember the deeds of the LORD; yes, I will [wholeheartedly] remember Your wonders of old. (Ps. 77:11 AMP)

TONIGHT I'M PRAYING THIS FOR _____

TONIGHT we pray for the dad who is in the middle of an important decision. He's dealt with finances, family issues, work schedules, and assorted illnesses. All his decisions have been important in some way. But some are more important than others, and he wants to make just the right choice now.

God wants us to make the right decisions based on what He desires. He always wants us to be dependent upon Him. As a dad, we sometimes take it upon ourselves to be self-sufficient, as if we shouldn't need the Lord because we've always been successful before. Sure, we have free will, but God wants us to obey Him with it. Our mind, will, and emotions are not nearly enough to trust in when big decisions are needed.

> *Lord, this dad needs Your wisdom tonight of all nights so he will be prepared for tomorrow's actions. Open his eyes to see the best path to take, and give him the courage to take that first step. In Jesus's name we pray. Amen.*

> If it is unacceptable in your sight to serve the Lord, choose for yourselves this day whom you will serve . . . ; but as for me and my house, we will serve the Lord. (Josh. 24:15 AMP)

TONIGHT I'M PRAYING THIS FOR _____

TONIGHT we pray for the dad who is unsure if he will make it another day. He's been up and he's been down. He got a good night's sleep, but the pressure of this morning was just overwhelming. He's one to finish what he starts, but the job is taking way too much of his emotional capital. He needs hope that there will be some real relief on its way.

We've all had times when the days feel twenty-five hours long, and when we fall into bed, tomorrow comes too soon. For those of us who have been there and done that, we know that the Lord promises us His help. He never slumbers or sleeps. He knows we're going to have days when we are physically and emotionally consumed. It doesn't matter why we're losing the battle or what the circumstances are, His strength is everlasting, and He makes the way straight and smooth for the next day.

Lord, this dad knows in his heart that he needs to look to You instead of trying to make it through this really tough challenge on his own. Help him realize just how much help You are in times of trouble. Restore him completely. Give him the resolve to press into Your presence. In Jesus's name we pray. Amen.

O Lord, do not stay far away! You are my strength; come quickly to my aid! (Ps. 22:19 NLT)

TONIGHT I'M PRAYING THIS FOR _____

TONIGHT we pray for the dad who focuses on giving real encouragement instead of getting results.

Most of us have brought home report cards with significantly less than perfect scores. In those instances, some of us were "encouraged" to never do that again. In some cases, our parents' "encouragement" made us not want to even go back to that class. But encouragement literally means "heart strength," and we believe that the Lord lives in our heart in the person of the Holy Spirit. When we are faced with a task, a project, an endeavor we might believe is beyond our grasp, the Lord reminds us that we can make it happen. Just as He encourages our heart for our responsibilities, so do we believe that for our family to prosper, we must encourage them totally. There is no right or wrong, only forward for them.

Lord, this dad knows that giving his love can't be about performance, and he gives all he has. Fill his heart with more than enough love. In Jesus's name we pray. Amen.

The LORD is my strength and my shield; my heart trusts in Him, and I am helped. (Ps. 28:7 HCSB)

TONIGHT I'M PRAYING THIS FOR _____

TONIGHT we pray for the dad who has children who still ask for one more story and one more drink of water.

When our children were younger, it was so much easier to provide for them. What did they need, really? Cheerios for breakfast, a little macaroni and cheese for lunch perhaps, and fish sticks for supper. A nap and a clean diaper and we're good to go, right? But oh so soon, they really need to know what we have to say. And we better be ready. If we're not now, when will we be? Whether we know it or not, the Lord has given us so much to say. He has filled our heart with stories that only we can tell. Tales of success and failure, of accomplishment and falling short. And our kids love us all the more when they hear that we got back up after getting knocked down.

Lord, this dad has lessons stored up for his kids, things he wants to teach them so that they can tell the stories to their children. One of those lessons is the gift of time. Bless him with more time tonight. In Jesus's name we pray. Amen.

These words that I command you today shall be on your heart. You shall teach them diligently to your children, and shall talk of them when you sit in your house, and when you walk by the way, and when you lie down, and when you rise. (Deut. 6:6–7)

TONIGHT I'M PRAYING THIS FOR _____

TONIGHT we pray for the dad who wants to know he can still climb that mountain. He believes he can achieve mighty goals with help from the Lord. He believes he can improve in certain areas of his life, and while it might take a while, he's convinced that he hasn't done all or been all he could be. He's sacrificed in the form of hard work and long hours. Yet he still believes he can do even more.

Maybe there's still that one true test we want to pass. It might be that dream career. It might be getting that degree to prove to ourselves we can do it. Maybe it's running that marathon after all the 10k's. And then there's the test of being a dad. For that, we sacrifice our very lives to be the best dad we can be. Yet, with everything we set our hands to and everything we hope to accomplish, our family is still at the top of the list. We never forget that our individual achievements pale into insignificance when compared to our family's hopes and dreams.

Lord, this dad believes there's more to him than just what people see. He wants to climb that mountain to be closer to You. Show him the desires of his heart. In Jesus's name we pray. Amen.

Go up on a high mountain. . . . Raise your voice loudly. Raise it, do not be afraid! Say to the cities of Judah, "Here is your God!" (Isa. 40:9 HCSB)

TONIGHT I'M PRAYING THIS FOR _____

213

TONIGHT we pray for the dad who tries harder. When things are going well, he wants them to be better. When life is throwing curves, he keeps swinging instead of giving up. When he comes home in anguish from his working conditions, he simply gets ready for the next day.

As much as our culture looks forward to retiring into a life of leisure as soon as possible, that's not God's plan. It's a hard sell, but God's plan was and is for a dad to work. He wants us to have the joy of achievement. Working is creating; working is producing. God provides work so that we can have the privilege of fulfilling His instructions, which carries with it the promise of provision for a dad and his family. When we look to God as the provider in our lives and use what He has provided, He returns to us provision and peace. He assures us that there will always be more than enough.

Lord, strengthen this dad's heart as he keeps going. He knows that very important people—his family—are always counting on him. Strengthen his hands and guide his feet to succeed. In Jesus's name we pray. Amen.

Whatever you do, work heartily, as for the Lord and not for men, knowing that from the Lord you will receive the inheritance as your reward. (Col. 3:23–24)

TONIGHT I'M PRAYING THIS FOR _____

TONIGHT we pray for the dad who is always thinking of ways for his family to make it. From the big ideas to the day-to-day responsibilities, or from near or far away, he's always working to keep them safe and secure.

When we believe that our security comes from the Lord, we can trust that what He provides is then what we are able to provide for our family. To the greatest extent possible, we endeavor to keep our family safe from the evils in this world, as well as from the natural calamities that occur in and near our community. While a certain amount of security is in the peace of adequate resources, it is a fool's game to trust in worldly riches, as if God blesses only those who are rich. Our determination may keep us going, but we need to keep our trust in God's provision.

Lord, as this dad is preparing for tomorrow, guide his hands and feet to make the way smooth for his family. In Jesus's name we pray. Amen.

Blessed [with spiritual security] is the man who believes and trusts in and relies on the Lord and whose hope and confident expectation is the Lord. (Jer. 17:7 AMP)

TONIGHT I'M PRAYING THIS FOR _____

TONIGHT we pray for the dad who is standing on the edge of something wonderful. He's been here before. He's ready to take that next step toward success for his family. But before he does, he makes sure to ask the Lord.

It's way too easy to jump into something just because it looks inviting or safe, and not have the success we're hoping for. If there's a rope swing hanging out over a lake, we can pretty much assume that someone has tested the strength of the rope and the depth of the water below. But we'd want to know for sure, right? There can be just a second between defeat and victory, between despair and rejoicing. And sometimes that second is needed to ask the Lord what He thinks about the endeavor.

Lord, this dad has been tested and refined. He's had his share of success by waiting that one second, and his share of failure by jumping too soon. He also knows that as long as he keeps going, he can achieve more than he might have hoped. Strengthen his resolve and remind him that You can meet every need and make every success possible. In Jesus's name we pray. Amen.

These are just the beginning of all that he does, merely a whisper of his power. (Job 26:14 NLT)

TONIGHT I'M PRAYING THIS FOR _____

TONIGHT we pray for the dad who would love a second chance. He's made a mistake or ten.

We've all gotten it wrong a few times, and like we always do, we turned around and set about trying again. The Lord has plenty of chances in His hands for the times we repent and acknowledge those mistakes we continue to make. We don't have to live in the failures of the past because He wants us to live in the successes of the future. Now, it's natural to think we are damaged goods and of no earthly use to the Lord. But He is actually closest when we fail. When our own children fall or fail, we want them to run to us as quickly as possible. The Lord wants us to do the same. We are not damaged goods. We are redeemable merchandise, called by the Lord to be used again and again and again.

Lord, You've seen the trials and setbacks this dad has had throughout his life. While he might reflect only upon his flaws, You see his destiny. Help him keep his spiritual perspective and his eyes forward to see what lies ahead with each chance he gets. In Jesus's name we pray. Amen.

Then the word of the LORD came to Jonah the second time, saying, "Arise, go to Nineveh, that great city." (Jon. 3:1–2)

TONIGHT I'M PRAYING THIS FOR _____

TONIGHT we pray for the dad who strives to be the best in everything he does. It's his thing. This dad wants to be the best at things no one else has even tried. He has been made in God's image, which means that God's character is a part of him.

We even want to be better than ourselves. When we're running on an empty track, not another soul in sight, we want to be faster than the day before. How many times do we play the same golf course, hoping we will do better than the last time? The only thing that holds us back is a sense of laziness or quitting before we're tired. There are times when we decide to settle for a little less—but that's not in our nature. We want to stay on the track, and at the end of the day, God gets the glory, showing us the way to achieve all His goals for us.

Lord, this dad is proud that his next step forward is always the right next step. He makes it his aim to always seek excellence in all his pursuits. Help this dad to keep going forward with courage in all circumstances. In Jesus's name we pray. Amen.

I will not set before my eyes anything that is worthless. I hate the work of those who fall away; it shall not cling to me. (Ps. 101:3)

TONIGHT I'M PRAYING THIS FOR _____

TONIGHT we pray for the dad who moves past his regrets. In the natural realm, he knows that those memories cannot change the past and they can only slow down the future. So he leads his family, trusting the promise of a better future instead of a worse one.

We all have scars, don't we? Haven't we all fallen off a bike or tripped while running and hit something immovable? Some scars are visible, some not so much. Some of us have mental scars or memories that we would just as soon forget. We remember the times we've fallen and just couldn't get up. Like when we didn't get that promised promotion, which would have solved all our financial difficulties. But there have also been times when we've fallen in the spiritual realm—fallen short of the glory of God. Those are heart scars, and they hurt. When we trip and fall against the Holy Spirit living in our heart, as they say, "It leaves a mark." Only the Lord can heal those regrets.

Lord, remind this dad that he has more triumphs coming when he wakes up tomorrow because he was ready today. In Jesus's name we pray. Amen.

"I will give you back your health and heal your wounds," says the Lord. (Jer. 30:17 NLT)

TONIGHT I'M PRAYING THIS FOR _____

TONIGHT **we pray for the dad who has seen the view from the mountaintop.** He's had joys and blessings that he thought might never end, that he wishes could last forever. He's been able to look out over the landscape and see a path to prosperity. But he discovered that in order to find that path, he had to leave the mountaintop to chart his family's course.

God didn't just let us get to the mountaintop for the sake of a great view of life. Those mountaintop highs are for us to have courage to do the hard work of raising the family He's given us. The real work is down in the valley of our regular experiences, where the path is rocky and dangerous. But since we know the mountaintop, we can trust and believe we're going there again to prepare for even greater challenges. So let's keep our eyes up to see the prize.

Lord, this dad's heart is strong and he's determined to experience Your glory. Take him to the mountaintop again. In Jesus's name we pray. Amen.

The LORD said to Moses, "Come up to me on the mountain and stay here, and I will give you the tablets of stone with the law and commandments I have written for their instruction." (Exod. 24:12 NIV)

TONIGHT I'M PRAYING THIS FOR _____

TONIGHT we pray for the dad who gets up every single time. He is committed to this life. It requires heart—a heart of faith, a heart of promise, a heart of hope. He arises not just to hang on for dear life. He's prepared to work deliberately every single day. There is no hitting the snooze button in the morning. When life happens, this dad gets up. Daycare closes—he gets up. Plumbing issues—he gets up. The truck's transmission fails—he gets up.

Even if the world throws haymakers, it is that heart of hope that gets us through the toughest times. When our company lays us off or the hospital calls with tough news, we don't have to stay down long. We can look up from the mat to the One who has all the resources, the One who can lift us up and stand us on our feet. With God's help, we know absolutely that what we seek we will find, that we will accomplish what we must and won't be conquered by our setbacks.

> *Lord, this dad is always ready to answer the bell for his next round. Fulfill Your promises as always. In Jesus's name we pray. Amen.*

> You need to persevere so that when you have done the will of God, you will receive what he has promised. (Heb. 10:36 NIV)

TONIGHT I'M PRAYING THIS FOR _____

TONIGHT we pray for the dad who does it all for joy. He operates in joy. When this dad works hard and takes those extra steps toward success, when he considers what the next day will hold, that's when he relies on that strength found in joy.

Joy is an attitude that cannot be disguised. Either we're living in joy or we're not. Many of us work at hard, tough, and often painful jobs. But joy can be the space we live in while we are accomplishing God's goals and feel His presence in them. Nehemiah 8:10 says, "The joy of the LORD is your strength," and that's the key. Unlike the peace of the Lord, which can and often does just fall upon us as His presence envelops us, joy comes when we feel His approval for our actions.

Lord, You probably won't hear this dad complain because he's not an "all eyes back to me" kind of dad. He believes that joy is available every morning, and he's always ready for his new challenges. Speak to him and keep his heart full of joy. In Jesus's name we pray. Amen.

Then he said to them, "Go your way. Eat the fat and drink sweet wine and send portions to anyone who has nothing ready, for this day is holy to our Lord. And do not be grieved, for the joy of the LORD is your strength." (Neh. 8:10)

TONIGHT I'M PRAYING THIS FOR _____

TONIGHT we pray for the dad who is committed to excellence. He always wants to be accomplishing something, getting things done. Sometimes circumstances and life keep him from finishing everything he starts. But he also believes he's a godly dad. And in order to live up to that, he knows he must be always growing, always learning, always chasing after God. It takes all his heart, mind, soul, and strength.

Sometimes doing our best at the end of our day, when we're at home, takes more energy and commitment than we might have left. But when we commit ourselves to who and what the Lord calls us to, we will find that we can accomplish way more than we might have thought. Our to-do list might have things left over for tomorrow, but that's just because the Lord came first today and now we're making sure our family is taken care of.

Lord, remind this dad that You have his back when he gives his all to You. Help him finish today's journey strong. In Jesus's name we pray. Amen.

You should be an example to the believers in speech, in conduct, in love, in faith, in purity. . . . Practice these things; be committed to them, so that your progress may be evident to all. (1 Tim. 4:12, 15 HCSB)

TONIGHT I'M PRAYING THIS FOR _____

TONIGHT we pray for the dad who always does his best because that's all he can do. Really, it's all he's ever done. However, it's not just about working hard. There is nothing that this dad cannot accomplish with the right attitude, the right commitment, and the right energy. All these things are just as important as the tools he picks up to begin his work.

We know everything we do should be done with a sense of God's purpose. That's why it is so important that the Lord is a full partner in our plans. And we don't work for what we hope to receive from the world. Those rewards are fleeting. But never doubt that God will reward our endeavors. That's His promise from the beginning. When we call on Him, He answers. When we do our best, we know that the outcome is in God's hands. We need to be willing to trust God and make sure our family knows we do.

Lord, continue to walk closely with this dad so his family can see You closely too. In Jesus's name we pray. Amen.

Let your light shine before men in such a way that they may see your good deeds and moral excellence, and [recognize and honor and] glorify your Father who is in heaven. (Matt. 5:16 AMP)

TONIGHT I'M PRAYING THIS FOR _____

TONIGHT we pray for the dad who is grateful for the gifts he's been given. He knows that not only has he received a wonderful wife and children from the Lord, but he has also been given exactly the right attributes, abilities, and attitudes to make his family prosperous and happy.

Gratitude springs from the heart. When we praise the Lord, such praise emanates from our heart. And while we are supposed to praise Him in all things, we are much more willing to praise Him for what we have received from Him. It's easy to be thankful for what we receive from others. A professional response from a bank teller or good service from a server—those are the types of things we are thankful for, and we tell others about them. Yet we are not truly pleased from our heart because, in some small way, we believe we are entitled to such things. But when we have gratitude, our heart is engaged because we are fairly certain that we have not deserved what we have been given.

> *Lord, You see this dad's heart. Continue to bless him with the confidence to lead his family along the right path that You have prepared. In Jesus's name we pray. Amen.*

Show me your ways, Lord, teach me your paths. Guide me in your truth and teach me, for you are God my Savior, and my hope is in you all day long. (Ps. 25:4–5 NIV)

TONIGHT I'M PRAYING THIS FOR _____

TONIGHT we pray for the dad who does all the dad things in every season.

Sometimes when mom is away, the mom things are also the dad things. Every couple can decide how they will split the responsibilities of parenthood. They may have made choices to be home with the kids at different times if necessary. And caring for our kids is an easy reach for a dad who listens to God. We work hard to make sure they have everything they need. When we're home with them, we make sure they have our attention. We may be the dad of take-out meals because we're just not as good in the kitchen as mom is, but we also remain the dad of strength and wisdom.

Lord, this dad is becoming the best dad he can be. He knows that his relationship with his children is singularly important, not just as a parent but as a true father in Your eyes. Open his heart to grow even more. In Jesus's name we pray. Amen.

For everything there is a season, and a time for every matter under heaven: . . . a time to cast away stones, and a time to gather stones together; a time to embrace, and a time to refrain from embracing. (Eccles. 3:1, 5)

TONIGHT I'M PRAYING THIS FOR _____

TONIGHT we pray for the dad who didn't make it home unscathed.

From time to time, many of us have felt like "offense magnets." Jesus told us that offenses would come and we should get used to it. When we feel offended, it's usually not that we've been physically harmed. It's more about our honor or our importance or our value being diminished, or someone thinking less of us than what we think we deserve. It's really all about us rather than the offender. Yet the Lord loves us, and our true value comes from Him. And as much as we chafe at it, He loves His disrespectful children as well. So we need to let Him discipline those who offend us.

> *Lord, this dad has had run-ins with unfeeling supervisors, bad actors on the streets of his city who act unkindly, and foolish and often less-than-helpful clerks. Yet he managed to keep his wits about him and prove that he is respectful and respected. He is a dad who is a role model for his kids, and he takes that responsibility very seriously. He has earned his restful place today. Help him keep going in the same way tomorrow. In Jesus's name we pray. Amen.*

Do nothing from selfish ambition or conceit, but in humility count others more significant than yourselves. (Phil. 2:3)

TONIGHT I'M PRAYING THIS FOR _____

TONIGHT we pray for the dad who is wondering about his purpose in life.

We want to believe that God has a purpose for each of us, and a select few of us are absolutely positive that the Lord Himself told us long ago what we were going to do. But there aren't very many of us who know why we do what we do or what the Lord's plans are. Many of us live our lives because circumstances dictated our choices, and we are safe and secure with those choices. We happily live with them to this day. But—shameless sports analogy to follow—most of us feel like the third-string quarterback on the football team, wondering if the coach is ever going to put us in the game. If it even matters that we're there. The answer is it does. We are all important in God's economy of life, and even the third-string quarterback has purpose.

Lord, assure this dad every day that You are with him on his journey. In Jesus's name we pray. Amen.

God has put the body together, giving greater honor to the less honorable, so that . . . the members would have the same concern for each other. . . . If one member is honored, all the members rejoice with it. (1 Cor. 12:24–26 HCSB)

TONIGHT I'M PRAYING THIS FOR _____

TONIGHT we pray for the dad who likes to get things done. He's a doer. No sitting around for this dad. He's always busy. When someone asks if he can do something, his answer is never "I'll try." He knows that triers try and doers do. He's usually willing to accomplish any task for someone who needs his help.

We have a mighty calling on our lives. The Lord uses us to uplift others. Whether we know it or not, we are often the answer to someone else's prayers, and our children also know this drill. They watch and believe they will have the same success when they grow up. It can be hard work, being a great dad. But we come by it honestly because we have sought the Lord and have made the choice to live a life of calling.

Lord, as long as this dad's breathing, he's working, and that working is answering a call of God. He's working to make a life for his family and helping others—the life You gave him. Give him even more strength, Lord. In Jesus's name we pray. Amen.

I will come down and talk with you there. And I will take some of the Spirit that is on you and put it on them, and they shall bear the burden of the people with you, so that you may not bear it yourself alone. (Num. 11:17)

TONIGHT I'M PRAYING THIS FOR _____

TONIGHT **we pray for the dad who waits for God's interventions.** He always leaves space for the Lord to move in his life.

We think we know what we're doing, right? We get really caught up in our own plans, our own procedures, our own lists of things to do. We know we shouldn't, but we do because we've been successful in the past. When we're locked into thinking that the plan is the plan and the Lord has okayed the whole undertaking, we can miss a massive change right up to the end of the program. Yet when we're hyperaware of His presence, we'll see those little changes that He's making for us throughout the project. The Lord is constantly crossing our path by sending His Holy Spirit through people with all sorts of questions that cause us to pause. We think we're being disturbed when in reality, that still small voice we often wonder about is whispering to us.

Lord, this dad trusts You in the major plans and the minor tasks. He sometimes doubts Your timing, but he knows You are still the Lord of times and seasons. Remind him that You are constantly making his path straight, if he will only watch where he's going. In Jesus's name we pray. Amen.

This is what the Lord says: "Stop at the crossroads and look around. Ask for the old, godly way, and walk in it. Travel its path, and you will find rest for your souls." (Jer. 6:16 NLT)

TONIGHT I'M PRAYING THIS FOR _____

TONIGHT **we pray for the dad who sets a spiritual standard for his children.** He's always known that he's expected to do his best, to make the best way for his children. So he prays that his very being will be the example of faith his children will remember when they think about their dad.

We're like that, aren't we? We work hard, pay the bills, love the kids' mother, be the type of model that we expect of ourselves. But there's more to what we model for our kids. Think of Jesus. People were moved just by His presence. He healed people, delivered them from spiritual bondage, and ultimately gave up His life as a sacrifice on behalf of all of us. And while the Lord is pleased with our efforts to be the best dad we can be on this side of heaven, He expects to be present *with* us so that we can be a heavenly example for our children.

> *Lord, this dad doesn't shy away from his spiritual responsibilities just because he works hard. He is better each day because his children are watching. Bless him tonight with even more wisdom for tomorrow. In Jesus's name we pray. Amen.*

Your wife will be like a fruitful vine within your house; your children will be like olive shoots around your table. Behold, thus shall the man be blessed who fears the LORD. (Ps. 128:3–4)

TONIGHT I'M PRAYING THIS FOR _____

TONIGHT we pray for the dad who is dedicated. He gives his all in everything he does. He lives his life in total love for his family and steadfastly perseveres with the Lord, because that's where his strength comes from. He also has the attitude "If it is to be, it's up to me." No matter where the Lord leads him, this dad is the one accomplishing His purposes at the end of the day.

We make the choice to live for our family. We've probably heard that Jesus had a servant's heart for His people. He taught his disciples that they should always be willing to serve. We understand those words as referring to how we treat those around us. But shouldn't we have a servant's heart for our family first? And if it truly is up to us, it's because we make the choice to serve. When we became a dad, we probably hoped fatherhood would be easier than it is. But because of our dedication, the cost just doesn't matter.

Lord, this dad gives everything he has or ever will have to secure the future for his family. You have many promises yet to be fulfilled in this family. Remind this dad that You are dedicated to them as well. In Jesus's name we pray. Amen.

Be devoted to one another with [authentic] brotherly affection [as members of one family], give preference to one another in honor. (Rom. 12:10 AMP)

TONIGHT I'M PRAYING THIS FOR _____

TONIGHT we pray for the dad who doesn't measure time by weeks and months but day by day by day. And he daily considers the Lord's timing in everything he does.

There have been so many events in our own lives, the success or failure of which has been determined by whether we consulted the Lord when it was necessary. That's how close the Lord wants to be in touch with us. We can't continue to believe that just because we get up and go to work at the same time every single day that the Lord doesn't have something new, different, or exciting in store for us on this particular day. We should have an expectation that each day will be different because the Lord is in it. His timing is impeccable.

> *Lord, this dad thinks about tomorrow and is certain that it will be better than today because he hears Your voice and moves in the direction You lead. He is trusting You for the success of his family. His faith in his own abilities together with the security of the promises in Your Word keep him going forward, ready for the new things You have for him. Awaken this dad with strength and an even better vision for tomorrow. In Jesus's name we pray. Amen.*

LORD, let me know my [life's] end and [to appreciate] the extent of my days; let me know how frail I am [how transient is my stay here]. (Ps. 39:4 AMP)

TONIGHT I'M PRAYING THIS FOR _____

TONIGHT we pray for the dad who feels like he's surviving. He's less desperate than he might have been in the past because he can see that the future still has potential. He just doesn't think he can get to it.

The Lord knows what is in store for us. He also knows the present, and He knows what it will take for us to move from the here and now to the "about to be." The Lord wants us to be a success at whatever we set our hands to so our future is full of hope. When we focus on the present challenges and weaknesses that so readily overcome us, we can limit the opportunities God has for us. It's a whole lot harder to see ourselves as mighty warriors when we're hiding from the defeats we've experienced in the past. In order to move from surviving to thriving, we have to believe that God actually has a plan and future in store for us. And pretty soon, our hope will turn into real options.

Lord, remind this dad to keep his eyes on You to see his blessings multiply. In Jesus's name we pray. Amen.

Ask me and I will tell you remarkable secrets you do not know about things to come. (Jer. 33:3 NLT)

TONIGHT I'M PRAYING THIS FOR _____

TONIGHT we pray for the dad who is struggling to remain noticed. He's well aware of his responsibilities, and he gladly takes them on every day. But some days he works really hard and the rewards just don't seem to cover his exhaustion. Despite his best efforts, that exhaustion follows him all the way home.

It can seem that our job is a collection of responsibilities that almost anyone can fulfill. We know it's not always enough to be highly skilled. It's not always enough to have the best credentials. Until it is pointed out, one can forget the very great difference that exists between a professional and even a great amateur.

Lord, this dad keeps going because he believes he should. Other dads are competing just like him. Between job and home, he's always playing catch-up with time. But he is not invisible to You. He holds a very special place in Your plan. Remove the blindness that keeps others from seeing what a difference he makes. Restore him and give him the energy he needs for tomorrow. In Jesus's name we pray. Amen.

Behold, the eye of the Lord is on those who fear him, on those who hope in his steadfast love. (Ps. 33:18)

TONIGHT I'M PRAYING THIS FOR _____

TONIGHT we pray for the dad who misses his sleep. He always hopes for the peace and security of a day well spent and a night to reflect upon the Lord's goodness waiting for tomorrow. Yet too often, he spends the evening worrying, anxious, falling asleep on the couch with the lights on, and trudging to the bedroom way too late in the night, looking for the bedside medication to ease the pain.

Wouldn't it be great if all our days were just peaceful and calm? If everything worked out and, when the doors were locked and the kids were safe, our time was our own? It would be. But nothing gets fixed by us simply staying awake. The Lord has determined that there should be a time when sleep is sweet because a rested dad is much more useful to Him than one working to the point of exhaustion.

Lord, this dad takes You at Your Word. When he lies down, he no longer considers the affairs of the day and allows sleep to do its work of refreshing his body and mind. Remind him that You are protecting all his endeavors even as he sleeps. In Jesus's name we pray. Amen.

In peace I will both lie down and sleep; for you alone, O LORD, make me dwell in safety. (Ps. 4:8)

TONIGHT I'M PRAYING THIS FOR _____

TONIGHT we pray for the dad who is trying to figure out his place in God's kingdom.

Most of us have noticed that the Lord doesn't just drop bags of money into our front yard for us to find. He wants us to search out His wonderful mysteries, not just stumble upon the physical blessings He has in store for us. Scripture tells us that Abraham left his home of peace and security, ostensibly to find the one true God. He had come to realize that God was greater than all his idols and carvings. And he was willing to exchange his comfortable life for one he did not know. Abraham's desire to find the one true God led him to the place where God could bless him. When we begin to search for God, He elevates our status to one who is worthy of glory like a king or queen.

Lord, this dad wants to feel Your presence, not just in the peace and joy that a healthy household can hold but also in the assurance that he will find You when he seeks You. There are blessings all around him that help him see You more clearly. Remind him that You love him for who he is and You are always available when he calls on You. In Jesus's name we pray. Amen.

It is the glory of God to conceal a matter, but the glory of kings is to search out a matter. (Prov. 25:2 AMP)

TONIGHT I'M PRAYING THIS FOR _____

TONIGHT we pray for the dad who is having a crisis of faith. He wonders why absolutely nothing is working out for him. He works day and night, and yet when he prays—if he prays at all—it seems no one is there. God is silent. No answers, no directions, no peace, no hope. Nothing. Everybody tells him that there is some hidden sin in his life keeping the Lord from being close to him.

That's not the way the Lord works. When the Lord seems distant, we're the ones who have moved. The Lord does not separate Himself when we have fallen. He remains steadfast for us, waiting for us to come to Him with open arms. What we need to do is look for Him in places we've never looked before. Remember when Job realized that while he was calling out to God in his greatest calamities, the Lord had been present all along in a whirlwind that Job could see and touch.

Lord, this dad has been confident that he was working Your plan and was on a path of peace and comfort in his home. Help him regain his confidence and assurance once again. Prove Yourself as You always have. In Jesus's name we pray. Amen.

The LORD, the LORD, a God merciful and gracious, slow to anger, and abounding in steadfast love and faithfulness, keeping steadfast love for thousands, forgiving iniquity and transgression and sin. (Exod. 34:6–7)

TONIGHT I'M PRAYING THIS FOR _____

238

TONIGHT we pray for the dad who is absent from his children way too often. His work hours are usually in flux, and he struggles with making plans with his family at home. He has to miss so many things that are important to his children, and he has only so much time. Because his hours vary, it can also be difficult to supplement his income. But this dad believes in himself and his ability to provide for his family. He is dedicated and devoted to providing for them.

Our God-given responsibility has always been to make the way for our family. But sometimes we have little peace in our life. We need assurance that God has a plan for us and our family. When we're on the road, we can remember that God is our fellow traveler and ever-present companion in all our journeys.

Lord, remind this dad of Your promises in all his circumstances as he travels the long road in the daytime and the weary road at night. Grant him peace in every storm of life, and remind him that You are protecting sensitive hearts. In Jesus's name we pray. Amen.

Then they said, "Ask God whether or not our journey will be successful."
 "Go in peace," the priest replied. "For the Lord is watching over your journey." (Judg. 18:5–6 NLT)

TONIGHT I'M PRAYING THIS FOR _____

TONIGHT we pray for the dad who is careful to remember the Lord.

There are times when our circumstances are so good, the blessings are so overwhelming, and the peace and security are so satisfying that we can actually overlook just how involved the Lord has been in our lives. We have a tendency to go down the road with the last best blessing we received, and that's where we leave Jesus. It can be easy to make a decision that we can take it from here with the blessings we've received. Remember the time Jesus healed ten lepers and only one returned to give glory to God? The Lord should always have our full attention. While we can be careless in our disregard for what the Lord has done in our life, we must never consider leaving Him, thinking that we can handle our circumstances for ourselves. We should always want to experience the very real blessing of salvation and security by returning to the scene of promise found in walking with Jesus.

Lord, two disciples once ran to the tomb where Jesus was laid so they could speak with Him again. This dad is running to You. He has seen all Your goodness, and he never wants to be separated from it. Assure him that You are never out of reach. In Jesus's name we pray. Amen.

He told him, "Get up and go on your way. Your faith has made you well." (Luke 17:19 HCSB)

TONIGHT I'M PRAYING THIS FOR _____

TONIGHT we pray for the dad who is suffering more than he thought he could. His body is not healing well.

All of us face pain and sickness. Many of us have experienced more physical pain than we ever thought we'd be able to endure. There is absolutely no way to adequately explain to anyone else, even a loved one who cares about our welfare, what we are going through. When our body is not healing correctly, it's hard to agree with the psalmist and say, "Yes, I'm suffering, but I have God." Yet our failing body is a big deal to the Lord, and this is exactly what the Lord would have us say . . . and mean it. Jesus did not heal every person He encountered during His sojourn, and He grieved for them because they were a big deal. We might doubt that God is enough, but He is—and we can lean all our weight on Him.

Lord, this dad is suffering right now. He's worried about how he's going to take care of his family. Give him the daily assurance that You will send the help he needs. In Jesus's name we pray. Amen.

My God, I cry by day, but You do not answer, by night, yet I have no rest. But You are holy, enthroned on the praises of Israel. Our fathers trusted in You; they trusted, and You rescued them. (Ps. 22:2–4 HCSB)

TONIGHT I'M PRAYING THIS FOR _____

TONIGHT **we pray for the dad who praises the Lord continually.** God has done many marvelous things in this dad's life, things he's prayed for and things that were totally unexpected. And for his part, he has felt like rejoicing.

Let us acknowledge that worship is a whole-body event. The Old Testament reflects this more clearly than the New Testament. In those Old Testament passages, God's physical presence, in the form of the ark of the covenant, always brought about boisterous celebration. The Lord would have us dance and sing, not as a requirement but because of the joy those actions represent.

Lord, this dad loves to be in Your presence. He has joy and peace in everything You are to him. He knows You have everything under control, and he worships because he knows that Your promises come to pass. Bless him as only a father can. In Jesus's name we pray. Amen.

David went and had the ark of God brought up from Obed-edom's house to the city of David with rejoicing. . . . David was dancing with all his might before the LORD. . . . He and the whole house of Israel were bringing up the ark of the LORD with shouts and the sound of the ram's horn. (2 Sam. 6:12, 14–15 HCSB)

TONIGHT I'M PRAYING THIS FOR _____

TONIGHT we pray for the dad who teaches his children to laugh.

How many times have we heard "Laughter is the best medicine"? We hear it often, but it's not the easiest response when trials and tribulations, sickness and disease are floating all around us. Yet laughter causes us to feel better because it triggers all sorts of physiological benefits, alters our brain chemistry, and manufactures "feel good" hormones. Most importantly, it allows us to experience trials and sicknesses differently by preventing the seemingly normal worry and anxiety we often attach to them. Laughter lets us view a heavy circumstance on its own without us carrying it as though it will last forever.

Lord, this dad's laughter overcomes his children's fears because they know he is not afraid that troubles will last forever. They trust him because he protects them against all their worries. When their dad is not afraid, they can live in confidence that everything is under control. You have done great things for this dad. Bless him with overflowing joy and Your peace in his heart. In Jesus's name we pray. Amen.

A happy heart is good medicine and a joyful mind causes healing, but a broken spirit dries up the bones. (Prov. 17:22 AMP)

TONIGHT I'M PRAYING THIS FOR _____

TONIGHT we pray for the dad who is there. Though some days he's on the road and some days he's putting in overtime or working that second (or third) job to pay the bills, his mind and heart are at home. He wants his family to always have a parent home for the kids. He knows the Lord does not promise us easy work, vacations, or normal hours. As long as he has his strength, he can accomplish almost anything.

We are responsible for how we spend our time, making sure it is well spent not only for the needs of our family but for ourselves as well. Overworking has a poor cost benefit. Wherever we are, home or away, let's make sure we also take care of ourselves.

Lord, grant this dad productive hours, purposeful work, and rest. Open the eyes of his supervisors to see the benefit and value of a man who gives his all to those in authority over him. Protect him as only You can as he gives his life away every day for his family. In Jesus's name we pray. Amen.

Our people must learn to do good deeds to meet necessary demands [whatever the occasion may require], so that they will not be unproductive. (Titus 3:14 AMP)

TONIGHT I'M PRAYING THIS FOR _____

TONIGHT we pray for the dad who has honest fears—the really subtle kind of fears that creep into his mind when, for no particular reason, things just don't go right. Things have always worked out before, and now they're not.

Work issues, family issues, health issues—there are times when some or all suddenly go south for us. We immediately go to the place where things will never be all right again. No more happy endings for us. We wonder if we're a good dad after all. And after we blame ourselves, we go directly to blaming the Lord, who we believe must secretly want us to experience suffering. But that's not true. Unfortunate things happen to righteous dads who walk with the Lord daily, and the Lord grieves with us when they happen. But the last thing we should ever do is blame Him and make Him the author of evil.

> *Lord, this dad knows You by name and trusts You in all things. He deals with these honest fears whenever they arise, and he remembers Your goodness in times past. He chooses not to let these fears interfere with his walk with You. Give him the faith to believe in himself and the hope to expect a good outcome to whatever he's facing. In Jesus's name we pray. Amen.*

Your eyes are too pure to approve evil, and You cannot look favorably on wickedness. (Hab. 1:13 AMP)

TONIGHT I'M PRAYING THIS FOR _____

TONIGHT we pray for the dad who is courageous.

There certainly have been times when our future looked daunting. We wondered if we had the strength and the willingness to move forward with plans we didn't fully understand. Not because of danger or dread necessarily, but because we were unsure about the steps we might need to take. Can we be willing to constantly and consistently put our prior life down and pick up a life of both adventure and uncertainty?

> *Lord, this dad deals with anxiety that comes from having to make just the right decision. He could be the most powerful, talented, successful, and admired man, and yet it often takes courage to step out in faith where others might not go. So while the world looks to him for answers, he continues to believe in You for the answers he might not have. With You, he moves forward with courage to care for the family You have given him. He has a big, big heart. Enlarge his heart even more. In Jesus's name we pray. Amen.*

Be strong and confident and courageous, for you will give this people as an inheritance the land which I swore to their fathers (ancestors) to give them. (Josh. 1:6 AMP)

TONIGHT I'M PRAYING THIS FOR _____

TONIGHT we pray for the dad who has made a mistake or two since he became a dad.

Too often we make mistakes in judgment, in accounting, in business acumen, and rather than learn from them and make conscious efforts not to repeat them, we double down and decide that our initial determination was the best one for the circumstances. But it's one thing to make a mistake. It's another thing altogether to brag about it. Circumstances in family life change far too quickly to allow stubbornness to rule the day. Of course, in the short term, we regret our setbacks and never stop trying to be the best dad we can be. But the words "I'm sorry" and "I was wrong" had better be words that roll off our tongue easily. That is the only way we can keep learning and moving forward for our family's sake. We must forgive ourselves for those past failures in order to succeed in the future.

Lord, remind this dad that You are always prepared to forgive his heavy heart. In Jesus's name we pray. Amen.

The fear of the LORD is the beginning of knowledge; fools despise wisdom and instruction. (Prov. 1:7)

TONIGHT I'M PRAYING THIS FOR _____

TONIGHT we pray for the dad who has stumbled more than once. Truth be told, sometimes he feels like it's just a way of life for him. He's made some really sorry choices, and then he manages to repeat them over and over. He just hasn't been able to believe in himself long enough to get a grip on his own reality.

We see opportunities come and go, and we're not the only dad who has fallen and couldn't get up. But that doesn't mean we quit. We can look back over the field of competition and remember the times we were almost there. Those are the times to be proud of—the times we got up, wiped our face, dug in, and got it done. The true test is not about failing. It's about trusting that we will succeed if we believe the One who gives us strength. The Lord wants us to have an abundant life.

Lord, this dad has achieved more than he could ever have dreamed possible and has kept going. The dad who has You has more than someone who has everything else. Lift him up tonight, and help him to make good choices. In Jesus's name we pray. Amen.

Since we are receiving a Kingdom that is unshakable, let us be thankful and please God by worshiping him with holy fear and awe. (Heb. 12:28 NLT)

TONIGHT I'M PRAYING THIS FOR _____

TONIGHT we pray for the dad who believes he is a somebody. He is probably not the most talented in terms of physical skills or abilities, but he works hard. He is probably not the most intellectual dad in the crowd who has stories about how he's changed the lives of all who know him, but he knows what it takes to keep his business going during times of crisis.

The Lord uses all kinds of people to accomplish His purposes. So we can confidently see ourselves as the Lord sees us and live up to our potential. We can encourage other dads, keeping them motivated and feeling confident in themselves even as we are. Life throws all sorts of things at us, but we can persevere because we know the Lord has made us who we are. And He delights in seeing us willingly take on the God-given responsibilities placed before us. We are the God-ordained parent of children He gave us to watch over. That makes us a somebody—a somebody God will use.

Lord, remind this dad to be ready when You call. In Jesus's name we pray. Amen.

Let each one live the life which the Lord has assigned him, and to which God has called him [for each person is unique and is accountable for his choices and conduct, let him walk in this way]. (1 Cor. 7:17 AMP)

TONIGHT I'M PRAYING THIS FOR _____

TONIGHT we pray for the dad who has never wanted the same old, same old. Even before he became a dad, he wasn't satisfied with just enough. He had dreams of success because nothing was impossible.

Everybody has desires, wants, and longings that should stay out of reach. Ever since Eve was enticed by the serpent to reach out for the forbidden fruit, we've been desiring more than we should. The difficulty we face is how to temper our natural desires to come into alignment with our spiritual responsibilities. We know dreams are important. It's those natural desires that keep us striving and reaching and longing for more. God made us that way. But He wants us to find satisfaction in Him even more. He wants those earthly desires to point to Him. And whatever we desire should be a testament of God's provision and goodness.

Lord, open this dad's eyes to the opportunities within his grasp, and give him the will and the determination to reach for them. In Jesus's name we pray. Amen.

Jesus replied to them, "I am the Bread of Life. The one who comes to Me will never be hungry, and the one who believes in Me [as Savior] will never be thirsty [for that one will be sustained spiritually]." (John 6:35 AMP)

TONIGHT I'M PRAYING THIS FOR _____

TONIGHT we pray for the dad who knows that winning has a price. The cost of true victory, by his choice to follow Jesus Christ, is his life.

For some, that cost means giving up things they love. They revere what they can hold in their hands, the things that make them happy, rather than turning to God for His reward. Taking up a cross, as it were, is hard work. As a dad, we know all about that. So we do what we have to do, willingly giving everything to God every day.

Lord, the dad who stays faithful and focused, who keeps going, who never quits, is the one who will be standing with You at the end of the day. That dad never loses because his eyes are on the prize that only You bestow. Bless his forever commitment. In Jesus's name we pray. Amen.

Jesus said to His disciples, "If anyone wishes to follow Me [as My disciple], he must deny himself [set aside selfish interests], and take up his cross [expressing a willingness to endure whatever may come] and follow Me [believing in Me, conforming to My example in living and, if need be, suffering or perhaps dying because of faith in Me]." (Matt. 16:24 AMP)

TONIGHT I'M PRAYING THIS FOR _____

TONIGHT we pray for the dad who rests in the Lord. He always wants to have a healthy relationship with the Lord. And while he's always striving to be better, he knows he needs to rest in what the Lord has already accomplished on his behalf. While he's learned that having possessions is all right, he's also learning he can't cling to what he owns. If he places too much emphasis on what he has achieved or the value of what he owns, he can't fully rest in the Lord's kindness and mercy.

We know this drill because we also are learning to place our full trust in everything the Lord has to offer. The Lord wants us to be 100 percent dependent upon Him. The minute we decide we can get it done without His help is when our rest fails.

Lord, this dad seeks Your face in his planning for the future. He seeks to spend as much time as possible with You so he can know that his decisions are Your decisions. Remind him that You are present at his every turn and he can rest in Your peace at all times. In Jesus's name we pray. Amen.

If the Lord delights in us, he will bring us into this land and give it to us, a land that flows with milk and honey. (Num. 14:8)

TONIGHT I'M PRAYING THIS FOR _____

TONIGHT we pray for the dad who has been down for longer than he'd like. He just doesn't seem to be able to accomplish the things he's been able to complete in the past. In some ways he feels guilty that someone else is doing his work.

That feeling is a dad thing. We were made to work, and the less we do, the more inadequate we feel. When someone carries or lifts something for us, we feel as though something has been taken from us. We've lost a part of our God-given responsibility to protect and provide.

Lord, this dad may have had a chronic illness, or maybe he was injured the way dads are—fixing the roof or just doing his job. He may be on the mend, but the bills have to be paid. He needs Your assurance that You have his well-being in Your hands. Help him continue to provide and protect as he always has while You provide his healing. In Jesus's name we pray. Amen.

He said to me, "My grace is sufficient for you, for my power is made perfect in weakness." Therefore I will boast all the more gladly about my weaknesses, so that Christ's power may rest on me. (2 Cor. 12:9 NIV)

TONIGHT I'M PRAYING THIS FOR _____

TONIGHT we pray for the dad who has been missing his children. Maybe he's out of the country. Maybe he's out of town. Or maybe he just works so many hours that they all can't get on the same schedule. Being a dad is what he wants to do most. He knows in his heart that his children are God's gifts. He knows that being a dad, a father, is a lifelong occupation.

It is God's plan that when we have children, we stop being children in our own right and become parents. Though making money is good and we have to feed the bulldog, our real life is about the kids. God says He will provide or make the way available for us to have the things we need to raise our children. He wants to make sure His children have a safe, loving, and peaceful environment.

> *Lord, this dad will need some peace. The kind of peace that helps him know he's doing a good job even if he's away, so that when he does get to reconnect, it's all good. Strengthen his heart and keep him safe wherever he is. In Jesus's name we pray. Amen.*

Behold, children are a heritage from the LORD, the fruit of the womb a reward. (Ps. 127:3)

TONIGHT I'M PRAYING THIS FOR _____

TONIGHT we pray for the dad who takes his role as a dad very seriously. He knew that once he became a dad, through birth, marriage, or adoption, he would always be a dad. His question has always been "What sort of dad will I be?"

Being a dad is not just about doing "dad things." It's about being the father God intends us to be. Becoming a father makes us examine ourselves and really take stock of who we are. We know that we need to give up bad habits. We realize that everything we do is going to impact how our children grow up. Our life has changed in ways we never thought possible. When we want to be the best dad for our children, that makes us the best dad of all.

Lord, this dad lives his life for his children. Remind him of how valued he is tonight so he can start again fresh tomorrow. In Jesus's name we pray. Amen.

Train up a child in the way he should go [teaching him to seek God's wisdom and will for his abilities and talents], even when he is old he will not depart from it. (Prov. 22:6 AMP)

TONIGHT I'M PRAYING THIS FOR _____

TONIGHT we pray for the dad who honors the Lord.

In its simplest sense, honor means treating someone else as more important than ourselves. How many times have we allowed someone to ease out into traffic or check out at the grocery store ahead of us? We are deferring to them as the Lord wants us to. There are also those in authority who are worthy of honor, and we respect them because we trust that God has placed them over us. When we do that, we honor Him. Jesus told us to love God with our whole selves and to love our neighbors as we love ourselves. When we follow these two commandments, we honor Him. It's not so much about obedience, because the Lord doesn't make us love anyone. It should be about our desire to give Him all the glory to which He is entitled. That's honor.

Lord, this dad loves his neighbors as himself because he knows You think they are worthy of honor as Your children. Bless him for his commitment to Your kingdom. In Jesus's name we pray. Amen.

My Father is glorified and honored by this, when you bear much fruit, and prove yourselves to be My [true] disciples. (John 15:8 AMP)

TONIGHT I'M PRAYING THIS FOR _____

TONIGHT we pray for the dad who takes his leadership role in the family seriously. He doesn't lord his expectations over his family. He wants them to trust him. He's the one with joy, knowing that the Lord blesses him when he acts with God's approval.

We know we have to be the ones to watch, see the dangers that arise all around us, and protect our family from them. At the end of the day, the Lord holds us accountable for our actions. He will ask, "What did you do with what I blessed you with?"

Lord, this dad is committed to accomplishing all the wonderful opportunities that a family can have together. He also knows that all success, all happiness, and all joy are only possible because he has dedicated his life and his family to You. In the midst of all his responsibilities, in his own way he leads. Watch over him as he carries his family on strong shoulders, and bless them all. In Jesus's name we pray. Amen.

Obey your leaders and submit to them, for they are keeping watch over your souls, as those who will have to give an account. Let them do this with joy and not with groaning, for that would be of no advantage to you. (Heb. 13:17)

TONIGHT I'M PRAYING THIS FOR _____

TONIGHT we pray for the dad who wants more than just enough for his family.

We all know about a "second mile" mentality. The Lord told his disciples to always be willing to give a little more, walk a little farther, engage with those who had greater needs. Jesus's words were about going beyond obligation without complaining or any word of reservation. About blessing those who might use our goodness against us. We have a tendency to think and act like going the second mile only applies to us when our neighbors are in difficulty. But it's also true when it comes to our family.

Lord, this dad knows that just enough means settling for a little less for his family. Aiming for more means a little less sleep and a little more sweat for him. It means a little more distance and a little less time together. More requires commitment, dedication, and perseverance. More is hard; enough is easy. And he wants more for his family because they are worth it. He goes extra miles every day. He needs good boots and a strong back and shade for his eyes. Prepare him for his extra miles tomorrow. In Jesus's name we pray. Amen.

May you be strengthened with all power, according to His glorious might, for all endurance and patience, with joy. (Col. 1:11 HCSB)

TONIGHT I'M PRAYING THIS FOR _____

TONIGHT we pray for the dad who is making plans for tomorrow. There have been some good days and some tough days, and the Lord has been in all of them. He has walked with this dad's family through lack and illness. He's been their protector through fears and their promise in joys to come.

God's promise of protection clearly does not guarantee that we will never know pain or loss. But the story of Job reminds us that God is able to deliver us out of every physical peril. Through all the afflictions of Job, God was protecting him from even greater harm. Even though we might not see God working, we can know and trust in His protection and believe that there are great promises coming.

Lord, thank You for all You have in store for this dad and his family. Thank You for the life that is to come. And thank You for the fulfillment of peace and security in his home. In Jesus's name we pray. Amen.

Have you no respect for me? Why don't you tremble in my presence? I, the LORD, define the ocean's sandy shoreline as an everlasting boundary that the waters cannot cross. The waves may toss and roar, but they can never pass the boundaries I set. (Jer. 5:22 NLT)

TONIGHT I'M PRAYING THIS FOR _____

TONIGHT we pray for the dad who thinks he is not keeping up. His children are growing up day by day, month by month, year by year, and the changes are real.

Whether they know it or not, we are learning more about our children every day. No matter how old they become, we are the ones watching them grow, so we do our best to keep up. We make sure we know where they are and who they are. Not so we can exercise some power or authority over them, but so we might always be present for them. In the same way, the Lord never abandons us and wants to always be present in our lives. Just as He never loses sight of who we are becoming, so too do we never lose sight of our own children.

Lord, as this dad grows in the image of God, he portrays You to his children. Remind him that his love for them is a picture of Your love for him, and give him peace. In Jesus's name we pray. Amen.

Why am I so depressed? Why this turmoil within me? Put your hope in God, for I will still praise Him, my Savior and my God. (Ps. 43:5 HCSB)

TONIGHT I'M PRAYING THIS FOR _____

TONIGHT we pray for the dad who faces challenges every single day. This dad lives in a high-stress world with low appreciation for the outcomes.

When everything we do seems to be dismissed, disregarded, and discounted, it's difficult to have faith for the day. When we approach our jobs with confidence and anticipation while those we work with belittle our value, the challenges of our daily responsibilities can become overwhelming. This fosters an attitude that our work is unimportant. But it is not overlooked by the Lord. He knows we have important work to do, and he knows the sacrifices we make to work hard, which take us away from our children, family, and friends.

> *Lord, this dad has courage to fight through any lack of resources and a disparaging environment and is determined to see the work completed. He chooses to serve You with his time and his talents, just as he does for his family. Give him a moment's peace and space amid the crises to rest just one time. In Jesus's name we pray. Amen.*

Whatever you do [no matter what it is] in word or deed, do everything in the name of the Lord Jesus [and in dependence on Him], giving thanks to God the Father through Him. (Col. 3:17 AMP)

TONIGHT I'M PRAYING THIS FOR _____

TONIGHT we pray for the dad who has some doubts. He has doubts about his ability to prioritize time with his family. He wonders if he could have made those last few minutes at home a little more special. He wonders if he is spending too much time at work and really could have made it home a little sooner. He has always believed that he was providing for his family the best he knew how, but somehow these thoughts of failure about being the best dad he can be keep creeping into his mind.

The Lord understands our struggles with all the responsibilities we have, and He wants us to look to Him in those struggles. What He does not ever want is for us to doubt His ability or desire to help us deal with those struggles. He is always here, always available, with unlimited access.

Lord, remind this dad it's these doubts that keep him honest and striving to be the best, but that he can count on You even when he doubts. In Jesus's name we pray. Amen.

Jesus said to him, . . . "All things are possible for one who believes." Immediately the father of the child cried out and said, "I believe; help my unbelief!" (Mark 9:23–24)

TONIGHT I'M PRAYING THIS FOR _____

TONIGHT we pray for the dad who is stressed to the max, where the tension is so thick at home it can be cut with a knife. Everyone is walking around wondering what's going to happen today, tomorrow, and next week.

We've all seen finances go south for a season, but sometimes they stay for the winter. Answering the phone is a challenge because the voices on the other end always seem to want more than we have, and there's just way too much month for the money.

Lord, this dad's been taking so many extra shifts away from home that his kids refer to him as "Mr. Dad." There's no quitting, for sure, but he knows that something has to change because he feels like he's drowning. He worries that answers to his prayers just aren't going to come soon enough. When he's struggling to keep going, he feels more like he's in this situation because he failed. He's swimming in a big ocean of expectation and carrying his family on his back. Bring them all to shore safely. In Jesus's name we pray. Amen.

O Lord, how long will you forget me? Forever? How long will you look the other way? . . . But I trust in your unfailing love. I will rejoice because you have rescued me. (Ps. 13:1, 5 NLT)

TONIGHT I'M PRAYING THIS FOR _____

TONIGHT we pray for the dad who needs a new perspective.

What we see is not all there will ever be. When we decide that our life will never change, we are adopting the negative view that God cannot help us. That is the time that our thoughts and emotions are capable of taking over our whole being and running our life into the ground. "We live where we live, my family is just the way it is, and this is just my job" are attitudes that we hold to tightly. We can never forget that following the Lord means He can change our circumstances for the better in an instant. Granted, welcoming God's constant presence can require a shift in our spiritual viewpoint. But this is how we can experience the peace He promises. It is only when we believe He can change our circumstances that we actually begin to see them change for the better.

Lord, this dad has been toiling for some time now, but he doesn't want to settle for what he sees. He believes he's capable of even more than what has been asked of him. Give him a deeper understanding of where he's been and where he's going tomorrow. In Jesus's name we pray. Amen.

From his fullness we have all received, grace upon grace. (John 1:16)

TONIGHT I'M PRAYING THIS FOR _____

TONIGHT we pray for the dad who worries that he has nothing left. This dad gives his all every day, but there are days when he thinks he may have run out of resources. Those are the days that fear sets in and doubt creeps into his mind and heart.

It is during our times of need, despair, and even frustration that we are moved to trust the Lord wholeheartedly. And we have to make the tough call that the things we thought we couldn't live without don't matter as much as we thought they did.

Lord, this dad has given his all so many times that he's lost count. He knows prosperity and he's been in scarce places. He can make it, of course, but he wants to be faithful with all he's been given. Show him that when his hands are empty, You have a miracle for him. Remind him that Your hands are never empty. In Jesus's name we pray. Amen.

This is what the Lord God of Israel says, "The flour jar will not become empty and the oil jug will not run dry until the day the Lord sends rain on the surface of the land." (1 Kings 17:14 HCSB)

TONIGHT I'M PRAYING THIS FOR _____

TONIGHT we pray for the dad who is unsure of himself as a father. He always wants to be in a position to help his children, but sometimes he doesn't know how. He knows that being a dad is not just a series of how-to tasks that are going to make everything better.

We all take stock of ourselves from time to time and realize we're just not making it as a dad. We work hard and pay the bills, but we know there are dad responsibilities we are just not meeting. We've read the books that tell us what to do and when, but seasons change and the kids—bless their hearts—are changing right out from under us. When we feel like we started behind the curve, so to speak, it makes our confidence shaky. But God is always prepared for our next conversation with Him to strengthen our faith and help us be a better dad.

Lord, this dad's own unbelief gets in the way of so many areas in his life. Some days he even wonders if You are listening to his prayers. Guide him to his place of confidence, especially for the answers that seem so hard to find. Increase his faith so he knows that You have made him the dad he is and he is enough. In Jesus's name we pray. Amen.

Many people say, "Who will show us better times?" Let your face smile on us, LORD. You have given me greater joy than those who have abundant harvests of grain and new wine. (Ps. 4:6–7 NLT)

TONIGHT I'M PRAYING THIS FOR _____

TONIGHT we pray for the dad who is trying to make it on his own.

We all think we can. We all think we know best. We're always being tempted to do things that are good only for us. And when it's just us making decisions, we can say, "Look how well I did." Especially when we've not always been on our own. But no matter how well we think we're doing, there hasn't been one time—not one—where we couldn't have done better with the Lord's help. The fact that we haven't fallen on our face yet often means the Lord was looking out for us.

Lord, this dad keeps going because he thinks he's the one who has to make it work. He goes to work, comes home when the shift is done, and fills the rest of the day or night with the kids. He doesn't make excuses. But at the end of the day, remind him to take that last best time to thank You for his success. Bless him in his determination and dedication to doing what's right. In Jesus's name we pray. Amen.

Let us, your servants, see you work again; let our children see your glory. And may the Lord our God show us his approval and make our efforts successful. (Ps. 90:16–17 NLT)

TONIGHT I'M PRAYING THIS FOR _____

TONIGHT we pray for the dad who makes his health a priority.

We can eat the right foods, abstain from those addictive behaviors that ruin our body, and get the right amount of sleep, and still leave our overall health in the dust because it's just too hard. It's one more thing to think about, one more thing to stress over, one more thing to do in a day that is already full to the brim. And aren't we supposed to focus on ourselves last, after the Lord, our wife, and our children? But if we take care of our truck with the best components and additives, why wouldn't we care for our body the best we can? The Lord is very clear that we are more important to Him than anything we own.

Lord, this dad knows he should make his physical health a priority. Just as You provide him with sleep, You desire for him to be healthy because he is better suited to the tasks at hand in Your kingdom if he is physically prepared for them. Remind him that he is worthy of care. In Jesus's name we pray. Amen.

Do you not know that your body is a temple of the Holy Spirit within you, whom you have from God? You are not your own, for you were bought with a price. So glorify God in your body. (1 Cor. 6:19–20)

TONIGHT I'M PRAYING THIS FOR _____

TONIGHT we pray for the dad who loves to be in God's presence. And he's done this before. Coming home from a trip or just a really long day while wearing stained and grimy clothes, with the kids and the wife inside waiting for him—maybe with dinner, maybe not—he stops and leans over the steering wheel and just thanks Jesus for a moment.

We don't know which moment is better—when we embrace our family or when we sit and give thanks to the Lord. While we probably don't address our heavenly Father as Dad or Daddy, when our children use that name for us, there is no better word in the English language. Our time set aside for the Lord is special to Him, and He welcomes us just as our family welcomes us into our home of peace and security.

> *Lord, this dad loves being with You in the quiet times and spaces with no one else around. When he's with You, he understands what his children feel when he holds them in his arms. Just as he is precious to You, so his children are precious to him. In Jesus's name we pray. Amen.*

A day in Your courts is better than a thousand [anywhere else]; I would rather stand [as a doorkeeper] at the threshold of the house of my God than to live [at ease] in the tents of wickedness. (Ps. 84:10 AMP)

TONIGHT I'M PRAYING THIS FOR _____

TONIGHT we pray for the dad who is always ready.

It is easy enough to prepare for the day-to-day schedules we all have. We have it down to a science, almost. Plan ahead for traffic on the way to work, make sure the kids' homework is done, check that the car is locked, set the alarm for tomorrow—we know the drill. It's our job; it's part of our protection plan. But we also must be spiritually attuned to what is happening around us to protect our family. God is at work in the world, and He wants us to understand the demands He has placed on us to watch and pray. That's why we pray for our earthly leaders, because they affect us in such an all-encompassing way.

> *Lord, the demands of work and family rarely take this dad by surprise. He's prepared for what comes next even if the requirements are sudden. But he also knows he needs to look beyond the right here and right now to maintain that level of vigilance. Open his spiritual eyes to see Your influence in the world while he manages his day with the needs of his family in mind. Guide him through the potential stumbles along his way, and keep him safe so he can keep his family safe. In Jesus's name we pray. Amen.*
>
> Above all else, guard your heart, for everything you do flows from it. . . . Let your eyes look straight ahead; fix your gaze directly before you. (Prov. 4:23, 25 NIV)

TONIGHT I'M PRAYING THIS FOR _____

TONIGHT we pray for the dad who believes that he and his family are on a path to prosperity. While he believes in his ability to achieve the best for them, he doesn't know the timeline for the best to come. He doesn't concern himself with *if* prosperity will come but rather *when* it will come. And that is totally up to the One who provides every good thing.

God is the ultimate rewarder of those who seek him diligently. We've seen Him work time and time again, especially in the rough places when the road seemed rocky and it would be so, so easy to stumble. Prosperity rarely comes easy for us, but we're willing to do what God asks. Whether our path is smooth or rough, our trust in God can increase day by day.

Lord, this dad knows You have carried him through hard times. He also trusts You for the promises that faith brings. He's struggled for a good portion of his life, and he's ready for the sweet rest that a job well done can bring. Assure him of Your truth tonight so he can move out in hope tomorrow. In Jesus's name we pray. Amen.

The Lord's blessing enriches, and struggle adds nothing to it. (Prov. 10:22 HCSB)

TONIGHT I'M PRAYING THIS FOR _____

TONIGHT we pray for the dad who needs a rest. We're talking *rest*. Not just sleep, not just a coffee break in the middle of the day, but rest. We've all seen what happens when we don't get it. Suddenly the love, joy, peace, patience, kindness, goodness, faithfulness, meekness, and self-control fly right out the window, never to return without it. This dad pushes himself. There's always something more to be done, he says.

The Lord knows our strengths and how much we've got left. He wants us to plan our rest just like we plan everything else. The seventh day should include what brings us the rest we need—sports, hiking, whatever we enjoy. So when we rest, we are resting in the knowledge that the Lord has our back.

> *Lord, this dad needs you today, tonight, and tomorrow. Sometimes he feels like he needs to seek permission to stop what he's doing in the kingdom and take a break. He's seen the calendar and he just can't get it all done in time. You have a plan to keep his family secure, so the two of you will work together to make it come to pass. Give him peace to trust in Your guidance as he rests tonight. In Jesus's name we pray. Amen.*

There remaineth therefore a rest to the people of God. For he that is entered into his rest, he also hath ceased from his own works, as God did from his. Let us labour therefore to enter into that rest, lest any man fall after the same example of unbelief. (Heb. 4:9–11 KJV)

TONIGHT I'M PRAYING THIS FOR _____

TONIGHT we pray for the dad who takes his title as dad seriously. He gives it his all every day. This dad is a hero no matter what his job description is because he never gives up, he never quits, and he comes through every time. He's a role model who inspires people to strive for excellence.

We can be heroes only to those we inspire, to those who want to be just like us. And as a dad, we hope we're a hero to our children. How do we become heroes? Our children are not particularly impressed by how hard we work, though we know that's important. But the spiritual attributes of love, joy, peace, patience, kindness, goodness, faithfulness, meekness, and self-control—these are the aspects of a dad who is a hero to his children.

> *Lord, the hardest work this dad will ever do is being a provider and protector for his family. You see his heart, and You lift him up for his children to see the fruit of Your Spirit in his life. He's confident in his heart that he knows the right path. Keep him focused. In Jesus's name we pray. Amen.*

We who are strong have an obligation to bear with the failings of the weak, and not to please ourselves. Let each of us please his neighbor for his good, to build him up. (Rom. 15:1–2)

TONIGHT I'M PRAYING THIS FOR _____

TONIGHT we pray for the dad who is battling an internal struggle. He has an ongoing health issue that has plagued him these last several weeks. There are mounting day-to-day pressures that keep him from fully functioning as the dad he knows he can be.

Stress is a killer in so many ways. It affects our minds and our emotions. We all have coping mechanisms, but when the stress inducer is not removed from our situations, it begins to affect us physically in the same way a disease might. Soon we are focusing on our physical symptoms rather than our other responsibilities. And this is where we must trust in the Lord's plan for us. It's not as though we must accept the stress in our life. Far from it. What we should do is keep Him present in those times and not allow the stress to manifest itself outside of that particular situation.

Lord, this dad keeps going because he just wants a fair shot at success. He has a strong heart. Strengthen his resolve and walk with him again tomorrow. In Jesus's name we pray. Amen.

Humbly accept the word God has planted in your hearts, for it has the power to save your souls. (James 1:21 NLT)

TONIGHT I'M PRAYING THIS FOR _____

TONIGHT we pray for the dad who knows war. He's fought and he's won, yet he knows others who have fought and lost. Some days it seems like his experiences are still occurring, and he wonders if his memories will ever end. He knows way too many friends whose experiences are just like his, and they struggle in exactly the same ways.

It's easy to feel overwhelmed by the chaos of our present lives, especially when the chaos includes the life we want to leave behind. It's in that chaos that we must trust in the Lord to fight the present-day battles and rehabilitate our memories from the battles that have already been fought. As He heals us from the past and prepares us for the future, we must always remember that He restores us for a reason greater than just our own lives. He heals us so that we might heal others.

> *Lord, this dad's life has been forever changed. Maybe it's the remembrances of the past. There are those who stay and those who come home. You have each dad, all dads, in Your heart. Not one escapes Your notice. This dad has a family he provides for, and he looks to You for fulfillment of Your promises. Keep him safe and bring him home, today and always. In Jesus's name we pray. Amen.*

This is what the Lord says to you: "Do not be afraid or discouraged because of this vast army. For the battle is not yours, but God's." (2 Chron. 20:15 NIV)

TONIGHT I'M PRAYING THIS FOR _____

TONIGHT we pray for the dad who often sees things in a whole new way. He's always been the pioneer, the one who makes the decisions when no one else has a clue. He knows which questions to ask and what the answers should be.

Life is sometimes complicated, and as a dad, we are the one who steers the ship. But there comes a time when we need to turn to the Lord, not out of desperation but with the sincere belief that He actually has *all* the answers. When we approach our life with humility, we will have a new vision and see not just the problems but the problem solver. Then we can look beyond the simple and the safe. We want more for those we love, and we will do what it takes, including trusting the Lord with all our heart.

Lord, this dad has Your heart because he wants whatever You have to give. Open his eyes to see all Your blessings, and show him how to multiply them for Your glory. In Jesus's name we pray. Amen.

Brothers, I do not consider myself to have taken hold of it. But one thing I do: Forgetting what is behind and reaching forward to what is ahead. (Phil. 3:13 HCSB)

TONIGHT I'M PRAYING THIS FOR _____

TONIGHT we pray for the dad who is in the path of the hurricane as he struggles to overcome his addictive behavior.

In a hurricane, there is always damage to lives and property. The same is true with the personal hurricanes that can sweep over us. When we engage in addictive behaviors such as drugs, gambling, and pornography, we set ourselves and our family up for failure. As with a natural hurricane, we are overwhelmed by suffering, both in our soul and in our physical body. And this doesn't even begin to address the toll taken on our family as they watch us beaten up by the hurricane's forces. The powerful winds of financial ruin shake us from side to side, and the storm surge of addiction consumes everything in its path and our body as well. And the tide overwhelms our loved ones as they attempt to hold everything together.

Lord, You have called this dad to protect his family in all things and with all his strength. He is determined to keep them safe. Calm the storm. Slow the tide. Abate the surge. Declare peace over this dad's body and soul. Place Your hand of protection over him and his family. In Jesus's name we pray. Amen.

You say, "I am allowed to do anything"—but not everything is good for you. And even though "I am allowed to do anything," I must not become a slave to anything. (1 Cor. 6:12 NLT)

TONIGHT I'M PRAYING THIS FOR _____

TONIGHT we pray for the dad who rises to the occasion.

Many of us have experienced circumstances where more was expected of us than even we ourselves thought possible. On the one hand, we want to believe we can accomplish anything. We also want to portray confidence to others that our beliefs are true. But then how do we respond? We believe that the Lord will not test us beyond what we are able to withstand. So we must trust Him to prepare us for the trials that may overwhelm us. Whenever we are experiencing a fiery trial, we can assume that the Lord is preparing us for something much larger. He wants to see what we're made of because He plans to use us in a place and time where we are needed.

Lord, this dad has risen to the occasion before. Remind him of his successes and prepare him for the day to come. In Jesus's name we pray. Amen.

Beloved, think it not strange concerning the fiery trial which is to try you, as though some strange thing happened unto you: But rejoice . . . that, when his glory shall be revealed, ye may be glad also with exceeding joy. (1 Pet. 4:12–13 KJV)

TONIGHT I'M PRAYING THIS FOR _____

TONIGHT we pray for the dad who ran his race today. When he started, he didn't know how far he would get. And when the day was done for this dad, he finished well. Maybe his race was to harvest a field. Maybe his race was to make it to the next city to bring the goods they needed. Maybe his race was to finish that report by day's end.

None of our races are competitions. They are responsibilities that the Lord has given each of us to accomplish. The accolade goes to he who runs, not necessarily just he who wins. It would be easy enough for any dad to sit down, to quit in the middle, because he's run *so many times*. But we know that if there are going to be any winners, there have to be runners. The real prize is knowing that our family has everything we bring with us as we run.

Lord, this dad prepares every day for the same race. Expand his vision to see the finish line a little closer tomorrow. In Jesus's name we pray. Amen.

I press on toward the goal for the prize of the upward call of God in Christ Jesus. (Phil. 3:14)

TONIGHT I'M PRAYING THIS FOR _____

TONIGHT we pray for the dad who is living a life he didn't expect. He never thought that a family like this would be possible. He worked hard as he was growing up, and he was pretty sure he would be a dad someday. He tried to put God first in his life, little by little. He was as committed to the hope of God's promises as he could be as a young man.

On the way to our dreams of a family, of course there were speed bumps that threatened to derail our plans. Maybe our family life wasn't perfect. Maybe a few things happened. Maybe a divorce. These are the types of things that can throw us off course and make us unsure that our hard work and steadfast dedication to a godly life will lead to success. But with the Lord's help, we can have confidence that every day has the potential to be even better than the day before.

Lord, this dad is looking forward to a great tomorrow. Give him that sweet sleep of assurance and peace. In Jesus's name we pray. Amen.

Only be strong and very courageous; be careful to do [everything] in accordance with the entire law . . . ; do not turn from it to the right or to the left, so that you may prosper and be successful wherever you go. (Josh. 1:7 AMP)

TONIGHT I'M PRAYING THIS FOR _____

TONIGHT **we pray for the dad who gives maximum effort.**
For him, it's not just about muscle memory and remembering what to do and how to do it. It's about understanding that our efforts are not ours alone and involving the Lord from the very beginning. It's about knowing that today will have challenges just like those of yesterday.

When the Lord is involved in our day-to-day activities from the beginning, the challenges that arise are much more easily solved. It takes practice, practice, practice to live in the presence of God. We gave our all yesterday, and we will have to be ready to give our all today and tomorrow. When game time comes, all the practice and muscle memory win the game. Sure, these game-time challenges require so much more effort because each one is different. But when the Lord is involved in the preparation, we can count on a successful outcome.

Lord, this dad's done all the expected things and a few more besides. He believes he is ready for whatever tomorrow brings. Remind him that he can do all the things You have strengthened him for. In Jesus's name we pray. Amen.

Commit everything you do to the Lord. Trust him, and he will help you. He will make your innocence radiate like the dawn, and the justice of your cause will shine like the noonday sun. (Ps. 37:5–6 NLT)

TONIGHT I'M PRAYING THIS FOR _____

TONIGHT **we pray for the dad who wants to be the very best.** He's driven, and he can't stop accumulating everything. Everything! He manicures his lawn with scissors because the lawn guy will never get it right. He's rocking his workout schedule, and he has maybe 4 percent body fat. He worries that if he's not the very best he can possibly be, everyone will wonder what happened to him.

We know this guy because we might have been him once. We were hurt or betrayed by someone we loved and who we thought loved us. We tried to hide the pain we felt that no one seemed to be looking out for us by doubling down on looking out for ourselves. We finally realized that we were just a little bit less than perfect and couldn't achieve perfection out of our hurt. That's when we discovered that Jesus loves us and we don't have to try so hard to love ourselves. He is always looking out for us.

> *Lord, this dad is hungry for a change in his mindset, but he doesn't know where to turn. Send Your Spirit to be a change agent in his life. In Jesus's name we pray. Amen.*

So then, brothers, we are not obligated to the flesh to live according to the flesh. (Rom. 8:12 HCSB)

TONIGHT I'M PRAYING THIS FOR _____

TONIGHT we pray for the dad who is facing an unavoidable change for his family.

We face changes in our lives all the time. As we try to stay close to the Lord, we realize that we don't know or understand everything, so our faith changes. We age, we love, we bear children, we survive tragedies, and all of those change us. But we really do appreciate a certain sameness, don't we? There is a certain peace that exists when we can anticipate what is next. The past is comforting but the future is uncertain, and it is that uncertainty that gives rise to anxiety and stress in our lives. When the future presents itself in an overwhelming way, we must take the lead as a father in our relationship with God and bring peace to our family's souls. We know that the Lord has a plan for our lives and our family's lives, and when the plans are different from anything we've seen before, we must lean into them even as we lean into Him.

Lord, this dad does not want to resist Your will and Your way. As much as he believes he's been on the right path, he also believes that You are in charge of his future and it is secure. Prepare the peace You have just for him. In Jesus's name we pray. Amen.

Listen to advice and accept instruction, that you may gain wisdom in the future. (Prov. 19:20)

TONIGHT I'M PRAYING THIS FOR _____

TONIGHT **we pray for the dad who knows his family's value,** not so much in dollars and cents but by his love and devotion to them. He protects them and sets them aside as special. He keeps his home as a sanctuary for his family to dwell in.

Most of us have things that we set aside, and sometimes we preserve and protect them in special places. China cabinets and hutches full of rare and fragile gifts of art are some examples. We keep valuable papers safely apart from our regular lives to protect them from accidents or theft. Of all the possessions that we might want to protect, we want to keep our family safest of all.

Lord, this dad is faithful to present his family to You in prayer, reminding You of Your Word to keep them safe in body, mind, and spirit. He steadfastly defends them against the wiles of the evil one. They are worth more than anything, and he daily gives his own life for theirs so they might have everything they need. Nothing can stand in his way when it comes to providing for his family. Remind him that they are always worth it. In Jesus's name we pray. Amen.

The kingdom of heaven is like a merchant in search of fine pearls, who, on finding one pearl of great value, went and sold all that he had and bought it. (Matt. 13:45–46)

TONIGHT I'M PRAYING THIS FOR _____

TONIGHT we pray for the dad who wants to have a greater place in the world around him. He believes that the more he is recognized as a man of interest in his community, the better he can provide financially for his family.

Wanting *so* much for our family can blind us to what the Lord calls us to do and be. This attitude can set us back in our desire to have a personal walk with Him, and it can interfere with our personal growth with Him as well. We must examine our lives, our goals, and our desires whenever we find ourselves focusing only on the physical needs of our family instead of their spiritual needs.

Lord, this dad has overcome the setbacks he's endured, for sure, and that is and has been hard work. He is still a warrior. He's won many battles, so he knows what he is made of and what he can still do. But he remembers that he has won those battles only with Your help. Prepare him for a new tomorrow. In Jesus's name we pray. Amen.

The kings of the Gentiles lord it over them; and those who exercise authority over them call themselves Benefactors. But you are not to be like that. (Luke 22:25–26 NIV)

TONIGHT I'M PRAYING THIS FOR _____

TONIGHT we pray for the dad who makes things happen. They happen because this dad is accustomed to keeping his eyes open for opportunities. This hoped-for event might have been in the works for days, weeks, months, or even years. It might have happened thirty minutes ago. But making things happen is what a dad does.

In order to be successful, we must listen carefully to God's heart as well as His voice. Sometimes we have to make critical decisions that make opportunities come to pass. In those moments, we need to know which choices might lead to failure and which ones might lead to success. We must also know when conditions are just right to achieve the greatest results. All successes were once opportunities, and we want to be ready for them.

Lord, You want this dad to see his surroundings and his circumstances and make the choice to always do good. As he keeps going, seeking that mountaintop, show him the way. In Jesus's name we pray. Amen.

This book of instruction must not depart from your mouth; you are to recite it day and night so that you may carefully observe everything written in it. For then you will prosper and succeed in whatever you do. (Josh. 1:8 HCSB)

TONIGHT I'M PRAYING THIS FOR _____

TONIGHT we pray for the dad who always wants to keep his children from harm.

The Lord promises to protect and defend His children, and our children as well. Does that mean no one in our family will ever suffer a broken bone or a car accident? Of course not! But God has taken our protection as His responsibility. That's our call as well. Our responsibility is to protect our children from the dangers that may overcome them. We protect them from themselves, in a fashion. We teach them how to do things safely. We help them grow from a very young age to become who the Lord would have them be.

Lord, this dad knows what his family needs, and he wants all those needs to be met. He has worked hard to make a straight and easier path for his family. Give him strength to carry on every day to protect those he loves. In Jesus's name we pray. Amen.

Because you have made the LORD . . . your dwelling place, no harm will come to you; no plague will come near your tent. (Ps. 91:9–10 HCSB)

TONIGHT I'M PRAYING THIS FOR _____

TONIGHT we pray for the dad who struggles with "Why not me?"

We have a tendency to look for things that will make us content. "If I only had . . ." and "If I only was . . ." and "If I only could . . ." are our cries to the Lord. We rail against the fact that there is someone who is "more" than us. And we most often complain to God about our lack of abundance or our inability to have what will make us happy. Scripture reminds us that God shall supply our needs, so when we complain about our needs not being met, there is a problem. We are telling God that we are not satisfied with what He has already bestowed on us. But He wants us to reach for Him instead of the next shiny object, which we will use and abandon once our desires have shifted.

Lord, this dad has it all, but he just doesn't know it. For a time, he has wished for something else when he has everything. You are the goodness in every aspect of his life. Remind him gently of all Your blessings, and open his eyes to see them. In Jesus's name we pray. Amen.

Where jealousy and selfish ambition exist, there will be disorder and every vile practice. (James 3:16)

TONIGHT I'M PRAYING THIS FOR _____

288

TONIGHT **we pray for the dad who has integrity.** He is the dad whose faith remains consistent, withstanding the slings and arrows of misfortune and hardship. He is, by all accounts, unchangeable. He never takes the easy way out. It seems like with everything thrown at him, the stronger he becomes. He believes in himself because he is absolutely positive that the Lord believes in him.

When we have integrity, darkness has no place in our lives. We can walk through life with the gospel of peace, fearing nothing because we are the living embodiment of God's promises. We walk in the knowledge that the Lord has blessed us and, because of this, we can bless others. Not only that, but we can trust Him to use us in the best way possible. There is not even a shadow of misunderstanding about our calling.

Lord, this dad is kingdom minded, with every assurance in the outcome of his decisions. He does what he does because it is the right thing to do. He is prepared for challenges when they arise because he embodies Your Holy Spirit and lives his life expecting to overcome those difficulties by Your Word. He always wants to portray Your confidence in his family's eyes. Strengthen him even more as he walks Your path for him. In Jesus's name we pray. Amen.

Walk in a manner worthy of the Lord, fully pleasing to him: bearing fruit in every good work and increasing in the knowledge of God. (Col. 1:10)

TONIGHT I'M PRAYING THIS FOR _____

TONIGHT we pray for the dad who wants to leave nothing to chance.

We all want to live according to God's way of life. Those who live closest to the Lord are the ones who have wisdom in all things. Not that wisdom comes right away, of course. It takes time because we are slow to learn. We are often "too soon old and too late smart." Too many of us are worldly wise when we should be heavenly wise. God wants us to think before we act, asking Him when to go and when to wait. Being in a hurry to make an important decision because we believe we know better doesn't always bring about the best outcome.

Lord, this dad takes care of the big and the little things. He might be taking a second job or just going the extra mile at his only job. He wants to go, go, go, but he listens carefully to what You have to say. He is strong in Your eyes, and You truly see him for all his efforts. Strengthen his heart and bless his determination. In Jesus's name we pray. Amen.

One who is wise is cautious and turns away from evil, but a fool is reckless and careless. (Prov. 14:16)

TONIGHT I'M PRAYING THIS FOR _____

TONIGHT we pray for the dad who searches for direction. He's been following the Lord for a long time, and he's fairly certain of the destinations that are prepared for him.

How many times have we prayed, "Lord, guide me to make the right decision"? We know where we're going; we just aren't always sure how to get there. It's hard to make tough decisions on our own. Many of us have engaged in financial and legal opportunities in which the circumstances changed at the last minute. We sought the Lord up to that point and were confident that the transactions were fair and aboveboard. We looked ahead to the successful completion of our plans because the path had been smooth. But, as can happen sometimes, the details caused the plans to go awry. Now suddenly life-altering negotiations are of no consequence. Bankruptcy is on the table and time is of the essence. It's at this moment that we must ask, "Lord, what great blessing do You have for me in this disruption?"

> *Lord, this dad is willing to hear Your voice in all circumstances, even when the destination seems sure. He wants to have every step be in Your perfect plan. Remind him of Your presence in the tough choices. In Jesus's name we pray. Amen.*

This is what the LORD says—your Redeemer, the Holy One of Israel: "I am the LORD your God, who teaches you what is best for you, who directs you in the way you should go." (Isa. 48:17 NIV)

TONIGHT I'M PRAYING THIS FOR _____

TONIGHT we pray for the dad who holds his fire.

Many of us are familiar with the phrase "Law for thee, grace for me." We know what that means, right? God loves us so much that He should overlook our transgressions even though we sometimes believe that others should be dealt with more harshly. That really shouldn't be our story, should it? We're called to be the example rather than the exception. Judging should not be a part of our actions or even our vocabulary.

> *Lord, this dad who holds his fire is remarkable because he does not judge anyone at all. He knows that if anyone is worthy of judgment, it's him. He believes You are the only One who can discern the hearts of people and can rightfully judge his motives when he acts on Your behalf. This dad deals fairly in all things, and he holds himself accountable for his words and actions. He wants others to know they can count on him. Open his eyes to see Your road of virtue in his daily life. In Jesus's name we pray. Amen.*

Judge not, that you be not judged. For with the judgment you pronounce you will be judged, and with the measure you use it will be measured to you. (Matt. 7:1–2)

TONIGHT I'M PRAYING THIS FOR _____

TONIGHT we pray for the dad who wants to reconnect with his children. They are growing up and growing older. As they mature, they need him less and less. No longer are they babies or toddlers or even preschoolers. They are coming of age, and they have their own ideas, their own experiences, their own views on life. Unfortunately, they are fairly certain that their need for their dad is going by the wayside.

The Lord would have us know that we can experience the reconciliation we seek as we remember that Jesus's closest followers abandoned Him. Even His connection with His heavenly Father was broken. But the Lord heals broken things, and He can heal our emotional wounds and our relationships.

Lord, this dad always wants to be in relationship with his children. He wants them to know they can have the peace and joy he has through You. No matter where they are or what their circumstances might be, he is always looking for the best way to help them grow from day to day. Bring his family closer to each other and to You as well. In Jesus's name we pray. Amen.

You keep track of all my sorrows. You have collected all my tears in your bottle. You have recorded each one in your book. (Ps. 56:8 NLT)

TONIGHT I'M PRAYING THIS FOR _____

TONIGHT **we pray for the dad who knows his own strength.** He also knows that once he starts relying on himself, he gets on that slippery slope of wondering where the Lord is when his own strength and confidence fail.

How many times have we faced a trial and been confident that we knew exactly what to do? Our confidence in ourselves must always be tempered, however, because what do we do when we face a crisis of conscience? When we are faced with someone whose views do not line up with ours and we are required to make moral and spiritual decisions that affect our own livelihood? This battle is a spiritual one about God's authority, and the Lord wants us to rely not on our strength but His. We put on the breastplate of righteousness every day in every way. Remember that God's plan will be accomplished in the warfare, even if the battles prove daunting.

Lord, this dad knows he is responsible for doing everything necessary to provide for and protect his family. He knows he has gifts and talents You have blessed him with. Give him the courage to invoke Your name in his situation and to rely on Your strength to overcome all the pitfalls. In Jesus's name we pray. Amen.

For this reason I remind you to fan into flame the gift of God, which is in you. (2 Tim. 1:6)

TONIGHT I'M PRAYING THIS FOR _____

TONIGHT we pray for the dad who has his commission.

We are all aware that our children are watching us, and probably more than we might think. We hope we are conducting ourselves in a manner pleasing to the Lord even when they're not watching. Our life should be an example of who the Lord is at all times, and the example we set should make others want what we have—a living God dwelling within us. Let's get creative with when and how we model the Lord's presence in our life. While we often think of modeling in home groups or Sunday school rooms, the Lord invited people to come closer on mountainsides and in boats on the water. He encouraged others to partake of His blessings while walking on a road and enjoying a meal. We can do the same!

Lord, this dad knows that he's been called to reach out to others in Your name. He signed up in Your army, and there are responsibilities for his office and rank. He may not have been as steadfast as he should be, but he takes his position seriously. Show him where his opportunities for ministry can be found. In Jesus's name we pray. Amen.

Therefore, as we have opportunity, we must work for the good of all, especially for those who belong to the household of faith. (Gal. 6:10 HCSB)

TONIGHT I'M PRAYING THIS FOR _____

TONIGHT we pray for the dad who lives within his means. He knows what it's like to not have quite enough. He makes do with what he has. When the trials come, he's prepared because he understands exactly what is needed. He does what must be done to keep his family safe in a crisis. But there have been times when the crisis seemed to last forever. When the hurricane destroyed his business. Suddenly the crisis turned into a lifestyle change.

When we go through times of crisis, when the insurance agent stops taking our calls, we wonder if we'll be able to make it to the end of the month with enough money. Those are the days when it's hard to get up in the morning because everything we've known, everything we've worked and planned for, has been blown away. It's one thing to take a little and make it into a lot, but when even the little is gone, where do we go? We have to see ourselves the way the Lord sees us, as worthy of His protection and provision.

Lord, this dad is accustomed to getting the job done. Tomorrow, when the job seems too big to handle, remind him that he is mighty in Your sight. In Jesus's name we pray. Amen.

The angel of the Lord appeared to him and said to him, "The Lord is with you, O mighty man of valor." (Judg. 6:12)

TONIGHT I'M PRAYING THIS FOR _____

TONIGHT we pray for the dad who speaks the truth. He is willing to speak forthrightly about who Jesus is in the toughest of circumstances, and that gives him confidence that he can speak the truth in his professional life as well.

Most of us know the Truth. It is He, the Lord Jesus Christ. We recognize Him in every form and every circumstance. We are totally committed to Him. When He says "Go," we go, and when He says "Come," we come. We not only speak Jesus, but we make sure nothing stands in the way of Jesus doing what He says He will do. This is not to say that Jesus needs defending when He is confronted with unbelief. Far from it. But we are to be prepared for how the world responds when faced with the Truth. Jesus was never politically correct, and when He asked the disciples what people thought of Him, one disciple answered with the truth—that He is the Messiah, the Son of the living God. The Lord confirmed that all of heaven would recognize that disciple for his words.

Lord, You and this dad are on a first-name basis. Continue to give him the courage to know the truth and to speak it. In Jesus's name we pray. Amen.

Simon Peter replied, "You are the Christ, the Son of the living God." (Matt. 16:16)

TONIGHT I'M PRAYING THIS FOR _____

TONIGHT **we pray for the dad who needs friends.** This dad wants to be his very best in serving the Lord. He knows in his heart that the Lord loves him, that He wants the best for him and moves heaven and earth when he prays. But sometimes he feels alone, fighting internal wars with himself, wondering if he's measuring up to the calling God has given him.

Even the most dedicated dad can have challenging days. In those instances, we believe we are stronger together than alone. God designed us to be interdependent, which defines the body of Christ. Within that body are dads who have different gifts, talents, and opportunities but who also have much in common. There is strength in friends who will walk among and with us for God's purposes, in good times and bad.

Lord, this dad needs a friend who will hold him accountable to being his best self. He recognizes his need for support in his walk with You. Bless him as he commits himself to growing in friendship with other dads. Continue to provide dads to help him along the way. In Jesus's name we pray. Amen.

A friend is always loyal, and a brother is born to help in time of need. (Prov. 17:17 NLT)

TONIGHT I'M PRAYING THIS FOR _____

TONIGHT we pray for the dad who believes in God's promises. This dad has read God's Word and knows it will help him overcome all his trials and tribulations. He's confident that God's promises will always appear just when they should.

So often we think that, in the sweet by-and-by, everything will work out fine. That we can just go with the flow, anticipating that God will handle everything. However, it's another thing altogether to actually plan a life around God's promises. That's real faith, isn't it? Scripture tells us that the great people of faith acted on God's promises and found exactly what they believed they would. When God told Abraham that He would meet him in a place he had never been and wonderful promises would come to pass, Abraham packed up his whole family. And though he went from "more" to "less," the Lord made his less into more.

Lord, this dad keeps dreams in his heart because he trusts You. When You declare that a promise will be fulfilled, he is already moving in that direction. He believes You have a destiny for him in Your promises. Guide him as he boldly follows You. In Jesus's name we pray. Amen.

I wait [patiently] for the LORD, my soul [expectantly] waits, and in His word do I hope. My soul waits for the Lord more than the watchmen for the morning; more than the watchmen for the morning. (Ps. 130:5–6 AMP).

TONIGHT I'M PRAYING THIS FOR _____

TONIGHT we pray for the dad who seeks the Lord. He discovered long ago that if there was something to be gained—more than riches, more than fame, more than any goal he might achieve—it would be the promise of the love of his heavenly Father.

As long as we seek Him, God will fulfill our heart's desire. He wants to fulfill our desires to be healed from past wrongdoing, to be free from accusation and attacks, and to be forgiven for our own shortcomings. When we seek God, we can be free in our mind, spirit, and body, free to live a life of peace in the presence of almighty God. We must seek Him before we can know Him. There can be no delay. Tomorrow is promised to no one, so to find Him, we must seek Him today.

> *Lord, this dad believes that Your Son Jesus is the One his heart seeks after. He believes Jesus is the Lamb of God who can take away his sins. And he believes there is a resurrection to life and peace in Your presence. Grant him security so he might have abundant life. In Jesus's name we pray. Amen.*

Delight yourself in the LORD, and He will give you the desires and petitions of your heart. (Ps. 37:4 AMP)

TONIGHT I'M PRAYING THIS FOR _____

300

TONIGHT we pray for the dad who still has hopes and dreams for his family. Sometimes it feels like the world and circumstances rob them of peace.

We remember that peace is often defined as provision of adequate resources. We must also acknowledge that every single child of God has faced, is facing, or will face trials. These are the types of trials that seem to keep us back on our heels, unable to really go forward in life. But God is in control of *everything*. He makes a way for us to have everything we need, to have peace and joy and rest in His provision. When we find satisfaction in the One who has all wealth in His hands *and* can be content with what we have, we will have real peace and prosperity.

> *Lord, this dad isn't working for Your benevolence in his life but instead trusts You for everything. Guide his steps to help bring Your peace to pass. In Jesus's name we pray. Amen.*

Not that I am speaking of being in need, for I have learned in whatever situation I am to be content. . . . I have learned the secret of facing plenty and hunger, abundance and need. I can do all things through him who strengthens me. (Phil. 4:11–13)

TONIGHT I'M PRAYING THIS FOR _____

TONIGHT we pray for the dad who does all he can do. He has doubts as he raises his children, because being a dad is hard work. He's an authority in his children's lives, but he doesn't want that authority to appear absolute. He is not the king and his children are not his subjects. He has adult experiences, and he wants his children to look to him for answers, guidance, and direction.

We are always shaping and influencing our children's lives. We have flaws, and we are a little less perfect than we would like to be. It's critical that our children see who we really are, that we be transparent and acknowledge our own insufficiencies. But in order for the wise dad to succeed, he needs to make sure his relationship with the Lord can provide the answers, guidance, and direction his children need.

Lord, this dad's children are his whole life, and he wants them to prosper today and know they can prosper tomorrow as well. Strengthen his heart as he dedicates himself to his children. In Jesus's name we pray. Amen.

Show yourself in all respects to be a model of good works, and in your teaching show integrity, dignity. (Titus 2:7)

TONIGHT I'M PRAYING THIS FOR _____

TONIGHT we pray for the dad who walks that sometimes fine line between panic and prosperity. Change is all around him, and he has to balance faith and wisdom to get from day to day. This dad does not concern himself with what might happen when trials come or when calamities are the rule. Rather, he looks at the perils that often present themselves and determines that the Lord is for him.

Where the world might ask "What if . . ." or "What are you going to do?," the Lord would have us respond with "So what?" and "I will follow the Lord." We do not just throw caution to the wind. We take our steps one day at a time. By following the Lord, we'll always find a safe place to land.

Lord, only You know the end from the beginning. The dad who trusts You will overcome every obstacle. And even if he stumbles, he knows it will not keep him from the prize. Strengthen his dedication and resolve to lead his family well in changing times. In Jesus's name we pray. Amen.

Don't fear sudden danger or the ruin of the wicked when it comes, for the LORD will be your confidence and will keep your foot from a snare. (Prov. 3:25–26 HCSB)

TONIGHT I'M PRAYING THIS FOR _____

TONIGHT we pray for the dad who is new to this role of fatherhood. He's a dad! And he's going to be a dad forever. This dad's been an adult for quite a while, yet he's never "adulted" like this before.

Scripture says that God created the heavens and the earth. When we look at that new son or daughter—helpless and at the same time demanding—they may as well be all of creation looking back at us. The attributes of helpless and demanding are going to continue for a very long time, but at the same time, our heart is just exploding every time our child laughs or cries or makes all kinds of messes, because we know we're their dad.

Lord, this dad may have just brought his first child home, or he may have a new little one to provide for and help to raise. Give him everything he needs for this journey. Remind him that You will be with him every step of the way. Bless him with your peace. In Jesus's name we pray. Amen.

You have not received a spirit that makes you fearful slaves. Instead, you received God's Spirit when he adopted you as his own children. Now we call him, "Abba, Father." (Rom. 8:15 NLT)

TONIGHT I'M PRAYING THIS FOR _____

TONIGHT we pray for the dad who remembers when things were less stressful at home. Things were good. He's never been accustomed to looking back, but the circumstances nowadays are hard to get used to. He realizes that it can be hard to be a Christian dad sometimes.

In difficult times, people often think only of themselves. Even parents and children can be at odds when they were always generous and grateful before. When we know the steps to take and still our plan does not come to pass, it's important to remain steadfast to what we've always known. The Lord will reward our faithfulness as we look to Him for every promise.

> *Lord, this dad never gave up, even in those sleepless nights as he wondered if the sun was coming up. Now he's ready for the good days again. He's ready to take his resources and use them as You make plain, as he always has. Fill him to overflowing with everything he needs. In Jesus's name we pray. Amen.*

People will be lovers of self, lovers of money, boastful, proud, blasphemers, disobedient to parents, ungrateful, unholy, . . . lovers of pleasure rather than lovers of God, holding to the form of godliness but denying its power. Avoid these people! (2 Tim. 3:2, 4–5 HCSB)

TONIGHT I'M PRAYING THIS FOR _____

TONIGHT we pray for the dad who has a responsibility to keep his family and his community safe.

We know that we can't survive without a connection to others in a community. We dwell with them, we work with them, we share our lives with them. Relationships with others are required for a healthy existence. And when we willingly share our lives, we are giving a gift to others. Every dad in public service knows that when the phone rings, he's going to have to do a job for someone. God desires for each of us to live for others. He blesses us when we go into situations where our lives may be on the line to save those who cannot save themselves.

Lord, this dad hopes to be an example of peace as he protects those around him as well as the people and families he knows and loves. He needs Your protection as he does the job he has been called to do. Keep him safe as he also exhibits Your wisdom in everything he says and does. In Jesus's name we pray. Amen.

Speak up for those who cannot speak for themselves, for the rights of all who are destitute. (Prov. 31:8 NIV)

TONIGHT I'M PRAYING THIS FOR _____

TONIGHT we pray for the dad who doesn't concern himself with what might have been. He focuses only on what can be. He sheds failure like he would an old coat in the summer and always puts on success when he walks out the door. The more he relies on God, the stronger he becomes. This dad never allows his current situations to inhibit his closeness with God. He doesn't go to the Lord only when things are tough. He maintains an attitude of gratitude that God has prepared his way in all things.

God is not bound to answer us in the ways we expect. And it is only when we are close enough to Him that we can recognize the sometimes subtle changes in His countenance. We need to be humble enough to wait and listen to God's still small voice, and wise enough to know we cannot force our way through and expect to have good success.

Lord, this dad's family always expects him to return with the prize he has sought and You have promised. Show him that when he keeps his eyes focused on You and Your presence, he will achieve all You have for him and his family. In Jesus's name we pray. Amen.

Such things were written in the Scriptures long ago to teach us . . . as we wait patiently for God's promises to be fulfilled. (Rom. 15:4 NLT)

TONIGHT I'M PRAYING THIS FOR _____

TONIGHT we pray for the dad who is looking for one more chance to live the life he remembers from his youth.

We remember the days when we could go on and on, seemingly forever. Whether it was some physical endeavor or just a sense of desire to accomplish all our goals as soon as possible, we still look back longingly on those heart-pumping, adrenaline-producing crises that made us want to be the best we could be. We loved reaching out to God, feeling His overwhelming presence, and expecting to see not just good results but the best results. It was habit-forming, like a drug, really, and we would jump into opportunities to see God do marvelous things.

> *Lord, this dad is still suited up with all his skills and abilities, ready for Your call. He knows that not every call is a four-alarm fire, but he's ready for the emergencies as they arise, just as he's always been. Give him the patience to wait for Your call even as he has kept the faith and lived his life for You every single day. Bless his dedication and his determination to win the fights You give him. In Jesus's name we pray. Amen.*

Be ready when the time is right and even when it is not [keep your sense of urgency, whether the opportunity seems favorable or unfavorable, whether convenient or inconvenient, whether welcome or unwelcome]. (2 Tim. 4:2, AMP)

TONIGHT I'M PRAYING THIS FOR _____

TONIGHT we pray for the dad who is trying to keep his good perspective. He's not a four-year-old who is "all eyes back to me." He's not a teenager, believing that he hasn't, doesn't, and won't ever make mistakes. He's a man who has always known he would have a family someday. He has made it his life goal to be sound in his judgment and to look for wisdom in every circumstance.

There's always some change for our family. The kids are getting older, needing more resources. Maybe Grandma needs extra care. Sometimes financial difficulties are all too real. We might be working two jobs, which means we might have to be late or away for dinner. But we can be the face of hope for our family, as they need stability and strength to get through whatever comes up. We can lean on the Lord and be confident that we can keep them safe and prosperous.

Lord, right now this dad is determined to lead his family. He's dedicated to the idea that by following You, they will all be better for tomorrow. He's learning every day that having confidence in You brings peace to his family, regardless of his circumstances. Show him that he's right to trust in You. In Jesus's name we pray. Amen.

My health may fail, and my spirit may grow weak, but God remains the strength of my heart; he is mine forever. (Ps. 73:26 NLT)

TONIGHT I'M PRAYING THIS FOR _____

TONIGHT we pray for the dad who is handy. He is building a life for his family. The Lord sees what he is building as a work of art in its own right because God has made him to be one as well.

Some dads can see how things fit together. They are the dads who build, who construct, who form things out of the whole cloth, as it were. They are the artists we've never been because they see things we just can't see. Yet the Lord intends for us all to be builders, whether we build cars or buildings or careers. Even if we do not recognize our value because it seems as though we are going through the motions of our lives, we know intuitively, in our spirit, that we are God's workmanship. While in some circumstances He is the potter and we are the clay, in other circumstances we take His creative abilities and make lives of handiwork different from every other dad.

Lord, this dad has every tool he needs to build what You have given him to build. You have given him a strategy to create something wonderful in his life. Expand his vision to see the finished product clearly. In Jesus's name we pray. Amen.

The LORD has chosen Bezalel . . . and he has filled him with the Spirit of God, with wisdom, with understanding, with knowledge and with all kinds of skills. . . . And he has given both him and Oholiab . . . the ability to teach others. He has filled them with skill to do all kinds of work . . . all of them skilled workers and designers. (Exod. 35:30–31, 34–35 NIV)

TONIGHT I'M PRAYING THIS FOR _____

TONIGHT we pray for the dad who is tempted. He has seen something he wants, and his soul has determined he should have it. Truth be told, this is not the first time he has had such thoughts.

Sometimes as we're working real hard, the life we're living can just seem unfair after a while. When we come up short on what we normally expect of ourselves, it's tempting to believe that maybe it would be okay, just once, if we cut the corner a little sharper. We know our integrity would be at risk if we did that, but the thought of that new ride is oh so enticing. And we've waited so long for a break that just hasn't come. So in those circumstances, it's good to know we can make that call to the friend who has bailed us out a time or two before, the one who has kept us out of the trouble we might have fallen into.

Lord, this dad has had thoughts of taking a path he knows he would regret later. He's been on the straight and narrow for so long, and Your Word has kept him strong up to now. He needs that strong word from a strong dad who will remind him of everything he has to lose and what little he has to gain. Send the messenger who will protect him from himself. In Jesus's name we pray. Amen.

When tempted, no one should say, "God is tempting me." . . . But each person is tempted when they are dragged away by their own evil desire and enticed. (James 1:13–14 NIV)

TONIGHT I'M PRAYING THIS FOR _____

TONIGHT we pray for the dad who wonders if he has enough time.

We all hear that clock ticking, don't we? One minute the kids are in diapers, and the next minute they're asking for the keys to the car, or their own car, even. We wonder if we've had any real impact on them at all in those early years. But the Lord promises that whatever time we have used to provide for and protect our children, He will multiply to their benefit (Isa. 54:13). That's not to say we shouldn't take stock of what our years of parenting have consisted of. We should do that all the more often. But the promise is that this time is never wasted. We've all missed out on milestones at one time or another while we were just trying to keep a roof over our kids' heads. But instead of looking back with regret, we should always look forward to tomorrow. Yesterday has only the power over us that we give it. Tomorrow always holds the promise of what we can achieve and what the Lord has in store for us.

Lord, this dad has been looking backward, and he wonders if his time is past. Remind him that there is still joy to be found in whatever season he and his children are in right now. In Jesus's name we pray. Amen.

The fear of the LORD is the beginning of wisdom, and knowledge of the Holy One is understanding. For through wisdom your days will be many, and years will be added to your life. (Prov. 9:10–11 NIV)

TONIGHT I'M PRAYING THIS FOR _____

TONIGHT we pray for the dad who has experienced the best and the worst. The joys don't last very long and sorrows last way too long. He keeps going because he knows that the Lord will always bring him to a higher place, but the road is rocky much of the time. Still, his family is with him because he's always come through.

We all know that the difficulty of our walk is based upon how well prepared we are for it. Walking the Pacific Crest Trail in sneakers with a school lunch will likely lead to sorrow and defeat, while having a well-provisioned backpack and climbing boots will usually get us to our destination. The Lord knows what our requirements are, where we've been, and where we're going. In order for us to know that we will succeed, we must be in a continual state of expectancy and preparation for what the Lord is going to do. We cannot go about moving mountains if we are only guessing that those mountains are going to move.

> *Lord, this dad knows that the best and the worst are only seconds apart. Circumstances can convince him he cannot win. But he is determined to look for and see Your victory as he continues his journey. Prepare him for the road ahead. In Jesus's name we pray. Amen.*

Therefore, with your minds ready for action, be serious and set your hope completely on the grace to be brought to you at the revelation of Jesus Christ. (1 Pet. 1:13 HCSB)

TONIGHT I'M PRAYING THIS FOR _____

TONIGHT we pray for the dad who may be wondering where his next meal is coming from, who may be wondering how he is going to take care of his family, and who sometimes wonders if God still hears him. This dad previously had plenty. He saw his life in prosperity and peace. And suddenly life became harder than it had ever been.

When we are tempted to say God cannot deliver us from these seemingly instant hardships that have arisen or He doesn't care about us or our family, we must remember that He is not surprised by our circumstances. He knows exactly where we are. We've been dependent upon God in the good times, and He wants us to continue to rely upon Him in the tough times. Remember that God can, and often does, change anything and everything in an instant.

Lord, there are miracles in store for this dad. Remind him of Your continual promises for his family. In Jesus's name we pray. Amen.

Whom have I in heaven but thee? and there is none upon earth that I desire beside thee. My flesh and my heart faileth: but God is the strength of my heart, and my portion forever. (Ps. 73:25–26 KJV)

TONIGHT I'M PRAYING THIS FOR _____

TONIGHT we pray for the dad who gets it done. His trial is just one more challenge to overcome, and he solves it his way, but not his way alone. He's in the habit of listening to the Lord's voice, whether it's a still small voice or a booming voice like thunder.

Scripture reminds us that after Adam sinned in the garden of Eden, the voice of the Lord was with him. The voice of God, His presence, was with Adam even as he was hiding in the garden. That's what we do when we feel overcome by circumstances, don't we? We hide. We feel discouraged and overwhelmed. But when we recognize the Lord's voice, we can overcome adversity and even stand strong in the midst of it. We know we can win because with the Lord, losing is not an option. At the end of the day, our reward is the knowledge that we are prepared for tomorrow.

Lord, because You are with him, this dad is being renewed every day for what lies ahead. Let him have well-deserved peace tonight. In Jesus's name we pray. Amen.

He only is my rock and my salvation; my fortress and my defense, I will not be shaken or discouraged. (Ps. 62:6 AMP)

TONIGHT I'M PRAYING THIS FOR _____

TONIGHT we pray for the dad who intends to win. He doesn't always win, mind you. He struggles too often for that to be true. But he works to win, he plays to win, and his children expect him to win. And he wins a lot because he doesn't fear defeat. He's seen it before, and every time he does, he addresses it head-on with the words "Is that all you've got?"

To a dad, defeat is merely a speed bump on the way to victory. When we lose, we don't dial back on our expectations. We don't rally around a mountain of defeats. We move on. The more we win, the better we become at it. More importantly, however, neither winning nor losing affects our self-worth. We know who we are in Jesus Christ, and that He died and rose again to redeem us from a human-centered way of life. Our victories are all in Christ.

Lord, assure this dad that he can win because You also stand with him. Bless him with prosperity and peace. In Jesus's name we pray. Amen.

I don't mean to say that I have already achieved these things or that I have already reached perfection. But I press on to possess that perfection for which Christ Jesus first possessed me. (Phil. 3:12 NLT)

TONIGHT I'M PRAYING THIS FOR _____

TONIGHT we pray for the dad who knows he's needed. He's had to make hard choices to give his children what they need, to train them well. Sometimes he's had to be away to provide financially. And sometimes he's chosen to be closer, even though it limits his job opportunities, so he can provide great support at home. Either way, he's needed.

The Lord instructs us to instruct our children in the ways of God. We are divinely appointed leaders of our home, modeling Christ's servant leadership. God has given us the responsibility to nurture and train our children (Eph. 6:4). We are the spiritual trainers, along with mothers. We tend to allow mothers to make home and hearth choices while we manage our children's outside worlds. But we must never shirk our spiritual responsibility. Children need their dad in every area of their lives.

Lord, please remember this dad and his children. Bring them always closer together. In Jesus's name we pray. Amen.

You know that we dealt with each of you as a father deals with his own children, encouraging, comforting and urging you to live lives worthy of God. (1 Thess. 2:11–12 NIV)

TONIGHT I'M PRAYING THIS FOR _____

TONIGHT we pray for the dad who sees God's richest blessings in his family's lives right now. He's prayed, believed, stayed the course that the Lord has directed, and steered his ship to a land of opportunity.

When Jesus traveled with His disciples across the Sea of Galilee, the waters were initially calm. But sometimes we must overcome hardships while sailing to the destination the Lord intends. When our daily responsibilities demand an inordinate amount of time and energy, we can lose our strength. During these times, it's easy to be overwhelmed and exhausted. Pretty soon we're wasting time on things that are not improving the quality of our life or our family's lives. Then, when more serious circumstances arise, we feel defeated rather than prevailing over them. It's best to realize that perils, difficulties, and struggles require a laser-focused approach to make sure that our family remains safe and sound.

Lord, thank You for supporting this dad who kept rowing, who believed You would come. Show him exactly the right course to steer toward for tomorrow so Your blessings will shower him as he goes. In Jesus's name we pray. Amen.

Therefore, submit to God. But resist the Devil, and he will flee from you. Draw near to God, and He will draw near to you. (James 4:7–8 HCSB)

TONIGHT I'M PRAYING THIS FOR _____

TONIGHT we pray for the dad who is part of a family, but not just the one that lives in his home and drives his car. No, this dad has a "family" that he sees regularly, shares a cup of coffee with, and knows will be honest with him in every single situation.

Unity, trust, love, and connections are the hallmarks of a strong group of friends who become like family. It's a gift to have friends who will ask us the hard questions and not let up until we've told the whole truth and nothing but the truth. We will keep each other's confidence, so what happens in the group stays in the group. With friends like this, we can all grow up together in the Lord.

Lord, this dad loves his family of friends. He needs this family. They've been through a lot together. They've learned to lean on each other. Protect this relationship to the end so this dad's life will be pleasing in Your sight. In Jesus's name we pray. Amen.

If we walk in the light, as he is in the light, we have fellowship with one another, and the blood of Jesus his Son cleanses us from all sin. (1 John 1:7)

TONIGHT I'M PRAYING THIS FOR _____

TONIGHT we pray for the dad who seeks after fellowship.

The Lord never intends for us to be alone. If we look at the Ten Commandments, we notice that at least half of them are focused on relationships with others. Fellowship with other Christians is necessary for us to enjoy a healthy life. It is only when we decide we can manage our own problems that we discover we are poor managers. The Lord desires us to be vulnerable with each other so we might have contentment and grow stronger together. Remember that the Lord sent the disciples out two by two so each of them could strengthen the other and make a unified front for those who were being discipled.

Lord, this dad knows that each of his friends has a different personality and different opinions about life. He also knows that differences often cause emotional sparks that can have lasting effects. But at the end of the day, he believes he can bring his friends together for fellowship. Show Your love to this dad and his friends, and smooth over the rough places in their lives. In Jesus's name we pray. Amen.

Holy Father, protect them by the power of your name, the name you gave me, so that they may be one as we are one. (John 17:11 NIV)

TONIGHT I'M PRAYING THIS FOR _____

TONIGHT we pray for the dad who is aware of his own shortcomings.

No matter how often we engage in self-reflection, we tend to look at our flaws and failures and start to make excuses: There wasn't anything we couldn't have done if given half a chance, and the only reason we didn't succeed was because someone else jumped the line, or the dog ate our homework so many years ago, or the test was unfair. The truth is most of us weren't the very best in much of anything. But rather than acknowledge that truth, we minimize the accomplishments of those who actually were the best and hide our own insecurities. We can take heart, though. The Lord knows us better than we know ourselves, and He is all right with exactly who we are. He isn't finished with us yet. He wants to heal us of our imperfections and those fears of failure that hold us back in life.

> *Lord, this dad loves You with his whole heart. He wants You to change him to be more like You every day. Give him the confidence to go forward. In Jesus's name we pray. Amen.*

> You, therefore, will be perfect [growing into spiritual maturity both in mind and character, actively integrating godly values into your daily life], as your heavenly Father is perfect. (Matt. 5:48 AMP)

TONIGHT I'M PRAYING THIS FOR _____

TONIGHT we pray for the dad who always looks forward to tomorrow. The dad who believes that no matter how good or how bad today has been, tomorrow has a chance to be better. It hasn't always been that way. There was a time when he thought "today" would never end, that the trials he was facing were simply going to last forever.

It is hard to trust in the Lord when our suffering is not alleviated. When our plans mean absolutely nothing and our life is just not our own anymore. But then, God! The phone rings and tomorrow comes. The longtime prayer is answered. Suddenly the Lord is even more present in our lives than He ever was. And we see Him for who He is: a God who plans for prosperity and not poverty, for health and not sickness. As we sleep tonight, our prayer can be "Thank You, Lord, for tomorrow."

Lord, it takes courage to trust You in all circumstances, but this dad does. He works the plan, he prospers, he overcomes. And when a bad day comes, he still trusts in You. Hear his prayers and honor Your promises tonight for tomorrow. In Jesus's name we pray. Amen.

The LORD is good. His unfailing love continues forever, and his faithfulness continues to each generation. (Ps. 100:5 NLT)

TONIGHT I'M PRAYING THIS FOR _____

TONIGHT **we pray for the dad who believes that he and his family are on a path to prosperity.** This dad believes in his ability to achieve the best for his family. He doesn't have a schedule or agenda for God's best to come to pass. He knows that prosperity rarely comes easy, but he's willing to do the hard work to trust in the Lord and see the victory.

God wants us to have enough to fulfill our every need and enough to bless others. And prosperity is so much more than just money; it's a variety of good things that also includes our finances.

> *Lord, this dad is seeking after You in everything he does. He has struggled for a good portion of his life, and he's ready for the rest that a job well done can bring. He trusts You for the promises of rewards and blessings that faith brings. Assure him of Your truth tonight so he can move out in hope tomorrow. In Jesus's name we pray. Amen.*

Blessed is the one . . . whose delight is in the law of the LORD, and who meditates on his law day and night. That person is like a tree planted by streams of water, which yields its fruit in season and whose leaf does not wither—whatever they do prospers. (Ps. 1:1–3 NIV)

TONIGHT I'M PRAYING THIS FOR _____

TONIGHT we pray for the dad who has seen a great success come to pass in his family. He knows that before he was able to experience success or failure, God ordained and planned his very life.

Most of us are familiar with the notions that God has counted every hair on our heads and He knows when a sparrow falls from the sky. He knows our circumstances, right down to the last dollar in our bank accounts and the last tear our children have cried. No two fingerprints are alike because no two humans are alike. God knows who we are because we are made in His image. So when we experience gain or loss, it's not because we stumble upon it. When we pray, plan, and follow through with the messages the Lord has spoken, we receive the blessings of the Lord. We receive our blessings, not someone else's. And what do these blessings portend? That we have been made for a purpose and our life has meaning.

Lord, grant this dad the assurance that all his successes will follow because he honors You. In Jesus's name we pray. Amen.

Your eyes saw me when I was formless; all my days were written in Your book and planned before a single one of them began. (Ps. 139:16 HCSB)

TONIGHT I'M PRAYING THIS FOR _____

TONIGHT we pray for the dad who looks toward changing for the better. He's always tried hard to accomplish what he believed was his destiny. But there were too many impediments to his success.

We try not to think of our past, but it almost always rises up and smacks us in the face: We didn't have the opportunities other dads had. Our family struggled emotionally. We didn't have the positive emotional influences some of our friends had. Obstacles seemed unassailable. But the Lord wants to use the dad we are capable of becoming. The best way to move forward is to continue to look forward. No matter who we've been in the past, we are capable of emotional and spiritual growth. We are not defined by who we were but by who we choose to be.

Lord, this dad has made some poor decisions that have affected his life and livelihood. But You know he is changing for the better as he relies on Your answers to his problems. You were in his past, and You are certainly in his present and his future. Give him a vision of what the future holds so he can live today in confidence. In Jesus's name we pray. Amen.

The plans of the diligent lead surely to abundance and advantage, but everyone who acts in haste comes surely to poverty. (Prov. 21:5 AMP)

TONIGHT I'M PRAYING THIS FOR _____

TONIGHT **we pray for the dad who is lonely.** He believes that no one has endured what he has endured and cannot possibly understand what he feels.

Many of us have some idea about what it means to be alone. Sunup to sundown on a tractor is fairly isolating. Sixteen hours a day in a tractor trailer is about as solitary as it gets. But in a very real sense, being alone and feeling lonely are two entirely different inclinations. When we are alone for a time, we somehow have a sense that there is someone looking after us or waiting for us to return. But the lonely person feels as though neither of the above is applicable. Maybe they have just gone off to college and a tragedy befalls their parents. Maybe a long-term marriage falls apart. Or maybe the children are living their own lives far, far away. That's what it's like to be lonely, not just alone.

> *Lord, this dad wasn't prepared for the separation that has taken his life away. He needs to know You are with him in those quiet hours, that You hear his prayers. Make sure he wakes to Your providence and slumbers with Your peace in every single minute You give him. In Jesus's name we pray. Amen.*

> Thus said the Lord God, the Holy One of Israel, "In returning and rest you shall be saved; in quietness and in trust shall be your strength." (Isa. 30:15)

TONIGHT I'M PRAYING THIS FOR _____

TONIGHT we pray for the dad whose heart is set on the Lord. This dad believes that if he puts his trust in the Lord, the Lord will continue to strengthen his heart and give him peace.

It's a wonderful attribute, peace. It's what God wants us to experience at all times. It is simply the provision of adequate resources. At all times, in all places, regardless of the circumstances, God wants us to know that His peace is available to us. It is unknowable until we know it. It is un-understandable by any human means. We usually think of adequate resources as financial safety. True enough, but peace is not measured only by financial resources. The widow who donated two mites in the Bible had peace, not because she had extra to give from her household but because she knew there would always be enough in her cupboard to give what she had.

> *Lord, this dad knows that peace will allow him to provide for and protect his family. He knows that he really can't hold peace in his hands as much as he holds it in his heart. You are the perfect provider for this dad's family. Remind him that he can trust in You in all things. In Jesus's name we pray. Amen.*

The eyes of all look to you in hope; you give them their food as they need it. When you open your hand, you satisfy the hunger and thirst of every living thing. (Ps. 145:15–16 NLT)

TONIGHT I'M PRAYING THIS FOR _____

TONIGHT we pray for the dad who needs his friends.

There are some of us who just aren't handy. We bear the expectation of what should be, so we try to do everything by ourselves. We'd love to see ourselves as invincible, but we're just not. Aren't we the ones who are supposed to do the helping? We reach the top shelf, we get rid of spiders, and we open the jar. But there's always a faucet that needs to be fixed or a water heater that needs to be installed or a fence gate that needs to be built. If we are wise, we will reach out to a buddy who knows us and is well aware of our inability to hammer a straight nail.

Lord, this dad has always been a winner. He's won battles with Your strength. He's had to learn that there is always help available, even when he hasn't accepted it. You have resources that will meet his needs, and he believes You will send them exactly when they are required. Open his eyes to see those opportunities. In Jesus's name we pray. Amen.

Whenever Moses held up his hand, Israel prevailed. . . . But Moses' hands grew weary, so . . . Aaron and Hur held up his hands, one on one side, and the other on the other side. (Exod. 17:11–12)

TONIGHT I'M PRAYING THIS FOR _____

328

TONIGHT **we pray for the dad who is optimistic.** The moment he became a dad, his entire worldview changed. No matter what he believed about his life, his goals, and his aspirations, they changed with the arrival of his first child. His own successes and failures took a back seat to the promise of a new life, a life he is responsible for.

As a dad, we have the opportunity to create a new and different kind of success. No longer do we live for ourselves; we live for our children. If we never believed it before, we must now believe that the Lord loves us and has prepared us to take care of the children He has blessed us with. The Lord wants us to believe that since our children will change the world, it is up to us to help fulfill His destiny in them.

Lord, this dad has hopes for his children. He believes in them and would move heaven and earth to see them succeed. He knows that it is up to him to guide them into a closer walk with You, where their own hopes and dreams lie. Give this dad peace as he hopes and believes for every good thing. In Jesus's name we pray. Amen.

Now all glory to God, who is able, through his mighty power at work within us, to accomplish infinitely more than we might ask or think. (Eph. 3:20 NLT)

TONIGHT I'M PRAYING THIS FOR _____

TONIGHT we pray for the dad who has had his share of want. He's had plenty as well, and like most of us, he likes plenty better. He wants to be seen as faithful and ready to contribute to the work of the Lord, but he just doesn't feel like he measures up. His quarter in the plate and the extra hours he has to work during the week make him wonder how the Lord looks at his spiritual condition.

It's way too easy to believe that our service to the Lord is based upon what we do or do not have. But if riches were the measure that the success of the church depended on, the church would have failed centuries ago. Rest assured, we have value in the kingdom of God, regardless of our wealth.

> *Lord, this dad is always looking for a way to succeed. He knows that You have placed blessings in his life in order for him to bless others. Remind him that You know his condition and You can use him in places where he can do the most good. Help him see just how much he has to share. In Jesus's name we pray. Amen.*

Have nothing to do with godless myths and old wives' tales; rather, train yourself to be godly. For . . . godliness has value for all things, holding promise for both the present life and the life to come. (1 Tim. 4:7–8 NIV)

TONIGHT I'M PRAYING THIS FOR _____

TONIGHT we pray for the dad who knows how to make good choices.

Between two or more equally viable options, don't we always want to make the best possible choice? Of course. We do our research and conduct our cost-benefit analysis and decide what to do. We're accustomed to making these decisions on our own. But what about those choices we might make if circumstances were different? The kinds of choices that involve our character? Like choosing to go home instead of staying out all night. Like choosing to be honest with an employer instead of having an unequal balance in the books. To be that dad, we need to actually go out into the world and meet it head-on with honor and integrity. To return to our home to keep it safe. And we choose to repeat that process every single day.

Lord, bless this dad who, by his actions, has chosen to serve You this day. In Jesus's name we pray. Amen.

Be glad in the LORD and rejoice, you righteous [who actively seek right standing with Him]; shout for joy, all you upright in heart. (Ps. 32:11 AMP)

TONIGHT I'M PRAYING THIS FOR _____

TONIGHT we pray for the dad who can usually do it all. He can make eggs and mac and cheese *and* reverse grill a steak. He can do new math *and* make sure all the bills are paid. He can fold a fitted sheet *and* manage a two-year-old single-handedly. He can still skateboard down the street *and* play a decent game of HORSE.

Sometimes we overestimate our skills and abilities, as though everything will work out just because it always has. But we know that isn't always true, and if we're wise, we must still rely on the Lord. Sometimes the bills don't get paid and the Lord steps in. Sometimes the doctor's report is bad and the Lord heals. We're supposed to expect problems. And no matter what we're good at, tough times build good character. That's what the Lord is after. Adversity brings challenges, and challenges bring future success.

Lord, this dad still looks to You for the hard decisions. He knows not everything is easy. But he can do easy and he can do hard. Protect him and guide him during the hard times. In Jesus's name we pray. Amen.

You, Lord, are a compassionate and gracious God, slow to anger and rich in faithful love and truth. (Ps. 86:15 HCSB)

TONIGHT I'M PRAYING THIS FOR _____

TONIGHT we pray for the dad who worries that there won't be enough time.

A dad who knows what to do when life gets overwhelming can carry a heavy burden. Everyone looks to the dad in times of crisis and expects him to know exactly what to do and when to do it. But if we spend too much time on one endeavor, will there ever be enough time for all the other responsibilities? For work? For family? Will we ever make up the difference? At times like this, it's easy to begin to rely solely on ourselves, and we can become prisoners to the perfect choice for the perfect outcome. But how can we know which is the best choice without consulting the One who gave us the choice in the first place?

> *Lord, remind this dad that every day is different from the one before. He is not bound by yesterday's actions. Help him to make the best decisions each day for that day, and the courage to carry them out. In Jesus's name we pray. Amen.*

Trust in and rely confidently on the LORD with all your heart and do not rely on your own insight or understanding. In all your ways know and acknowledge and recognize Him, and He will make your paths straight and smooth [removing obstacles that block your way]. (Prov. 3:5–6 AMP)

TONIGHT I'M PRAYING THIS FOR _____

333

TONIGHT we pray for the dad who believes he has a destiny.

"The kingdom of God is at hand," Jesus says in the Gospel of Mark (1:15). It is in the future, but the time has come to reach for it, He says. When we choose to repent and change ourselves and our way of thinking, that kingdom will draw ever closer. There is no greater choice, no greater opportunity, than to repent of our earthly-minded character and look to the possibility, the destiny, of the kingdom of God. And once we've repented, the Lord will bring to our mind and remembrance what He has shown us in the past so we may count on His future for us. The Lord knows our frame (Ps. 103:14), and He is fully prepared to reward us because of the treasure He sees in us. He knows our passions and our personalities because He knows us better than we know ourselves, and He can use every bit of us to accomplish His purpose.

Lord, all of this dad's successes are carrying him to this place. None of the trials he has suffered can prevent him from achieving what You have prepared for him and his family. He can accomplish exactly what You have promised because he is dedicated to You and determined to see it through. Bring all the good things to pass for this dad and those he cares for. In Jesus's name we pray. Amen.

Humble yourselves before the Lord, and he will exalt you. (James 4:10)

TONIGHT I'M PRAYING THIS FOR _____

TONIGHT we pray for the dad who still thinks his hard work is all that matters. It's a belief that can make each day exhausting.

Sure, hard work generally yields superior results. But ultimately, simply working hard makes for a tired dad. The world creates obstacles that distract us and take our attention away from what is important. Then all we can see is a lack of success in our efforts. And then come discouragement and an inability to complete tasks. At times like this, we need to know we're valuable to God in our own right. Work is not supposed to be prison. God does not hold us accountable for what we do so much as He looks to who we become in our labor. He has given us a destiny of success that is greater than the intensity and diligence of our labor. It is our character—our dedication to family that means more than the tasks we complete.

> *Lord, this dad needs a new outlook to take his family where they need to go. Open his eyes to the prize right in front of him. In Jesus's name we pray. Amen.*

Do the will of God with all your heart. Work with enthusiasm, as though you were working for the Lord rather than for people. Remember that the Lord will reward each one of us for the good we do, whether we are slaves or free. (Eph. 6:6–8 NLT)

TONIGHT I'M PRAYING THIS FOR _____

TONIGHT we pray for the dad who tries to set the tone for expectations in his home. He leads by example. He's industrious and makes sure that what needs to be done is, in fact, completed. There's enough for everyone to do, and he's always at the head of the line because his day is managed by the Lord. All of this dad's responsibilities have been ordained by the One who blesses him with energy, commitment, and the attitude to keep going. He chooses to serve his family because that's where their success lives. And since his success comes from being prepared in all things, his family has peace and security for their lives.

There's an awful lot of day-to-day living that can deaden our preparedness for sudden changes. But it's our responsibility to constantly be on the lookout for impending adverse events. When we are prepared for life, when the prep work is behind us, we can keep our eyes forward to keep our family safe.

Lord, this dad makes sure the easy jobs are done so he can focus on what lies ahead. He knows life can be a challenge, but he is determined to be prepared for the sake of his family. Since he takes care of business every single day, strengthen him as he prepares for tomorrow. In Jesus's name we pray. Amen.

Don't begin until you count the cost. For who would begin construction of a building without first calculating the cost to see if there is enough money to finish it? (Luke 14:28 NLT)

TONIGHT I'M PRAYING THIS FOR _____

TONIGHT we pray for the dad who fixes broken things. He knows sometimes he has to take the walls down to the studs in order to restore a bathroom. He knows he has to remove the engine from the car to fix it. And he knows that what he rebuilds will have greater value than what he began with.

When parts of our lives need repair, the Lord will remind us before everything comes to an abrupt halt. It's at that time we listen carefully to the Holy Spirit, consult the owner's manual, and collect all the tools necessary to rebuild what needs to be fixed.

> *Lord, this dad's life is in disrepair. He knows that You can and will give him everything he needs to put the pieces back together. He's living his life one day at a time, and he believes that the Holy Spirit will repair his broken heart and his broken life. Bring him to a place of peace where he can rest in the assurance of tomorrow's promises. In Jesus's name we pray. Amen.*

The Spirit of the Lord God is upon me . . . to bring good news to the poor; he has sent me to bind up the brokenhearted, to proclaim liberty to the captives. (Isa. 61:1)

TONIGHT I'M PRAYING THIS FOR _____

TONIGHT we pray for the dad who honors his parents.

Our culture is changing around us and suggests that our extended families are less than necessary for us to thrive. We want to have what we have and keep it because we have earned it. A more secure dad will know that we are responsible for our own accomplishments. On the other hand, we might want to attribute part of the responsibility for our failures to those who came before. However, the Lord makes no allowance for choosing not to honor our parents. They were charged with the responsibility of providing for our needs—even if they did their job poorly. We do not get to honor them only if they have been honorable to us.

> *Lord, this dad loves his parents. He knows You expect him to honor them and continually recognize their importance in his life. He knows their needs will increase and they will need his physical and spiritual strength sooner rather than later. Remind him also that honoring them means taking the lead in providing for them. In Jesus's name we pray. Amen.*

Each of you shall respect his mother and his father, and you shall keep My Sabbaths; I am the Lord your God. (Lev. 19:3 AMP)

TONIGHT I'M PRAYING THIS FOR _____

TONIGHT we pray for the dad who depends upon the Lord. He might look like a dad who isn't ready for the rough-and-tumble of parenting, but when he remembers who his own provider is and how he is armored up, he knows that he can mix it up with any spiritual forces that might arise.

We know that our success comes from the Lord. When we have victories, our confidence level rises. We can look back at our achievements and know that we have the resolve to defend what needs to be protected.

> *Lord, this dad counts on You for everything. He's had successes and failures, and You have always seen him through to the end of the path he's taking. He knows You will carry him to his next endeavor with power and authority. Remind him of the victories and that the giants in the land are no match for him with You by his side. In Jesus's name we pray. Amen.*

When a lion or a bear comes to steal a lamb from the flock, I go after it with a club and rescue the lamb from its mouth.... The LORD who rescued me from the claws of the lion and the bear will rescue me. (1 Sam. 17:34–35, 37 NLT)

TONIGHT I'M PRAYING THIS FOR _____

TONIGHT we pray for the dad who works with his hands.

The wonderful part of working with our hands is that we get to see our success immediately. Remember how the Lord created the heavens and the earth and declared each day to be good before He was finished. Think of the great artists or sculptors who are finished with their work only when they say they are finished and not before. Think of the engineers and architects who construct roads and bridges as well as homes and skyscrapers. But never forget that the labor is all-encompassing. We are never far away from our work, seeing the finished projects in every waking hour until they are completed. Dawn to dusk is not uncommon for us. The Lord's creativity is evident in those of us who make what we see in the Spirit and complete the plan the Lord has for us.

Lord, this dad never shies away from hard physical labor. He knows he has been created to accomplish great things and impart great value to what he creates. Strengthen his hands and heart to want to labor for You. In Jesus's name we pray. Amen.

In the beginning God created the heaven and the earth. . . . And the Spirit of God moved upon the face of the waters. . . . God saw every thing that he had made, and, behold, it was very good. (Gen. 1:1, 31 KJV)

TONIGHT I'M PRAYING THIS FOR _____

TONIGHT **we pray for the dad who is grateful even in the tough times.** This dad's life is not all about easy. He knows that life is not a smooth path.

We are to remain grateful in any and all circumstances, in the trials as well as in the blessings that we hope will overtake us. How can we be grateful in the trials? Because we see the Lord and His goodness in every single thing. This is counterintuitive, for sure. And it takes training. But we don't want to just get by; we want to prosper, which happens when we are committed to an expectation of God's promises. When we trust God for everything we have as well as everything we will receive, that trust keeps us going and makes us confident there's a good tomorrow coming.

Lord, this dad looks for You in everything he tries and sees You in everything he achieves. He is ready for anything, and when those tough times do show up, he's already thanking You for the better day ahead. Show him that no matter how long they last, the tough times will end in Your perfect timing. In Jesus's name we pray. Amen.

Give thanks in all circumstances; for this is the will of God in Christ Jesus for you. (1 Thess. 5:18)

TONIGHT I'M PRAYING THIS FOR _____

TONIGHT we pray for the dad who often wonders if he's doing it right. We can't help it. There are always others in our families who believe that their strategies for raising children two generations ago are still good today. We want to be supportive and appreciative of them, but we all know that the times, they are a-changin'. Rather than blindly criticizing our parents or other relatives when they disagree with what we think are appropriate actions, we should ask them, "When you were raising me, what part of God's Word did you rely on heavily?" In this way, we bring God's teaching into the conversation and can share what we rely on as well.

Lord, this dad wants to be a faithful dad, and he has questions about how he should parent a toddler and a preteen. Your Holy Spirit is ever present in his heart and mind, and He has an answer at the ready. Give this dad wisdom and guide him to Your Word so he can make the right choices. In Jesus's name we pray. Amen.

Hear this, ye old men, and give ear, all ye inhabitants of the land. Hath this been in your days, or even in the days of your fathers? Tell ye your children of it, and let your children tell their children, and their children another generation. (Joel 1:2–3 KJV)

TONIGHT I'M PRAYING THIS FOR _____

TONIGHT we pray for the dad who faithfully searches for answers. This dad has realized that whenever he asks the Lord for anything, the Lord makes Himself known.

God knows everything we don't. There is nothing beyond His purview, and the Holy Spirit brings to our mind and remembrance everything the Lord wants us to know. He wants us to experience His heart and His mind. He breathed into us the breath of life, meaning all of Himself was given to us at creation. Now, we've managed to lose all or most of His gifts to us since the fall. But since He gave Himself to us once, He's more than happy to share with us again. He's a good Father and He doesn't hold our ignorance against us, nor does He wonder why we haven't asked for what we needed sooner. You see, everything we want is found in God. True wealth, peace, security—all those things are wrapped up in His presence. So when we ask for anything, He shows up with everything.

Lord, this dad's life is stressful, and he needs Your presence to bring him peace. Show him the best outcome for his choices. In Jesus's name we pray. Amen.

You will have plenty to eat and be satisfied and praise the name of the Lord your God who has dealt wondrously with you. (Joel 2:26 AMP)

TONIGHT I'M PRAYING THIS FOR _____

TONIGHT we pray for the dad who is neither too old nor too young to have a dream.

We all have more wisdom today than we did yesterday—on purpose. The Lord intends for us to always be growing and maturing. There is no set time when He decides that suddenly we are no longer valuable in His kingdom. Scripture is very clear that the Lord always has a plan for us, and only when we leave this planet is that plan completed. He is no respecter of persons, Scripture relates, and the dreams we have are not time challenged. We may be less physically able to complete the plans the Lord has for us, but they are always available whenever we seek Him and discover the blueprint for our lives. And our dream can be something we've always wanted because when we were young we believed it represented fulfillment. For one dad, it might be a new home. For another dad, it might be finally overcoming the difficulty that's held him back for so long.

Lord, this dad wants to have a life that he is proud of. Grant him the strength to pursue the dream and the life You've promised. In Jesus's name we pray. Amen.

The counsel of the Lord stands forever, the plans of his heart to all generations. (Ps. 33:11)

TONIGHT I'M PRAYING THIS FOR _____

TONIGHT we pray for the dad who is looking forward to a new opportunity. As with most opportunities, it's well within what this dad can accomplish.

Though God is in charge of all our opportunities, sometimes the temptation is to do things on our own. God will never ask us to do something we cannot do. He is with us, and He always wants us to join Him in His endeavors. But it requires us to sense His leading every single day. That's difficult when we are accustomed to leading our own lives successfully. While waiting on the Lord and following him might cost some ease and convenience, it will give us and our family greater peace in our lives. And we must always remember that even in our willingness to serve the Lord, we can't accomplish everything we might wish to. He will lead us into what He needs from us in His time.

Lord, You are the Creator of all good things. You lead, guide, and direct this dad because he believes in that goodness. Now he needs Your assurance that he should take that next step. Confirm Your promise in his life. In Jesus's name we pray. Amen.

As it is, they desire a better country, that is, a heavenly one. Therefore God is not ashamed to be called their God, for he has prepared for them a city. (Heb. 11:16)

TONIGHT I'M PRAYING THIS FOR _____

TONIGHT we pray for the dad who makes a maximum effort every day. He's been doing his best for as long as he can remember. It's an attitude he was raised with.

We may have learned long ago that there's no sense in getting up in the morning if we don't plan to make it a good day. Someone once said that making one's first words encouraging will set the tone for the entire day. And the best days are the ones spent in conversation with the Lord from beginning to end. That doesn't mean just acknowledging His presence. We should lean into praying *with* Him, not *to* Him. A discussion with a friend about Babe Ruth is never limited to his stats but about how great a player he was. Likewise, the Lord wants to have a conversation about why we might need something, not just about what we need.

Lord, this dad knows that in all things he can't just rest on a good yesterday or a good last week. He's too important to the family. He wouldn't coast at work or home. He wants his kids to know him as the dad who always tries. But he also wants to show his children that You are important to him at all times. It's the heart that matters, and he has a big heart. Give him a good night's rest after doing his best today. In Jesus's name we pray. Amen.

Trust in Him at all times, you people; pour out your hearts before Him. God is our refuge. (Ps. 62:8 HCSB)

TONIGHT I'M PRAYING THIS FOR _____

TONIGHT we pray for the dad who has a chance to have what his heart truly desires. He really wants the best God has to offer him. That's his heart talking. That's his heart's true desire.

What we usually want is a whole lot more of what we already have. That's our natural desire talking, right? Sure it is. And aren't we fairly certain that sometimes what we want is not exactly what the Lord wants for us? Yes, that's probably true too, because the Lord is just not that into things. He knows we can and will grow tired of "too much." He also knows we can use up what we have in our hands. And we've done that all before. We've had money and spent it. We've had success and found out all glory is fleeting. We've had freedom and discovered we were lonely. Instead of things, God is much more into love, joy, and peace for us. These gifts remain after we've spent our lives on things.

Lord, reward this dad with his family, where peace reigns and life begins, every single day. Extend his arms tonight so that he may reach around and hold his family together, all at once, and keep them safe. In Jesus's name we pray. Amen.

The eternal God is your refuge, and his everlasting arms are under you. (Deut. 33:27 NLT)

TONIGHT I'M PRAYING THIS FOR _____

TONIGHT we pray for the dad who sometimes feels as though he will never catch up.

How many times have we felt like everyone is moving on without us? We pray, we give, we repent of our sins on an almost daily basis, and yet others are prospering more than we are. We wonder if we've missed our calling since things seem to be happening to everyone but us. We want to level the playing field, have a new start to our life. And guess what? God is all about giving us a new sense of purpose as our relationship with Him grows. Anytime is the time to move directly to the Lord. Often in our haste to succeed, we've trusted ourselves instead of Him.

Lord, this dad works long hours and does hard work. He never quits and he always gives it his all. But he's really tired and still wants to finish strong today. He is looking forward to a fresh outlook on where he's going and how he's getting there. Remove his fears and show him the clear path before him. In Jesus's name we pray. Amen.

With all my heart I have sought You, [inquiring of You and longing for You]; do not let me wander from Your commandments [neither through ignorance nor by willful disobedience]. (Ps. 119:10 AMP)

TONIGHT I'M PRAYING THIS FOR _____

TONIGHT we pray for the dad who remembers his first child.

Wow, what a great feeling we had when our first child came home. The awesome responsibility we had steeled ourselves for was finally coming to pass. We'd thought about it, prayed about it, and, if we're honest, fretted about it, but when that first child came into our home, there just wasn't anything like it. And we've always wanted to keep that memory sacred. The Lord would have it that way. He sees all His children with that very memory all the time, and He wants each of us to keep that memory ourselves. To always see our children in that moment, perfect and loved. To always put their failures as far away as the east is from the west, the way He does for us.

Lord, this dad takes his role as a father seriously, and he wears the mantle proudly and gladly. Remind him that fatherhood is a joy and not just a series of tasks and responsibilities. Strengthen him every day so he might rise to the challenge he's been given. In Jesus's name we pray. Amen.

Behold, I and the children whom the Lord has given me are signs and portents in Israel from the Lord of hosts, who dwells on Mount Zion. (Isa. 8:18)

TONIGHT I'M PRAYING THIS FOR _____

TONIGHT we pray for the dad who never gives up. He has seen some impossible tasks, tasks that he thought he'd never be able to accomplish. He's waded right into the midst of them, not really thinking about how hard they might turn out to be. The Lord always seems to have a sense of humor, because it's been those jobs that have had the greatest rewards, for both this dad's body and his spirit.

We are exactly suited to what we are called to accomplish. The Lord is always going to be at the completion of the task, waiting for us to experience the joy of finishing a job well done and seeing His face as we finish the race. If we look for the path of least resistance instead, we'll miss the greatest blessings. Let's not shirk responsibilities and tough assignments—it's the uphill climb that proves the engine.

Lord, this dad wants Your guidance every day. Give him Your strength to accept every assignment, no matter how hard. In Jesus's name we pray. Amen.

The Lord said to Abram, "Go from your country. . . . And I will make of you a great nation, and I will bless you and make your name great." (Gen. 12:1–2)

TONIGHT I'M PRAYING THIS FOR _____

350

TONIGHT we pray for the dad who holds his tongue.

In these constantly changing political times and with the proliferation of social media, we discover that everyone has an opinion. For good or ill, whatever we say has enormous reach, far beyond what James, the brother of Jesus, might have envisioned in his epistle (chap. 3). Our words are like feathers released from a pillow in a high wind, and trying to put them back before they offend someone is so very difficult. Our default is often not to bless others with our words but rather to judge and define them with our attitudes. We value our convictions and are willing to defend them to the death, it seems. But if the first words someone hears from us are used to belittle the thoughts and aspirations of a person we barely know, the listener will have forever heard our heart and no longer consider what we have to say as valuable. We only get one chance to make a good first impression.

> *Lord, this dad wants to speak life. Out of the abundance of his heart his mouth speaks. Help him to use his words wisely so Your Spirit might spring forth in his life. In Jesus's name we pray. Amen.*

So also the tongue is a small member, yet it boasts of great things. How great a forest is set ablaze by such a small fire! And the tongue is a fire, a world of unrighteousness. The tongue is set among our members, staining the whole body, setting on fire the entire course of life, and set on fire by hell. (James 3:5–6)

TONIGHT I'M PRAYING THIS FOR _____

TONIGHT we pray for the dad who wonders if things will really get better.

All of us have our own situations of joy and sorrow. The things that happen, for good or ill, are not surprises to God. While He is not in the business of causing accidents, He always takes the affairs of the day and uses them to bring good to the world. Although we almost never complain about the blessings that happen to us (say, the really good used car that gets us from place to place for a great price and all it has against it is a very noticeable dent in the fender), we often wonder where God is in our big and small tribulations. We can rest assured that He knows where all His children are at any given moment.

Lord, this dad knows You care for the world and You have a plan for his life as well. Despite all the misfortunes that have befallen him, he knows You are restoring all Your children to complete wholeness, regardless of their situation or circumstance. Strengthen him as he looks out for the world You have created for him. In Jesus's name we pray. Amen.

I am not ashamed, for I know whom I have believed, and I am convinced that he is able to guard until that day what has been entrusted to me. (2 Tim. 1:12)

TONIGHT I'M PRAYING THIS FOR _____

TONIGHT we pray for the dad who doesn't wait to be happy. He makes his own breaks. When what seems like an insurmountable obstacle arises, this dad immediately places his trust in God to move the mountain. He doesn't rely on his own willpower to overcome the stress and anxiety that come from unforeseen difficulties. No, he smiles and moves on.

Some of us worry that good things haven't happened, aren't happening, or maybe never will happen. Once we are trapped in worry, we will never achieve what God has in store for us. Living in the past is self-defeating. Instead, going forward, God wants us to trust Him every minute of every day. When we are trusting Him, we don't have time to worry about what has or hasn't been done. And we can make decisions that take care of our family, knowing what they need because we trust the Lord in all things.

Lord, this dad has powerful faith, and he believes in You. Give him the courage to always act on that faith. In Jesus's name we pray. Amen.

Be still in the presence of the LORD, and wait patiently for him to act. Don't worry about evil people who prosper or fret about their wicked schemes. (Ps. 37:7 NLT)

TONIGHT I'M PRAYING THIS FOR _____

353

TONIGHT we pray for the dad who believes in the Lord all the time. He knows the Lord is always working to supply his every need.

Not everybody does believe this. We kind of pick and choose what we believe about God. Maybe He heals this but doesn't heal that, and sometimes He provides, unless we really don't need it. But God is in every single word we speak in prayer, and He is always moving behind the scenes to bring to pass the miracle we seem to need. And we are often the hands and feet of a miracle someone else needs. Someone else who believes in the Lord might just be counting on us to be faithful to receive what He has for us and for them.

Lord, this dad understands and lives in the miracle of his salvation. He knows that You have saved him to great things and great works in Your name. He remembers that what You have given him is supposed to be a gift to others. He knows a miracle and a changed life are possible when he shares Your love, peace, and provision with others. Fill this faithful dad's hands with more than enough. In Jesus's name we pray. Amen.

How amazing are the deeds of the Lord! All who delight in him should ponder them. . . . All he does is just and good, and all his commandments are trustworthy. They are forever true, to be obeyed faithfully and with integrity. (Ps. 111:2, 7–8 NLT)

TONIGHT I'M PRAYING THIS FOR _____

354

TONIGHT we pray for the dad who has missed out on far too much. This dad has seen the mess of his life, and he believes he can be remembered for who he could become and not just who he has been.

We know that God has a plan for our lives. We also know that His plan is intimately connected to His Son, Jesus Christ. When we turned our eyes to see Him, to know Him, and to trust Him, the plan of God began to unfold for us and our family. He gives good things to all His children whenever they call upon His name.

Lord, this dad absolutely knows that he is lost. His life is a shambles, and he knows it's because he has made really poor choices even in the face of opportunities to pick a God-given path. He knows that only Jesus can save his life and bring him back to the land of the living. Remind this dad that Jesus is looking for that opportunity to connect with him and bring him peace. In Jesus's name we pray. Amen.

If you declare with your mouth, "Jesus is Lord," and believe in your heart that God raised him from the dead, you will be saved. (Rom. 10:9 NIV)

TONIGHT I'M PRAYING THIS FOR _____

TONIGHT we pray for the dad who has children suffering through a divorce.

While statistics tell us most of us will not go through a divorce, some of us have or will. And our children are so vulnerable. When their dad is no longer married to their mom, the family they grew up in no longer exists. It is their lives that experience the most upheaval. We may not remember that our parents were the tether to reality that we had in order to make our way in the world that was not yet ours. When we understand just how much we suffer while being separated from our children, we will also understand that the emotional trauma to our children is multiplied exponentially because of the life changes they have yet to experience. The Lord weeps for all His children in these difficult times, no matter how young or old they are.

Lord, as a father Yourself, You have placed the awesome responsibility on this dad of protecting his children. He needs Your understanding to help him keep his children emotionally safe through this ordeal. Guide his hands, mind, and heart so he can give them what they need. In Jesus's name we pray. Amen.

In My Father's house are many dwelling places. If it were not so, I would have told you, because I am going there to prepare a place for you. And if I go and prepare a place for you, I will come back again and I will take you to Myself, so that where I am you may be also. (John 14:2–3 AMP)

TONIGHT I'M PRAYING THIS FOR _____

TONIGHT we pray for the dad who wants to leave a legacy for his children. What this dad does for God matters.

We all want our children to have more than enough in their lives. We work hard so they can have everything they need. Even more importantly, we want them to see us for our character—not just what we achieved but *how* we accomplished our dreams and aspirations. Money dwindles, glory is fleeting, but the dad who influences his children in the ways of the Lord is remembered forever.

Lord, this dad loves his children and wants them to know that he made the right choices for them. He lives his life in such a way that they can understand the godly influence in their lives. He knows You have shaped his life from beginning to end and You will be faithful to protect them as well. Enlarge his heart to overflowing so his children might see You in his life every day. In Jesus's name we pray. Amen.

The people of Israel went each to his inheritance to take possession of the land. And the people served the Lord all the days of Joshua, and all the days of the elders who outlived Joshua, who had seen all the great work that the Lord had done for Israel. (Judg. 2:6–7)

TONIGHT I'M PRAYING THIS FOR _____

357

TONIGHT we pray for the dad who is dealing with a critical illness in his family. When he wakes up in the morning, it's happening. When he closes his eyes at night, praying for the peace that sleep can bring, it's still happening.

When illness affects our own child, our prayers reflect an intensity that is unfathomable. We never realize how much our heart can ache when our child suffers and our supernatural fatherly desire to protect them is thwarted. Why is this happening? Who is to blame? God, how come? We ask the questions that only the God of heaven and earth can answer. Knowing that He is aware of our grief and wants to be as close to us as we need to be to Him, we can be confident that He loves us and He loves our child. He has never been absent from them, and He has always been closer to us than we realized.

Lord, in the darkest hours of the night, You have promised that we can count on Your hand of mercy in the morning. Wipe away this dad's tears as he looks forward to a new day trusting in Your goodness. In Jesus's name we pray. Amen.

The LORD is close to the brokenhearted; he rescues those whose spirits are crushed. The righteous person faces many troubles, but the LORD comes to the rescue each time. (Ps. 34:18–19 NLT)

TONIGHT I'M PRAYING THIS FOR _____

TONIGHT we pray for the dad who is thankful for his livelihood. He knows that he doesn't just labor day to day at a job or a profession but that he's extremely good at what he does.

Accomplishing goals with our hands gives us a wonderful sense of well-being at the end of the day. Scripture reminds us that the Lord not only will supply every need but will place in our hands the necessary tools to enlarge what we have (Phil. 4:19). We may not part the Red Sea, but we can and will perform miracles in people's lives when we use our skills, tools, and talents for His glory.

Lord, this dad has used every available means to provide for his family. You have gifted him remarkably to make use of his talents and wisdom for them. Not only is he a provider and protector, but he also makes use of what he has and does to prosper the community. Give this dad even greater confidence in his calling and the strength to see it through. In Jesus's name we pray. Amen.

The Lord will open for you His abundant storehouse, the sky, to give your land rain in its season and to bless all the work of your hands. (Deut. 28:12 HCSB)

TONIGHT I'M PRAYING THIS FOR _____

359

TONIGHT we pray for the dad who understands the importance of prayer. This dad doesn't know how prayer works, exactly, but he knows that when he prays, things go better for him and his family.

We don't know how the Lord works everything for our good, especially when things are a mess, but we can trust Him to make that happen when we pray. Spending a moment or two in quiet reflection, thanking the Lord for everything we've received, brings about a peace we just can't explain. As a dad, we know our life isn't always the best. Sometimes we stumble, lose our temper, get things wrong at work. But connecting with the Lord sometime during the day—morning, noon, or night—sure seems to keep the wheels from falling off our life the next day.

Lord, this dad wants to see what You see and know what You know. He believes in You even if he's stepped away at times. Help him to make prayer the first thing in his life, trusting in You to bring about Your promises for him. In Jesus's name we pray. Amen.

"You must love the Lord your God with all your heart, all your soul, and all your mind." This is the first and greatest commandment. (Matt. 22:37–38 NLT)

TONIGHT I'M PRAYING THIS FOR _____

360

TONIGHT we pray for the dad who doesn't know what he's going to do tomorrow. Each time he's experienced loss, the Lord has been faithful to bring him up above the waves and place him on solid ground. But now . . . now he's wondering if God is still there for him.

We've all had struggles, because they're a fact of life. We've picked ourselves up and moved on—a little less sound or a little less fortunate, but we kept going just the same. We've experienced all manner of emotional loss as well. Each loss is heartbreaking, no matter to whom it befalls. Although the losses might cause us to question God's provision and protection, since we have come through them time and again, we remember that He sees all our needs and keeps our heart safe.

> *Lord, this dad is wondering if he's made some awful mistake and it's now catching up to him. He wonders if he's a man You can still bless. He's never needed You more to help him reconstruct the ruins of his life. Show this questioning dad how he can lean on others to be his hands and feet today and tomorrow. In Jesus's name we pray. Amen.*

You caused me to experience many troubles and misfortunes, but You will revive me again. You will bring me up again, even from the depths of the earth. (Ps. 71:20 HCSB)

TONIGHT I'M PRAYING THIS FOR _____

TONIGHT we pray for the dad who loves his job as a father.

Somehow we all think that being a father shouldn't be a job, that it should be a mission or an endeavor or a work of the heart. Those are nice words, pleasant words. But it is a job, one we gladly applied for and one we always made sure we kept. We fully understand that this job is to provide for and protect the children we are raising. It is made up of a million small and seemingly insignificant moments, each of which can have eternal consequences. The Lord completed his mission on this planet only after He had fulfilled every single prophecy as Messiah. We have a similar undertaking to fulfill our spiritual responsibilities, and there will be a lifetime achievement award for us if we hold fast and keep the faith. Our reward will be greeting our children's children with all the hope of the tomorrows we have prayed for.

Lord, each day has new possibilities for this dad. He's been given today, and he plans to take care of it for his children. He wants them to understand how important they are to him, whether he is near or far away. That is his daily prayer. Remind him that You are with him every step along the way. In Jesus's name we pray. Amen.

I have singled him out so that he will direct his sons and their families to keep the way of the Lord by doing what is right and just. Then I will do for Abraham all that I have promised. (Gen. 18:19 NLT)

TONIGHT I'M PRAYING THIS FOR _____

TONIGHT we pray for the dad who always wants a close walk with the Lord.

There really are no easy answers to being a dad. It would be nice to think that all we have to do is check a few boxes and everyone will be happy—get a job, keep a job, be present, *bingo!* That all we have to do is compartmentalize our lives and we'll have this fatherhood thing down. But what about our spiritual lives, the place where all the connection begins and ends? We even segregate our time with the Lord, keep Him in the space where He can easily be reached if we need Him. If we're not connected to the Lord in some form or fashion, seeking His love and His peace, there will be precious little of either of those in our home. Then what fatherhood becomes is simply a dad daycare. We all need time daily to experience the Lord's presence.

Lord, as this dad is protecting his children, he makes wise choices to know how best to take care of them every day. He provides for them by loving their hearts and minds. Bless this wise dad in every season of his life. In Jesus's name we pray. Amen.

He will be the sure foundation for your times, a rich store of salvation and wisdom and knowledge; the fear of the LORD is the key to this treasure. (Isa. 33:6 NIV)

TONIGHT I'M PRAYING THIS FOR _____

TONIGHT we pray for the dad who has questions. Why was there an unexpected malady in his family today? Why were there catastrophes in his community recently? How come his coworker received a raise when he has been working just as hard for just as long?

We have a tendency to think that when we are faithful to pray for the peace and security of our family and events take place that are out of our control, the Lord must not hear our prayers. What good does it do to pray if the things we pray for will only every once in a while come to pass? Deep down, we want it to be true that when we pray, God is working everything in creation for our good. We rely on Romans 8:28, which says everything is going to work out. But sometimes it doesn't seem like it. This is the hardest aspect to understand about our relationship with God—that He is managing all the events in our lives, and our responsibility is to understand what measure of His goodness is involved in the unexpected events.

Lord, this dad believes that You have all the real answers to the questions in his life. Remind him that You are never out of reach when he prays. In Jesus's name we pray. Amen.

Nicodemus said to him, "How can these things be?" Jesus answered him, "Are you the teacher of Israel and yet you do not understand these things?" (John 3:9–10)

TONIGHT I'M PRAYING THIS FOR _____

TONIGHT we pray for the dad who knows God as his **Father.** He knows it's important to have a relationship with his heavenly Father in order to portray Him to his children as their Father. He wants to be a model to them of how a father should be.

When we know God as Father, we understand who we are as a dad. This is not just about what we do and how we act and react to situations; it's also about our identity as a dad. The creation story in Genesis reminds us that when God breathed into Adam, He held nothing back. Adam became a truly living being, with many of God's qualities. "Father" is one of God's living attributes, and He breathed that same attribute into us at the beginning. How wonderful it is to know that we are truly fathers as well.

Lord, this dad prays using Jesus's words when he says, "Our Father in heaven." Help him to know the joy and power and goodness of that relationship in every way, every day. Show him how to capture Your heart for his life. In Jesus's name we pray. Amen.

See how very much our Father loves us, for he calls us his children, and that is what we are! (1 John 3:1 NLT)

TONIGHT I'M PRAYING THIS FOR _____

TONIGHT we pray for the dad who believes he can make things better. Where there might have been strife in his family, he longs for communication. He's coming to know that while he might be able to generate good on his own, only the Lord can provide the better and the best.

The Holy Spirit can guide our words in a way that brings peace into our home. We do not need to concern ourselves with the "better" job because the Lord always provides more than enough and plenty left over to share with others. Where there might be lack, the Spirit can provide plenty. Where there might be absence, the Spirit can help bring about connection with our family. We know that the Lord earnestly desires to have a relationship with His wayward children like us. Likewise, as a dad we can seek reconciliation with our own children to always have our family whole.

Lord, in any or all of these things, this dad believes he can achieve peace in his home. That is what his heart desires for his family. Make his dreams come true for them. In Jesus's name we pray. Amen.

Behold, I stand at the door and knock. If anyone hears my voice and opens the door, I will come in to him and eat with him, and he with me. (Rev. 3:20)

TONIGHT I'M PRAYING THIS FOR _____

SUBJECT INDEX BY DAY

acceptance, 23, 174
accountability, 291
addiction, 276
adversity, 54, 76, 113, 155, 162, 336
becoming a better dad, 30, 54, 78, 102, 152, 201, 212, 225, 253, 265, 301, 341
calling, 294
challenges, 79, 167
changes, 165, 195, 282
children, 1, 17, 35, 49, 63, 77, 109, 121, 137, 153, 167, 181, 196, 211, 242, 259, 272, 286, 292, 303, 311, 328, 356
  faith of, 230, 316
  leaving home, 204
choices, 7, 50, 90, 128, 158, 169, 193, 208, 250, 289, 290, 330, 332
commitment, 6, 7, 9, 13, 44, 104, 150, 151, 213, 222, 231, 250, 257
community, 13, 57, 105, 156, 203, 255, 305, 353
confidence, 6, 56
contentment, 180, 287
courage, 3, 245

difficult times, 8, 16, 20, 26, 41, 62, 64, 98, 107, 110, 138, 145, 198, 209, 220, 233, 260, 264, 302, 304, 313, 332, 340
direction, 185
discouragement, 25, 54, 65, 99, 144, 154, 161, 176, 252
divorce, 59, 355
doubt, 158, 261, 360
evangelism, 296
excellence, 48, 217
expectations, 48, 52, 277
faith, 92, 96, 135, 237, 299
family changes, 51, 179
family life, 28, 283
fathers, importance of, 32, 75, 117, 139, 254, 348, 361, 364
fear, 73, 127, 166, 244, 320
finances, 27, 64, 84, 143, 182, 207, 262, 264, 284, 290, 313
first responders, 43, 71, 140
forgiveness
  of my sins, 85, 148, 218, 246, 333
  of others, 94, 226
friendship, 80, 205, 297, 318, 319, 327

future plans, 14, 22, 37, 60, 83, 103, 124, 147, 156, 168, 189, 212, 233, 258, 263, 279, 300, 321, 323, 324, 343, 344
generosity, 39, 329
God
  favor of, 114
  faithfulness of, 59, 154
  guidance from, 110, 131, 342, 344
  love of, 23, 68, 99, 119, 129, 281
  presence of, 19, 45, 52, 97, 120, 126, 188, 221, 236, 266, 314, 345, 347, 362
  promises of, 2, 42, 149, 232, 298, 322
  provision of, 23, 36, 40, 53, 62, 84, 88, 107, 122, 157, 173, 190, 191, 214, 238, 239, 317, 351
gratitude, 31, 164, 224, 340
health, 153, 267
hearing from God, 229
hope, 98, 200
humility, 78, 125
illness, 89, 159, 240, 273, 357
integrity, 288
joy, 55, 160, 221, 241, 352
leadership, 33, 56, 88, 106, 256, 294, 335
loneliness, 41, 325
loss of a child, 61
military dad, 274
new dad, 10, 303
opportunities, 86, 170, 344
parenting, 210
parents, caring for, 18, 337
past mistakes, 38, 136, 172, 216, 247, 324, 354
peace, 15, 36, 73, 95, 118, 168, 204, 238, 253, 279, 300, 326
perseverance, 11, 81, 108, 134, 176, 202, 220, 278, 308, 349

prayer, 24, 47, 91, 133, 141, 190, 268, 269, 345, 359, 363
prosperity, 15, 68, 118, 171, 219, 270, 300, 321, 322
purpose, 39, 68, 82, 112, 178, 227, 284, 323
responsibility, 70, 115, 184
rest, 199, 271
sacrifice, 34, 192
self-worth, 130, 132, 194, 207, 234, 309, 315
service, 44, 104, 206
significance, 5, 142, 234, 248
silence, 306
single dad, 35
sleep, 101, 235
speech, 350
spiritual battles, 147, 163, 293, 338
stepdad, 49
strength, 2, 21, 22, 58, 74, 87, 102, 123, 134, 177, 186, 191, 202, 228, 280, 331
stress, 66, 262
success, 20, 53, 55, 87, 108, 116, 150, 166, 182, 183, 215, 249, 285, 306, 312, 315, 346
temptation, 310
times of crisis, 65, 69, 175, 295
trust, 21, 46, 58, 72, 93, 111, 119, 145, 146, 173, 175, 197, 214, 223, 229, 232, 251, 275, 302, 326, 352, 365
wisdom, 208, 289, 308
words, power of, 67, 350
work, 16, 58, 100, 186, 243, 358
  and family balance, 12, 29, 136, 187, 238, 261, 332, 334
  loss of, 36
  travel for, 157
  value of, 4, 213, 334, 339

SCRIPTURE INDEX BY DAY

GENESIS
1:1, 31 339
12:1–2 349
15:1 114
18:19 361

EXODUS
4:10–12 174
4:14–15 205
17:11–12 327
20:12 18
24:12 219
34:6–7 237
35:30–31, 34–35 309

LEVITICUS
19:3 337

NUMBERS
11:17 228
14:8 251

DEUTERONOMY
6:6–7 211
8:17–18 68
28:12 358
31:6 140
33:27 346

JOSHUA
1:6 245
1:7 279
1:8 285
1:9 41
24:14 5
24:15 208

JUDGES
2:6–7 356
6:12 295
18:5–6 238

1 SAMUEL
16:7 161
17:34–35, 37 338

2 SAMUEL
6:12, 14–15 241

1 KINGS
17:14 264
19:11–12 128

1 CHRONICLES
29:17 76

2 CHRONICLES
20:15 274
20:17 117

NEHEMIAH
8:10 221

JOB
1:5 1
26:14 215
38:1, 12–13 173
42:2, 5–6 54

PSALMS
1:1–3 322
2:4 112
3:5 101
4:6–7 265
4:7 126
4:8 23, 235
13:1, 5 262
16:11 55
18:35 135
19:1–3 19
22:19 209
22:2–4 240
25:4–5 224
27:3 69
27:13 157
28:7 210
29:1, 4 193
29:10–11 8
30:5–7 97
31:14–15 65
31:19 164
32:11 330
33:11 343
33:18 234
34:4–6, 8 82
34:18–19 357
37:4 299
37:5–6 280
37:7 352
39:4 232
40:1 66
43:5 259
46:1–3 138
55:22 162
56:8 292
61:2–3 98
62:6 314
62:8 345
69:14–15 198
71:20 360
73:25–26 313
73:26 308
77:11 207
84:10 268
86:15 331
90:12 187
90:16–17 266
91:9–10 286
95:1 194

100:5 321
101:3 217
103:13 64
111:2, 7–8 353
112:1–2 147
118:5 149
119:10 347
123:1–2 192
127:3 253
128:2 170
128:3–4 230
130:5–6 298
139:16 323
142:1–2 85
142:7 148
143:3 45
145:15–16 326

PROVERBS
1:7 246
3:5–6 332
3:25–26 302
4:23, 25 269
4:26–27 185
9:10–11 311
10:22 270
13:4 151
14:16 289
16:2–3 28
16:9 163
16:32 108
17:17 297
17:22 242
18:24 204
19:20 282
19:21 14
20:7 26
20:24 186
21:5 103, 324
22:4 201
22:6 254
23:24 10
24:16 202

25:2 236
31:8 305

ECCLESIASTES
3:1, 5 225
7:8 195
12:1 111
12:13 92

ISAIAH
8:18 348
26:3–4 145
28:16 146
30:15 325
30:20–21 107
32:17 56
33:6 362
40:9 212
40:31 46
41:9 93
41:10 2
42:13 88
43:16 176
43:18–19 36
48:17 290
54:13 32
61:1 336

JEREMIAH
1:12 156
5:22 258
6:16 229
17:7 214
20:9 84
29:11 25
30:17 218
33:3 233
33:6 159

LAMENTATIONS
5:19, 21 59

EZEKIEL
3:21 70

DANIEL
2:21 21

JOEL
1:2–3 341
2:26 342

JONAH
3:1–2 216

MICAH
6:8 125

NAHUM
1:7 165

HABAKKUK
1:13 244
2:2–3 183
3:19 22

ZEPHANIAH
3:17 52

MATTHEW
5:16 223
5:48 320
6:6 4
6:14 94
6:21 196
6:33 72
6:34 120
7:1–2 291
7:7–8 47
10:26 3
11:28–29 177
13:45–46 283
16:16 296
16:21 113
16:24 250
16:25–26 11
18:3 181
18:14 61
22:37–38 359
25:23 104

25:29 115
26:41 200

MARK
4:35, 37–39 16
6:31 15
9:23–24 261
11:24 91

LUKE
3:22 139
6:38 57
12:6–7 153
14:28 335
15:20 167
17:19 239
21:36 133
22:25–26 284
24:15, 31 110

JOHN
1:16 263
3:9–10 363
4:35 86
6:35 249
8:31 42
10:14–15 203
14:2–3 355
14:17 188
14:27 62
15:7 155
15:8 255
15:13 71
16:33 29
17:11 319
17:26 152
21:22 197

ACTS
3:16 129
13:2–3 206
20:24 81

ROMANS
5:3–4 43
8:6 131
8:12 281
8:15 303
8:28 154
10:9 354
12:1 34
12:2 51
12:10 231
14:5–6 199
15:1–2 272
15:4 306

1 CORINTHIANS
1:5 53
2:7 17
2:9 99
6:12 276
6:19–20 267
7:17 248
9:24 87
10:31 50
12:24–26 227
14:33 96
15:58 74
16:14 30

2 CORINTHIANS
3:2–3 75
3:5 63
3:18 119
5:7 90
5:17 38
5:18 130
6:16, 18 12
8:11 6
9:7–8 39
12:9 252

GALATIANS
5:13 105
5:16 189
6:4 150
6:8–9 123
6:10 294

EPHESIANS
2:10 171
3:12 190
3:18–19 168
3:20 328
4:2 109
4:29 37
4:31–32 33
5:15–17 136
5:18–20 31
6:6–8 334
6:10 102
6:12 191

PHILIPPIANS
1:6 134
2:3 226
2:4 106
2:13 79
3:3 184
3:12 315
3:13 275
3:13–14 278
4:4 160
4:6–7 24
4:11–13 300
4:19 182

COLOSSIANS
1:10 288
1:11 257
1:17 89
1:28–29 142
2:8 178
3:17 260
3:23–24 213

1 THESSALONIANS
2:11–12 316
4:10–11 95
5:18 340
5:23 27

2 THESSALONIANS
2:13–14 48
3:16 77

1 TIMOTHY
4:4 132
4:7–8 329
4:12, 15 222
5:8 49
6:6 180
6:11 83
6:17–18 122

2 TIMOTHY
1:6 293
1:7 166
1:12 351
2:4–5 116
3:2, 4–5 304
4:2 307

TITUS
2:7 301
3:14 243

HEBREWS
4:9–11 271
4:16 7
6:10 100
10:35 144
10:36 220
11:1–2 58
11:6 44
11:16 344
12:1–2 40
12:9 137
12:28 247
13:5 143
13:17 256

JAMES
1:2–4 20
1:5–6 169
1:13–14 310
1:21 273
3:5–6 350
3:16 287
4:7–8 317
4:10 333
4:13–15 9
5:16 141

1 PETER
1:13 312
2:9 127
2:23 35
3:10–11 60
3:13–14 73
4:12–13 277
5:6 78

2 PETER
1:3 118
3:18 124

1 JOHN
1:7 318
1:9 172
3:1 364
3:16 80
4:7, 9, 11–12 13
5:2–3 121
5:14 37
5:15 158

3 JOHN
4 179
2 175

REVELATION
3:20 365

DR. MARK PITTS is the founder of the Midnight Dad Devotional community, the coauthor of *Midnight Dad Devotional*, and a pastor. His large and loyal audience of men looks to him for wisdom, prayer, and encouragement for their roles as husbands and fathers. Mark lives in Northwest Oklahoma with his wife, Susan.

CONNECT WITH MARK:

PastorMark.Pitts@gmail.com

Facebook @MidnightDadDevotional

A Note from the Publisher

Dear Reader,

Thank you for selecting a Revell book! We're so happy to be part of your life through this work.

Revell's mission is to publish books that offer hope and help for meeting life's challenges, and that bring comfort and inspiration. We know that the right words at the right time can make all the difference; it is our goal with every title to provide just the words you need.

We believe in building lasting relationships with readers, and we'd love to get to know you better. If you have any feedback, questions, or just want to chat about your experience reading this book, please email us directly at publisher@revellbooks.com. Your insights are incredibly important to us, and it would be our pleasure to hear how we can better serve you.

We look forward to hearing from you and having the chance to enhance your experience with Revell Books.

The Publishing Team at Revell Books
A Division of Baker Publishing Group
publisher@revellbooks.com